"Toil and Peaceful Life"

Doukhobor Village Settlement
in Saskatchewan, 1899-1918

"Toil and Peaceful Life"

Doukhobor Village Settlement in Saskatchewan, 1899-1918

Carl J. Tracie

Canadian Plains Research Center
University of Regina
1996

Copyright © Canadian Plains Research Center

Copyright Notice

All rights reserved. No part of this work covered by the copyrights hereon may be reproduced or used in any form or by any means — graphic, electronic or mechanical — without the prior written permission of the publisher. Any request for photocopying, recording, taping or information storage and retrieval systems of any part of this book shall be directed in writing to the Canadian Reprography Collective.

Canadian Plains Research Center
University of Regina
Regina, Saskatchewan S4S 0A2
Canada

Canadian Cataloguing in Publication Data

Tracie, Carl J. (Carl Joseph), 1939-

"Toil and peaceful life" : Doukhobor village settlement in Saskatchewan 1899-1918

(Canadian plains studies, ISSN 0317-6290 : 34)

Includes bibliographical references and index.
ISBN 0-88977-100-6

1. Dukhobors - Saskatchewan - History. 2. Dukhobors - Saskatchewan - Social life and customs - History. 3. Dukhobors - Saskatchewan - Government relations - History. 4. Agricultural colonies - Saskatchewan - History. I. University of Regina. Canadian Plains Research Center. II. Title. III. Series

FC3550.D76T73 1996   305.6'89   C96-920141-9.
F1074.7.D76T73 1996

Cover Design: Agnes Bray, Donna Achtzehner and Brian Mlazgar
Cover photograph courtesy British Columbia Archives and Records Service HP96801.

Printed and bound in Canada by
Hignell Printing Limited, Winnipeg, Manitoba

Printed on acid-free paper.

For Darlene

"*The question is always a question of trace.
What remains of what does not remain?*"

— Rita Kleinhart

Contents

Introduction ix
Chapter 1: Preparation. 1
Chapter 2: Beginning - 1899 20
Chapter 3: The North Colony - 1899 44
Chapter 4: The South Colony and Annex - 1899 65
Chapter 5: The Saskatchewan Colony - 1899 84
Chapter 6: Flux - 1899-1905 95
Chapter 7: Stasis - 1905 125
Chapter 8: The North Colony - 1905 128
Chapter 9: The South Colony and Annex - 1905 135
Chapter 10: The Saskatchewan Colony - 1905 145
Chapter 11: Decline - 1906-1913 152
Chapter 12: Transition - 1913 169
Chapter 13: The North Colony - 1913 172
Chapter 14: The South Colony and Annex - 1913 183
Chapter 15: The Saskatchewan Colony - 1913 194
Chapter 16: Dissolution - 1913-1918 200
Chapter 17: Conclusion 207
Epilogue 213
A Note on Sources 215
Appendix A: Doukhobor Villages - Legal and File Location . . . 218
Appendix B: Surveyors' Notebooks 221
Bibliography 223
Index 227

Acknowledgements

It is a pleasure to acknowledge the help and encouragement I have received from many people in the course of bringing this book to completion. Staff at the National Archives of Canada, the Saskatchewan Archives Board, the British Columbia Archives and Records Service, the Glenbow-Alberta Archives, the University of Saskatchewan Library (Special Collections), and the University of British Columbia Library (Special Collections) have assisted greatly in the collection of primary material. Glen Hammond of the Legal Surveys Branch, SaskGeomatics (formerly Saskatchewan Property Management Corporation) was especially helpful in providing direction and space in reconstructing vegetation cover and village locations from the surveyors' notebooks. Among many individuals in the Doukhobor community who encouraged me along the way I would especially acknowledge Koozma Tarasoff, Larry Ewashen, and Mabel Androsoff.

I am grateful to two anonymous reviewers who at different stages read the manuscript and made useful comments which led to its improvement. Brian Mlazgar and Agnes Bray of the Canadian Plains Research Center guided the manuscript to publication; their careful and thoughtful reading eliminated a host of inconsistencies and infelicities and I want to record my appreciation for their professional and courteous direction. I am also grateful to the Social Sciences and Humanities Research Council of Canada for providing partial funding of the research through their block grant to Trinity Western University.

Finally, I thank my wife, Darlene, for her encouragement and understanding during the long gestation of this book.

Introduction

The 7,400 Doukhobors who came to Canada in 1899 were a small but significant part of the great wave of immigration which began under the creative impetus of Clifford Sifton in 1896. They were to provoke government frustration and public reaction far out of proportion to their numbers. Initially, both government and public were delighted with these sturdy "sons of the soil" and their equally sturdy wives and children. Here were experienced farmers who had persevered in the face of hardship and severe persecution. They would not only flourish in the freedom of their new home, but would confirm the settled security to be had by intending settlers in the still-available lands of the Canadian West. Public reaction was positive as well. The Doukhobors' modest, almost deferential, ways, their vitality, and their very "foreignness" appealed to public and press alike. They were well-behaved, and effusively grateful for every kindness shown to them. And the Doukhobors' skin-of-the-teeth escape from the heel and whip of the combined forces of the Russian state and the Orthodox Church, which had aroused and focussed international attention, gained Canadian sympathy as well.

For their part, the Doukhobors seemed pleased with their new home. They remarked on the absence of soldiers, the friendliness of the people, and despite their suspicion of government in general, seemed willing to believe that Canada would be a satisfactory refuge.

It was soon apparent, however, that things were not quite as they seemed. Conflicts between the Doukhobors and the government on such routine regulations as registering births and deaths, collecting census information, and registering for the homestead lands made both sides wonder what they had got themselves into. Peter Verigin temporarily remedied these conflicts when he joined his followers from his exile in Siberia in 1902, but the underlying conflict associated with permanently occupying these "free" lands could not be resolved. The Doukhobors faithful to Verigin would not compromise on what they held to be central tenets of Doukhoborism; the government would not adjust the homestead regulations to accommodate either the communal landholding system of the Doukhobors or their rejection of the oath of allegiance. Consequently, the Community Doukhobors abandoned their exotic farm villages scattered across the 750,000 acres of reserved land and, on purchased land in Saskatchewan and British Columbia, replaced them with settlements reflecting a more rigid communal organization. Others abandoned the villages to join the Independent Doukhobors who had earlier determined that communal living was not essential to true Doukhoborism. From initiation to abandonment, the process of village disintegration took less than two decades.

Today, the image of the Doukhobors, for those who have heard of them at all, is that of naked bodies, and flames in the night. It is of hunger strikes, protest marches, and public disobedience; of erratic, irrational, often bizarre, behaviour. Such is the nature of those media which mould public perception that the most outrageous (that is, newsworthy) actions of the radical fringe become stereotypical of the main group, particularly, it seems, when religious zeal is involved. It has been the lot of the Doukhobors to be characterized and stigmatized in the minds of the public by the actions of the Sons of Freedom, a small and radical fringe element which has never represented the beliefs or actions of the majority.

What is distressing about this misrepresentation is not just that it is unfair and untrue, but that it dismisses or overlooks the solid, if less newsworthy, achievements of a large group of settlers in the agricultural development of the West. It also makes the dispassionate assessment of the conflict between the values and goals of the Doukhobors and the host society more difficult. The basic beliefs of a group may provoke two quite different responses among its members, for example, arson and nudity by the Sons of Freedom and obdurate, almost unemotional, resistance by the Community Doukhobors. Society may deem one set of responses unacceptable and the other acceptable, but the beliefs are regularly associated with the unacceptable responses, and ultimately the beliefs themselves, and therefore the people who hold them, are belittled.

The work which follows is not concerned primarily with righting old wrongs or in changing the public perception of a much-misunderstood group of people, although I hope it will contribute to both. It is a work of historical geography, concerned with understanding past cultural landscapes — the distinctive marks on the land which people of differing cultures make in the process of occupying and managing varying physical environments. My purpose, then, is to provide a detailed description and analysis of the cultural landscapes of the Doukhobors, beginning with their earliest settlements in 1899, and to trace over the next two decades the flowering and fading of these distinctive landscapes in the grassland-forest fringe of what is now the province of Saskatchewan. I limit the geographical focus to the three blocks of land set aside for them by a government eager to attract experienced farmers, and I am concerned primarily with the Community Doukhobors — those fervent followers of Peter Vasilevich Verigin who set up a most remarkable communal enterprise in the West, and who were willing to abandon almost all their gains rather than compromise the beliefs they held to be essential to true Doukhoborism. Thus, although Community settlements persisted in Saskatchewan on purchased land until at least 1939, my treatment of their villages ends with the final dispersal of the government-held village lands in the original reserves in 1918. And, although during this period a significant portion of the original settlers left the Community and eventually took up land individually within, or surrounding, the original reserves as Independent Doukhobors, I have not followed their settlement except to note its impact on the viability of the villages which they left.

Since my primary focus is on describing and analyzing the cultural landscape as a reflection of a range of ideological and practical concerns, I have chosen a traditional approach in historical geography which combines cross sections or "stills" of the cultural landscape at significant points in time with a narrative treatment of intervening events and changes which explain and are reflected in the selected snapshots. This has been called, somewhat facetiously, the "Dagwood sandwich" approach: slices of substantive description interlayered with explanatory narrative.

I have chosen 1899, 1905 and 1913 as the critical years to "freeze" the cultural landscape for detailed description and analysis. The year 1899 focusses on the initial cultural landscape created by the Doukhobors as they established fifty-seven Old World villages and began the process of cultivating the land. The cultural landscape of 1905 reflects the changes and advances in settlements and cultivation at or near the peak of Community development. By 1913, the distinctive cultural landscapes of the Community Doukhobors were in decline: most of the villages had either been abandoned or were in the process of abandonment, and the government land base which had supported their agriculture had been decimated. Only small parcels of village land remained, and these would be disbursed in 1918, bringing to an end a unique cultural landscape. The cultural landscape which the Doukhobors established on purchased land in Saskatchewan, Alberta and British Columbia after 1918 reflected modified values within a different societal context and preserved little of the traditional elements reproduced in the earlier settlements.

A focus on the settlement landscapes of the Doukhobors enhances our understanding of the richness and variety of the cultural landscape itself as an expression of Doukhobor beliefs, values and traditions. This study reconstructs the pattern of original villages, traces the changes in village location in response to forces of consolidation and fragmentation within the Community, and identifies the pattern of village decline as the Community waned on government land. Analyzing the factors involved in changes in the cultural landscape highlights questions surrounding the eventual disappearance of this distinctive landscape in Saskatchewan. Did the government fail to carry through on promises which the Doukhobors took in good faith — did it betray their trust? Or was the government finally forced to deal firmly with a group that had tried its policy and its patience with stubborn and irrational behaviour?

In occupying their new lands, the Doukhobors worked toward goals common to all agricultural pioneers in the Canadian West: to make the raw land productive, first to survive, and then to prosper; and to transform unfamiliar landscapes into something akin to home. Like others, they struggled with a set of more or less unfamiliar external variables — physical, social and political — in attaining these goals. But, perhaps more than most, they were profoundly influenced by a testing of their individual and collective beliefs in the crucible of a new social environment. They were suspicious of government and government ways, and they were recent adherents to a communal way of life which idealistically held to a classless society — "we have no leader; no one is greater than the other" — but which was practically in thrall to a leader who was obeyed as a veritable Christ. These components, held in varying degrees by segments of the larger group, together with the very practical survival necessities of wood, water and agricultural suitability, found expression in the cultural landscape of 1899: in the location of villages and fields, in the structure and form of their villages and buildings, in their agricultural organization.

It says something about the central concerns of the two societies and governments that in Russia, the Doukhobors' pacifism and antiecclesiastical beliefs aroused the most extreme persecution, while in Canada, their communalism and resistance to sworn loyalty proved ultimately "undigestable." Spiritual individualism, the rejection of the authority and ritual of the Orthodox Church, and their refusal to bear arms brought them into inevitable conflict with the Church and State in Russia, while in Canada, economic communalism and rejection of allegiance ran against the grain of economic individualism and nationalistic fervour. The Doukhobors' unquestioned allegiance to a Christ-like leader (and their attempt to determine the *real* meaning of his pronouncements) only exacerbated their problems.

There are some ironies inherent in the Doukhobor experience. At the very time when the individual homesteader was struggling with the very real problems of isolation and loneliness, the Doukhobor settlements, whose compact form allayed these problems, were being dismantled by forces which could not accommodate the communal aspects of the group. Also, although the initial government concern was the survival of the Doukhobors, their very prosperity, based as it was on communal effort, may have worked against them since it illustrated the success of a system diametrically opposed to the individualistic system dictated by government policy and assumed by mainstream society. Finally, it was Sifton's focus on the peasant farmers of Central and Eastern Europe which made western Canada a welcome destination for the Russian Doukhobors, but the very success of his overall campaign ensured that the Doukhobors would not long remain isolated from other settlers and from the changing conditions that this flood of immigrants would produce. In western Canada, concern shifted from filling unsettled land to providing sufficient space for land-hungry immigrants, and national concern shifted from immigration to integration.[1] These shifts produced a new rigidity in applying homestead requirements (not only to the Doukhobors but to all homesteaders) and made the Doukhobors' failure to maintain their distinctive communal settlements all but inevitable.

---

1   See Doug Owram, *Promise of Eden* (Toronto: University of Toronto Press, 1980), 224; Howard Palmer, "Strangers and Stereotypes," in R.D. Francis and H. Palmer (eds.), *The Prairie West* (Edmonton: Pica Pica Press, 1985), 322. Hall notes that 1899 was a bad year for those who feared Anglo-Saxon submergence for the British immigration was overwhelmed by large numbers of Galicians and Doukhobors. That it did not precipitate any change in immigration policy he attributes to the historic open-door policy of the Liberals, and to the fact that most of these "foreign" immigrants did not stop in the central cities, but moved west, thus keeping the issue from the central political stage. Later, both the pressure of increased settlement and the behaviour of a segment of the Doukhobors themselves, brought the problem not only to the central political stage but to the world press. See D.J. Hall, *Clifford Sifton*, Vol. 1, *The Young Napoleon 1861-1900* (Vancouver: University of British Columbia Press, 1981), 263.

Chapter 1
Preparation

Midnight, 28 June 1895. Flames from huge bonfires of weapons leapt in the blackness of the Caucasus night, illuminating the sober faces of hundreds of men and women. A sombre, melancholy anthem rose and fell in the night air as members of the *Doukhobortsi* gathered in three remote locations to reaffirm their return to the truth, their solidarity against the evils of killing. This single act would weld together the most conservative of the Russian Doukhobor communities in protest, in persecution, and finally in flight to the prairies of western Canada, and would become the touchstone of modern Doukhobor identity.

The origins of the Doukhobors are obscure. While the rejection of the highly structured and institutionalized Church associated with the Reformation spawned many groups with beliefs broadly similar to those of the Doukhobors, it is likely that their basic tenets grew out of the spirit of peasant protest characterizing the *Raskol*, the Great Schism in the Russian Orthodox Church brought about by new ceremonial details introduced by Bishop Nikon in the mid-seventeenth century.[1] The "priestless" segment of the *Raskol* rejected many of the tenets of the Orthodox Church including intermediaries and icons. Priests or other intermediaries were unnecessary since each person was the bearer of the "spark of God" and could have direct contact with God individually, while icons were seen as idols rather than as aids to worship. The term *Ikonobors* was scornfully applied to those who rejected the icons, and in 1795, the term *Dukho-borets* or "spirit-wrestlers," an equally pejorative name, was applied to those "spiritual Christians" who would not conform to the practices and beliefs of the Orthodox Church. The Church maintained that these "Christians" wrestled *against* the Spirit of Christ. In a fashion which was to prove characteristic of the Doukhobors, they accepted the name but reversed its meaning: they indeed wrestled, but *in* and *for*, rather than against, the Spirit of Christ.[2] Over time, the distinctives

---

1   Koozma J. Tarasoff, *Plakun Trava* (Grand Forks, BC: Mir Publication Society, 1982), 1-2.
2   Ibid., 3.

of Doukhobor belief emerged — spiritual individualism (each person possessed a bit of the "divine spark," could individually hear the voice of God, and was individually responsible only to God as supreme authority), pacifism, and communalism (the practical expression of brotherly love), although only the first appears to have been held consistently throughout their history. They held all persons to be equal and rejected earthly authority where it opposed or contradicted their interpretation of the laws of God. Ironically, their own leaders were elevated to near-divine status and were obeyed unquestioningly by the faithful. While avoiding credal statements, the Doukhobor philosophy came to be expressed in two slogans: "toil and peaceful life" and "the welfare of the world is not worth the life of a single child."[3]

By rejecting both the spiritual authority of the Church and the secular authority of the Czar and his representatives, the small, scattered groups of Doukhobors were persecuted by both agencies. In 1802, Alexander I decided that the best way to deal with dissident groups was to concentrate them in one isolated region where their nonconformist ways would have little influence and where they could colonize lands at the edge of the empire. The Doukhobors prospered in the chosen area — the Milky Waters (Molochnaya River) region north of the Crimea — but after a "golden age" of forty years of relative peace and prosperity, they were again relocated to Russia's recently won Transcaucasus region to serve as human buffers along its border with Turkey.[4] Here again, the Doukhobors persistently carved out new settlements around the Wet Mountains centre of Tiflis, and around the more southerly settlements of Kars and Elizavetpol, the three areas which would identify both different origins and attitudes of those settling in western Canada. The Doukhobors prospered under the effective leadership of Luker'ia Kalmykova, but conflict with the marauding Tartars and compromises with the military weakened Doukhobor commitment to pacifism. Peter Verigin, Luker'ia's protégé and nominee for leader, was arrested and exiled immediately following his installation by the majority of the Doukhobors, but he began a long-distance renewal among his followers which culminated in the "burning of the arms" in 1895.

The Doukhobors' return to pacifism and their persistent rejection of the institutional Church brought renewed and intensified persecution. They were hounded and whipped and murdered. They were forcibly dispersed in the southern valleys of Georgia where, landless and poverty-stricken, they were decimated by disease. Their deplorable plight and persistent adherence to principle, as well as their attempt to live out the tenets of first-century Christian communalism, attracted the attention and sympathy of Lev Tolstoy, and of Christian pacifists and utopians in England and America.[5] Together, they publicized the atrocities committed against

---

3   A third slogan — "the Sons of God will not be the slaves of corruption" — was appropriated by the Sons of Freedom in the early twentieth century.

4   For a discussion of the reasons for this relocation, see George Woodcock and Ivan Avakumovic, *The Doukhobors* (1968; Toronto: McClelland and Stewart Ltd., 1977), 44-61.

5   Prominent among these sympathizers were the Society of Friends (Quakers) in the United States, England and Canada, and the Purleigh Colony in England.

the Doukhobors, persuaded the Russian government to allow them to emigrate, and worked at raising the funds necessary for their transport to a favourable destination. That destination was Canada.[6]

The Agreement

The Doukhobors came to Canada in four sailings of two refurbished freighters, the SS *Lake Huron* and the SS *Lake Superior*, from January to June of 1899 — the largest single body of intending settlers in Canada's history.[7] Their migration to Canada brought to completion, under quite vague conditions,[8] collaboration among representatives of the Doukhobors, the Canadian government, James Mavor,[9] and English and American Quakers and Tolstoyans. The arrangement seemed a happy coincidence of needs and resources: the Doukhobors were escaping fierce persecution by removing to a country which promised them freedom of religion and extensive farmlands; the Canadian government was receiving proven agriculturalists to fill and develop the still incompletely settled lands of the Canadian West. But the reality was quite different: as one astute assessment had it, "Both were perfectly satisfied with each other and neither realized how far they were from mutual understanding."[10] The accuracy of this statement would become quite clear within a matter of months, as the vaguely worded conditions, agreed to in haste, were interpreted quite differently by the Doukhobors and the Canadian government almost immediately after the Doukhobors' arrival. Woodcock and Avakumovic point

---

6   A group of the most desperate Doukhobors participated in a short-lived experiment on Cyprus, and then they too joined the others in Canada. For a full account of the preparations for these migrations and the experience on Cyprus see Woodcock and Avakumovic, *The Doukhobors*, 107-29.

7   Although the final numbers given vary in several sources, Woodcock's and Avakumovic's figure of 7,400 is a reasonable working number (Woodcock and Avakumovic, *The Doukhobors*, 148). Telegrams to the Department of Immigration give conflicting figures ranging from 7,365 — no doubt the source of Maude's figure of 7,363 (see below), since the telegram goes on to note that one adult and one child returned to Russia (National Archives of Canada (hereafter NA), Department of Immigration Papers, RG75, V200 F84930, McCreary to Smart, 15 August 1899) — to 7,603 for the four sailings, but the Department of the Interior summary figures record 7,427 people (NA, Department of the Interior Papers, RG15, V755 F494483, Pt. 6, N.O. Côté Memorandum, 24 November 1906); the discrepancy of about 200 appears to relate to some miscalculation of the number of passengers on the first boat. The earliest complete schedule of Doukhobor villages in the autumn of 1899 gives a total of 7,355 (NA, Immigration Branch Records, RG 76, V184 F65101, Pt. 5, "Doukhobor Statistics"). This latter is close to Maude's figure of 7,363. See Aylmer Maude, *A Peculiar People: The Doukhobors* (New York and London: Funk and Wagnall's Company, 1904), 74.

8   James Mavor described the agreement as "this rather indefinite undertaking." See James Mavor, *My Windows on the Street of the World*, 2 vols. (Toronto: J.M. Dent and Son, 1923), 2:3.

9   James Mavor, a University of Toronto Professor of Economics, was an admirer of the Doukhobors and was instrumental in negotiating the conditions under which they came to Canada. He maintained a close relationship throughout their migration and subsequent settlement, championed their cause when the group was in danger of losing their lands, and argued their claims for compensation when their homesteads were finally cancelled (ibid.).

10 Harry Snesarev (Harry Trevor), "The Doukhobors in British Columbia" (unpublished report for the University of British Columbia, 1931), 25.

out that the Liberal government and the railroad companies were so anxious to recruit the Doukhobors that

> they chose to waive formalities in the interests of haste. This lack of detailed written agreements between the principal parties involved in the arrangement was eventually productive of great misunderstanding, since it enabled the Doukhobors to claim rights they did not legally possess and Sifton's successors to act in ways not in the spirit of the understanding reached in 1898.[11]

The formal agreement between the Doukhobors and the Canadian government addressed in a general way conditions which, according to James Mavor, the Doukhobors had stipulated:

> 1. Land in a block or reserve similar to the Mennonite Reserve.
> 2. Some reasonable aid in establishing themselves in the country.
> 3. Some concession to their prejudices regarding education. They wish their children educated, but wish to be consulted as to the mode. Some arrangement like that with the Mennonites might be made in the first instance. I do not think this will turn out to be a practical difficulty.
> 4. Assurance that they will not be called upon to render military service. In fact generally, an arrangement similar to that entered into with the Mennonites.[12]

In an amplification of this allusion to the Mennonites which must have seemed ironic just a few years later, Mavor goes on to say that those who know the Doukhobors "say that they are in many ways superior to the Mennonites. They are not so obstinately non-adaptive. On the contrary they readily adapt themselves to new conditions."[13]

Three conditions appeared formally in the final agreement: 1) each eligible Doukhobor should receive "the usual Free Grant Homestead"; 2) the steamship company's bonus would be paid to the Doukhobors to help them establish themselves (the monies were not to be used for transportation but "must be expended entirely in the interests of the settlement of the Doukhobors"[14]); and 3) they would be exempt from military service.[15]

The soon-to-be contentious issue of the interplay between the type of agricultural organization and the conditions of taking up the land which was buried in the innocuous first condition was not detailed. It could be argued that uppermost in the minds of the Doukhobors was escape from their desperate conditions and that they

---

11   Woodcock and Avakumovic, *The Doukhobors*, 137.

12   NA, RG76, V183 F65101, Pt. 1, James Mavor to James Smart, 8 September 1898. As I will suggest later, the reference to similarities with the Mennonites may have led the government to assume their system of landholding was also similar.

13   Ibid.

14   Ibid., Smart to Mavor, 1 December 1898, in discussing the revised (and final?) agreement.

15   Woodcock and Avakumovic, *The Doukhobors*, 137; NA, RG76, V183 F65101, Pt. 1, Clifford Sifton to Governor-General, 30 November 1898; Maude, *A Peculiar People*, 327-28.

were perhaps willingly ignorant of any details that might interfere with that escape. On the other hand, the government may have unwisely assumed that the Doukhobors understood more about the requirements of acquiring the land than they actually did. In assessing the conflict between the Doukhobors' concept of property and the requirement of the Dominion Lands Act, Mavor later argued that the government was fully aware of the Doukhobors' communal way of life before they entered Canada,[16] and Peter Verigin made the same point about their rejection of oath-taking in his petition on behalf of the Doukhobors in 1907:

> Is it possible that you did not know why the incident [the loss of their lands in Russia] has taken place between us and the Russian government and why we left our country and migrated to your country, Canada? This happened only because we did not choose to take the oath of allegiance to Nicholas Alexandrovitch.[17]

The government maintained that the conditions of obtaining homestead land, including the matter of swearing allegiance to the Crown, were clear from the beginning.[18] Wherever the truth lies, it is evident that the agreement itself was imprecise and open to varying interpretations.

The Land

Although James Mavor later made the point that the Doukhobors had never asked for lands set apart for their sole use,[19] reserved land *en bloc* was a necessity for their communal way of life and was a major inducement offered by the government. Representatives of the Doukhobors and the government, assisted by Tolstoyan Aylmer Maude, a retired businessman, and Prince Hilkoff, a dispossessed Russian estate-holder and Doukhobor sympathizer, set about to locate a block of land which would accommodate the potential immigrants. Mavor suggested that the reserves be "as near as possible to the northern limits of practicable settlement"[20] so the Doukhobors could establish themselves in a self-contained manner while attracting other settlers to the intervening areas. The representatives found a suitable area near Beaver Lake, northeast of Edmonton, but had to abandon this location owing

---

16 Mavor, *My Windows*, 2:3.

17 Government of Canada, *Papers Relating to the Holding of Homestead Entries by Members of the Doukhobor Community* (Ottawa: Government Printing Bureau, 1907), 14.

18 "The Canadian authorities were quite explicit about the conditions on which the Doukhobors might come to Canada. They were to make entry for their homesteads individually, in the usual Canadian fashion." But Maude goes on to say that as an additional concession, they were allowed to cultivate an amount of land anywhere on their "township" equivalent to the total amount required, rather than on each individual quarter section, "thus facilitating their communal arrangements"(*A Peculiar People*, 61). As to the oath of allegiance, Woodcock and Avakumovic's research turned up nothing to indicate a specific reference to the need for pledging allegiance as a requirement for patenting the land. Their conclusion is that probably nobody thought to mention the issue (*The Doukhobors*, 134).

19 Mavor, *My Windows*, 2:4.

20 Ibid.

to strong opposition by Edmonton district residents to these very "foreign" settlers. They were forced to consider lands "in other, less tempting, parts of the country."[21] The Doukhobors were favourably impressed with a block of eleven townships near Wetaskiwin,[22] but Sifton thought it too small to accommodate the whole group.[23] Both William McCreary, the Commissioner for Immigration at Winnipeg, and James Smart, Deputy Minister of the Interior, championed a location in the Pipestone district just south of the Canadian Pacific Railway along the eastern edge of the District of Assiniboia,[24] but the Doukhobors showed little enthusiasm for it as it contained few trees, and Sifton thought it might be too small after all.[25]

The indecision of the Doukhobor representatives added to the difficulty of finding a large block of land which satisfied their requirements. As representatives of a group in which "all are equal, no one is better than the other," they did not feel empowered to make any final decisions, and so were unwilling to express firm preferences about any piece of land. Even Prince Hilkoff, who took the initiative in representing them, proved indecisive. William McCreary, described by Sulerzhitsky as a "lively, energetic, good-natured man,"[26] betrayed his frustration when he reported to his superiors that he was "pretty much going blindfolded" in the matter of locating the Doukhobors since Hilkoff "changes so often in his ideas."[27] Finally, after Hilkoff and the delegates had looked at lands in the Carrot River district and in northern Manitoba, they agreed to lands in the Yorkton-Swan River area. Two blocks of land comprised the initial reserves: the North Reserve (also called the Thunder Hill, or Swan River Reserve) and the South Reserve (Kamsack, Yorkton, or Whitesand Reserve), with a later addition to it known as the Devil's Lake (or, later, Good Spirit Lake) Annex.

Eventually, more than twice as many migrants came as originally expected.[28] As the government received news of more and more migrants, it made substitutions, modifications and additions to these reserves even as the Doukhobors were arriving. Even so, it was clear that the two reserves would not accommodate the last group of more than 2,000 Kars Doukhobors. Prince Hilkoff continued to favour lands east of Prince Albert, particularly those in the Carrot River and Leather River valleys, to

---

21   Maude, *A Peculiar People*, 51-52. Foreshadowing a later conflict, this opposition was led by Edmonton businessman Frank Oliver who was later to succeed Clifford Sifton as Minister of the Interior, and who was to show little regard for the "non-binding" modification of cultivation requirements negotiated by Sifton with the Doukhobors.

22   NA, RG76, V183 F65101, Pt. 1, William F. McCreary to James Smart, 11 October 1898.

23   Ibid., Smart to McCreary, 14 October 1898.

24   Ibid., Deputy Minister to Maude, 6 October 1898.

25   Ibid., Sifton to McCreary, 18 October 1898.

26   L.A. Sulerzhitsky, *To America With the Doukhobors* (Regina: Canadian Plains Research Center, 1982), 93.

27   NA, RG76, V183 F65101, Pt. 3, McCreary to Smart, 18 February 1899.

28   As late as the end of September, only 2,000 Doukhobors were expected during the winter (NA, RG76, V183 F65101, Pt.1, Maude to Smart, 27 September 1898).

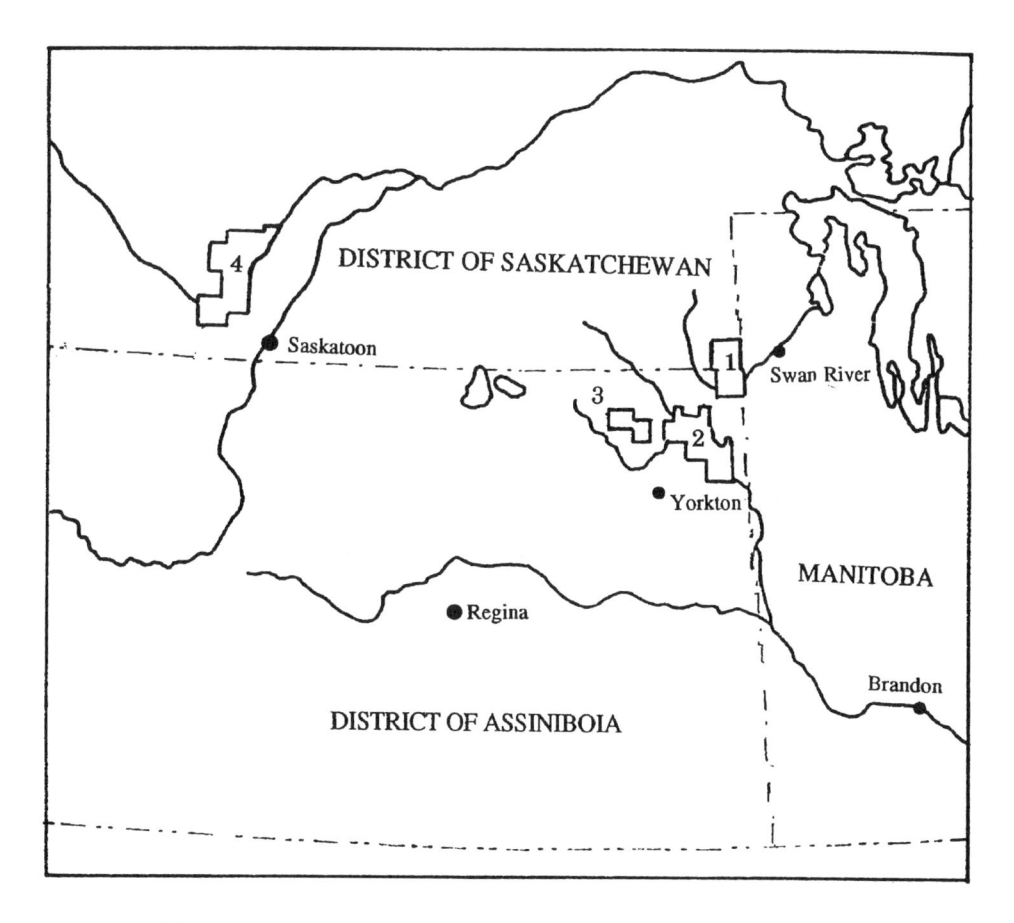

Map 1. Doukhobor Reserves: 1. North Colony; 2. South Colony; 3. Good Spirit Lake Annex; 4. Saskatchewan Colony.

accommodate this last group, but finally agreed to lands along the North Saskatchewan River some 204 miles north and west of the original reserves. In June 1899 the Saskatchewan Reserve (or Prince Albert Reserve)[29] was added to the others. The three reserves totalled nearly three-quarters of a million acres, a "magnificent endowment"[30] set aside by the Canadian government for the Doukhobors' sole use (see Map 1).

---

29 The lands in this region were almost totally in the Prince Albert Land District; a few of the southernmost townships were in the Regina District.
30 The phrase is James Mavor's (*My Windows*, 2:4).

The North Reserve

The first block of land set aside in the North (Thunder Hill) Reserve lay astride the Manitoba-District of Assiniboia boundary in Townships 34, 35 and 36 in Ranges 29, 30 and 31.[31] The confusion of having colonies under two different sets of school and municipal laws and the problem of pre-reservation entries on the land[32] led to the exchange of townships in Range 31 for those in Range 29, although timber for houses had been cut and two blockhouses had been erected in Range 29 (McVey's Camp).[33]

Township 33 in Ranges 30 and 31 was added later, making a final reservation of eight townships. Since Township 36, Range 31 was not used for agriculture (although a sawmill utilizing the timber was built there) and only the extreme southeastern margin of Township 36, Range 30 was settled, the effective reserve was only six townships.[34] These northern townships were to be reserved for the "Yakutians," a small number of exiles released in 1904 and 1905, but they chose more favourable land in the South Reserve, both because the agricultural capabilities were greater there, and, being of a more independent turn of mind than the communal North Colonists, they were more comfortable with the independent component in the Good Spirit Lake area.

The reserved area was a patchwork of prairie and forest (including much *brûlé*, or burn-over land), lakes and swamps[35] laced together with a network of creeks and rivers flowing from Duck Mountain and the Porcupine Hills, and from the local prominence that gave the colony its name — Thunder Hill. Sulerzhitsky described the trip from Cowan to the blockhouses near the Swan River through a forest ravaged by fire, with "huge, smooth trunks shining with a bluish light" as far as the eye could see. These "naked giants" thinned and gave way to more open country only as they came within sight of Thunder Hill. He likened the prairie country between the Swan River and Fort Pelly to the sea, "empty, bare, nothing to hold the eye," although the description appears to be more appropriate to the larger prairies near Fort Pelly than to the scrubby prairie patches in the Thunder Hill Reserve proper.[36]

---

31 The Department of the Interior files indicate that the initial reservation was for all lands in Townships 34, 35, 36 in Ranges 30 and 31; and "all available lands" in Townships 34, 35, 36 in Range 29. This latter qualification reflected pre-reservation settlement in Manitoba; there was apparently no homestead settlement on the Districts of Assiniboia and Saskatchewan side.

32 The census of 1901 records 121 people in two of the three townships in Manitoba, with Township 34 vacant (Canada, *Census of the Prairie Provinces*, 1906).

33 NA, RG15, V760 F502904, E.W. Hubbell to James Smart, 10 April 1899.

34 The nonagricultural northern townships were valuable for their timber. As late as April 1903, the Doukhobors resisted the government's proposal of taking these northern townships out of the reserve. A state-of-the-art sawmill was established in Township 36, Range 31 (NA, RG15, V755 F494483, Pt. 6, Stephenson, Inspector of Crown Timber Agencies, to Oliver, 26 June 1907).

35 Sulerzhitsky, *To America With the Doukhobors*, 121, 143.

36 Ibid., 121, 124.

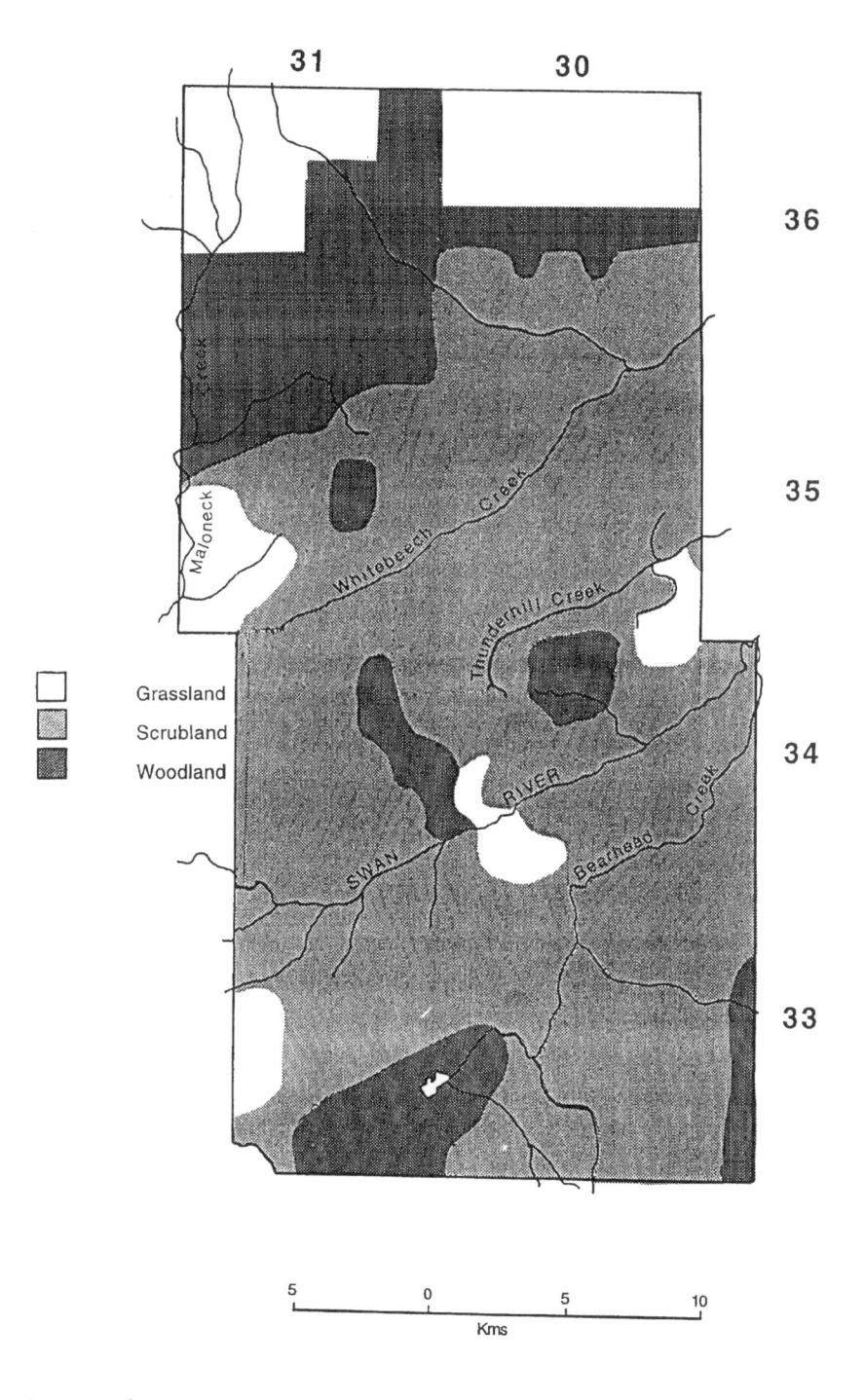

Map 2. Pre-settlement Vegetation, North Colony.

The surveyors who subdivided the Doukhobor lands provided a more detailed and comprehensive description of the vegetation cover (see Map 2).[37] They noted some areas of scrubby prairie, but identified most of the reserved lands as covered by second-growth willow, poplar, birch and spruce after earlier fires had razed the original forest. The surveyors characterized most of the cover as "scrub" and noted the evidence of *brûlé* either by that term, or by noting dry trees or windfall. They noted larger trees only in limited patches in the southern half of the reserve, often associated with muskeg, while forests covered considerably larger areas in the northern half of the reserve, especially in Townships 35 and 36, Range 31, and in the northern half of Township 36, Range 30.

The summary reports of the surveyors indicate that only a small portion of the reserve was first-class agricultural land. The east half of Township 35, Range 30 was broken up by Thunder Hill; Township 36 in Ranges 30 and 31 was heavily wooded and had light soil; nine sections of Township 34, Range 30 were of little agricultural value owing to hilly, stony areas or muskeg; while Township 33, Range 31 was described as "not very well adapted for farming purposes," although it was noted that it would be desirable country for stock raising. Agriculturally, the most favourable area was Township 33, Range 30 with excellent deep clay loam; Townships 34 and 35 in Range 31 and Township 35, Range 30 had first- and second-class soils. The valley bottom and more gently-sloping sides of the Swan River also were assessed as having good agricultural potential.

James Mavor's *Report to the Board of Trade* attempted to give some general indication of the agricultural potential of lands in the west; he included almost the whole reserve (excluding only Township 33, Range 31) as falling within "Areas not susceptible for wheat Cultivation; at present timbered and largely suitable only for pasturage even where cleared."[38]

Not much was known of the climate of the region, except that it was an area "in respect of which [the frost hazard to wheat] settlers were still somewhat doubtful" in Maude's cautious phrase.[39] This potential hazard seemed of little concern in the choice of lands, although Maude had noted that the Doukhobors had been forced to look for lands beyond the "safe" wheat-growing limit in their search for a block of land large enough to settle in a compact community.[40] On the contrary, the

---

37 The original surveyors' notebooks are kept by Geometrics (formerly the Central Survey and Mapping Agency of the Saskatchewan Property Management Corporation) in Regina. The notebooks used are as follows: #6041 — J.C. DesMeules, October 1898; #6118 — J.A. Belleau, August 1899; #6120 — J.A. Belleau, February-March 1899; #7072 — C.F. Aylsworth, March-April 1900; #7073 — C.F. Aylsworth, April-May 1900; #7395 — C.F. Aylsworth, August-September 1900; #7396 — C.F. Aylsworth, May-August 1900; #7397 — C.F. Aylsworth, July-August 1900; #14423 — G.P.J. Roy, November-December 1913.

38 James Mavor, *Report to the Board of Trade on the North West of Canada with Special Reference to Wheat Production for Export 1904* (London: His Majesty's Stationery Office, n.d. [1905]), Map.

39 Maude, *A Peculiar People*, 51-52.

40 Ibid., 50.

abundant crops of one or two earlier settlers were taken to augur well for the area as productive wheatland.[41] Damaging fall frosts were noted and then dismissed. After all, Sulerzhitsky observed, the Mennonites in southern Manitoba initially experienced hardships because of early fall frosts, but "with the increase in the area of cultivated land, the frosts become rarer, weaker and finally almost disappear."[42] He went on to say that the Doukhobors themselves had encountered this same amelioration in the Caucasus where "with the increased areas of fields, the frosts became less and did not prevent the Doukhobor settlements from becoming the wealthiest in the Caucasus."[43] To settlers from the chilly Caucasus highlands near Tiflis (later Tbilisi), this limitation must have been regarded as a temporary inconvenience.

The land which received these newcomers admirably met their essential requirements: a good water supply, accessible timber to build with, and reasonably close proximity to a railway.[44] Fred Fisher, an assistant to the Indian agent at the Côté Reserve who assisted in the search for land, noted: "They were looking for running water, wood and good soil, and they were not particular where it was as they intended to live within themselves."[45] The Swan River with its major tributaries, Bearshead [now Bear Head] Creek and the Woody River, provided a good water supply, and there was timber, both dry and green, for the construction of houses and barns.[46] Although at the time of settlement, the end of steel at Cowan was about fifty-four miles from Michaelovo, the first North Colony village, the railway was extended to Swan River and beyond in the summer of 1899, leaving the eastern part of the reserve only about eight miles from the railway. Although Fisher noted the Doukhobors' concern for good soil, even today, third-generation Doukhobors question the actual importance of this factor since they are now farming former village lands of quite modest agricultural capability.

---

41   Sulerzhitsky, *To America With the Doukhobors*, 144-45.

42   Sulerzhitsky was echoing the hopeful tone of many promoters of the Canadian West (ibid., 147). Maude himself expresses a similar sentiment (*A Peculiar People*, 51-52).

43   Sulerzhitsky, *To America With the Doukhobors*, 147. This supports Mavor's early evaluation that the Doukhobors would make excellent and successful settlers for western Canada owing to their experience with a similar environment: "There can be no doubt of the suitability of these Eastern European peasants for the climate of certain lands of the North West Territories and Manitoba. They are accustomed to the severe conditions of the steppes and can be readily acclimatized in a country whose conditions are analagous to those of their own" (NA, RG76, V183 F65101, Pt. 1, Mavor to Sifton, 26 July 1898).

44   Maude, *A Peculiar People*, 51.

45   Quoted in John Hawkes, *Saskatchewan and Its People*, 3 vols., (Regina: S.J. Clarke Publication Company, 1924), 2:724.

46   There were, however, numerous complaints related to the practice of cutting timber outside the reserves, especially by residents of Range 29. The uncertainty about the actual reserve boundaries exacerbated this problem.

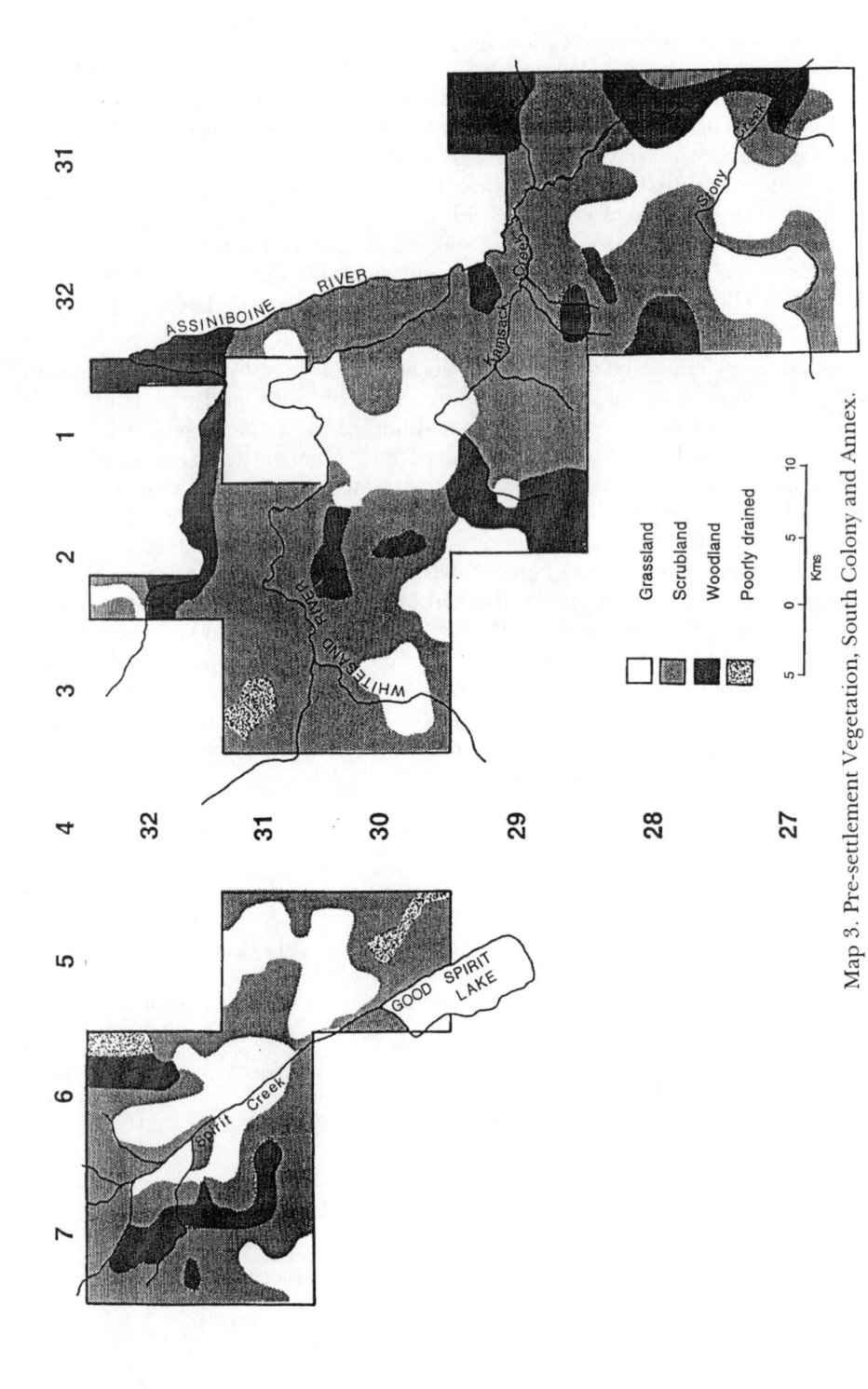

Map 3. Pre-settlement Vegetation, South Colony and Annex.

The South Reserve and Annex

The South Reserve proper was set aside in 1898, enlarged in 1899 and again in 1900.[47] The original reserve was made 16 November 1898 and seems to have included 8.5 townships between the Assiniboine River and Good Spirit Lake.[48] Negotiations to acquire a part of the Côté Indian Reserve fronting the Assiniboine River were begun in January, and were successfully concluded a short while later.[49] Further adjustments were made in March 1899 and sometime after May 1899,[50] adding five townships to the reserve — four of which had only the even-numbered sections reserved. A map prepared in the fall of 1905 shows an addition of three fractional townships around the Key Indian Reserve, two of which had only the even-numbered sections reserved. Range 33, a wedge of land between Range 32 west of the Prime Meridian and Range 1 west of the Second Meridian created by the convergence of the meridians, was also added to the reserve in Townships 27 to 33.

The Good Spirit Lake (Devil's Lake) Annex was set aside in March 1899 and initially was comprised of four townships (two of which were abbreviated, twenty-four-section townships). Following Hilkoff's suggestion, Township 30 in Ranges 5 and 6 was added so the Doukhobors could take advantage of village locations along Good Spirit Lake and Spirit Creek, and by May 1900, Township 32, Range 7 also had been added. Revisions by 3 May 1902 removed two full townships and added one twenty-four-section township,[51] leaving a reserve of three full townships and three twenty-four-section townships, one of the latter (Township 31, Range 5) having only the even-numbered sections reserved for the Doukhobors.

Surveyor E.W. Hubbell gave a general description of the lands in the South Colony: "Of this Reserve I have little to say; except that it is a fine tract of fairly level country, watered principally by the Assiniboine and Whitesand Rivers; the soil is generally good, but timber and firewood scarce .... Water is easily obtainable by

---

47 NA, RG15, V755 F494483, Pt. 5, J.W. Greenway to N.O. Côté, 24 November, 1906.

48 NA, RG15, V760 F502904, Map, "Doukhobor Reserves." The townships in Township 31 are "abbreviated" townships, having only twenty-four sections, so the original reserve would have encompassed 270 square miles rather than 306 square miles.

49 NA, RG76, V183 F65101, Pt. 2, Frank Pedley to James Smart, 26 January 1899.

50 Three townships were added 28 May 1901 according to notes attached to a response to a list of questions by Commissioner J.W.Greenway in November 1906 (NA, RG15, V755 F494483, Pt. 5); NA, RG76, V183 F65101, Pt. 3, D.A. Hilkoff to Smart, 20 May 1899. Hilkoff notes that the plan to have the Cyprus Doukhobors join their compatriots in the North Colony would not work as there was insufficient agricultural land there. His suggestion was to add four full townships (Townships 28 and 29, Ranges 31 and 32) and a quarter of a township (the northeast of Township 27, Range 31) south of the major Whitesand settlement for them. Township 29, Range 32 was already part of the reserve according to an early map (NA, RG15, V760 F502904, "Doukhobor Reserves," n.d.). The Department went along with this suggestion and added these townships and two others (Township 27 in Ranges 31 and 32).

51 NA, RG15, V754 F494483, Pt. 2, James Crerar to J. Turriff, 3 May 1902; Map, "Map Shewing Doukhobor Homesteads and Disposition of Same, (Yorkton District)," Ottawa: Interior Department, 1 August 1907.

digging wells; generally at a depth of six to twenty feet is sufficient."[52] The surveyors who outlined and subdivided the reserved lands supported these generalizations and provided considerable detail in terms of surface configuration and cover, drainage and soils (see Map 3). In general, the reserve contained quite extensive areas of prairie dotted with bluffs of small poplar and clumps of willow. These areas were generally well drained and had a black loam to clay loam soil well suited to grain growing. Broken land, associated with the Whitesand and Assiniboine Rivers and numerous small tributaries, interrupted the otherwise level to gently rolling terrain. Along the streams and around Good Spirit Lake, fringing belts of larger trees — poplar, balm-of-Gilead, and occasionally, birch and spruce — provided the major source of building timber on the reserve. The larger trees on the slopes of Duck Mountain also provided building timber and fuel for the settlers in Township 29, Range 31.

The western part of the South Colony and the lands of the Good Spirit Lake Annex were particularly well suited to mixed farming and stock raising, according to the surveyors. The grasses of extensive hay meadows and small, fire-created prairie openings — "the greatest portion of this township [30-5-W2] is dry marshes in which grass grows from three to five feet high and which keeps green till late in the fall of the year"[53]— numerous streams and ponds for water, and rolling terrain covered with sheltering bush and trees, combined to produce an environment particularly well suited to cattle raising. James Mavor, in fact, designated the whole of the South Colony and Annex as "Areas in which wheat is a less certain crop and in which mixed farming is likely to be profitable than exclusive wheat growing."[54] In these more broken areas, timber for building was often available; in the larger portion of the reserve, however, it was in short supply. This deficiency was to influence the types of structures which the Doukhobors built in their initial villages, particularly in the southern portion of the reserve.

The South Reserve and Annex again provided the essentials for the Doukhobors: water, wood, and good agricultural soils. In comparison to the North Reserve, surface water was more widely available from numerous streams and from Good Spirit Lake, the soils on the whole were more generally suited to agricultural pursuits (there is very little mention of lands unsuited to agriculture in the individual surveyor's notes), but building timber was more restricted.

The Saskatchewan Reserve

Originally, the fourth and final shipload of Doukhobors from the Kars region of Transcaucasia was to join the Kars people already located in the South Colony; however, as the lands filled up, it was clear that another block of land would have to be found. As late as May 1899, just two weeks before the last boatload was to arrive,

---

52 NA, RG15, V760 F502904, Hubbell to Smart, 10 April 1899.
53 F. Vincent, Surveyor's Notebook #5462, 1890.
54 Mavor, *Report to the Board of Trade*, Map.

Hilkoff was urging the Department to set aside land in the Carrot River area for these last arrivals, although he also noted the difficulties that might arise from splitting the Kars Doukhobors. In the end he agreed to lands within the bend of the North Saskatchewan River, some 204 miles northwest of the South Colony.

Twelve townships were set aside in June and July 1899, with two of the townships almost wholly south of the North Saskatchewan River and the rest north and west of the river. By 1904, the reserve was enlarged to nineteen townships (two of these were fractional townships divided by the North Saskatchewan River),[55] and two more townships were added by 1907.[56] Although the village of Spasofka was located in the southern part of Township 45, Range 5, it does not seem to have been part of the reserved land; only Tarasoff includes it, though the 1907 map indicates Doukhobor homestead lands in that township.[57] Unlike most of the North and South Reserves, only the even-numbered sections (with the exception of the Hudson's Bay Company sections) were reserved for the Doukhobors throughout the Saskatchewan Reserve. Since all but the extreme southern portion was in the Prince Albert Land District, the reserve, despite its distance from that settlement, was usually known by that name.

The physical character of the Saskatchewan Reserve was extremely varied. Sections of first-class agricultural lands were interpersed with sand hills, stony areas, numerous swamps, sloughs and ponds, and rough, broken land associated with the North Saskatchewan River and the ravines running into it. Two large lakes (Redberry Lake and Blaine Lake) and numerous smaller lakes and ponds provided extensive areas of surface water, although much of this was alkaline. The Saskatchewan Reserve was much more open than either the North or South Reserves with a surface characterized by rolling prairie, with poplar and willow brush (see Map 4). The prairie on the reserve south of the river was more open with fewer clumps of poplar and willow as compared to the "bushier" prairie north of the river. Only around the edges of the lakes and along the banks and ravines of the North Saskatchewan River was timber of sufficient size or extent for building.

The climate and agricultural potential of this more northerly area was better known than the other reserves. Agriculturalists had settled the land immediately east of the Saskatchewan Reserve, between the North and South Saskatchewan Rivers, several years before the Doukhobors came, and all indications appeared quite positive. Still, the rolling character of the reserve lands with numerous low-lying depressions was somewhat different from the successfully settled land. While surveyors did not normally comment on the climate, Walter Beatty apparently felt the need to allay some concerns that may have been present — in two cases he noted the absence of summer frosts: "the climate is good and early summer frost is

---

55 NA, RG76, V184 F65101, Pt. 7, C.W. Speers to W.W. Cory, 15 June, 1904.
56 Canada, "Map Shewing Doukhobor Homesteads and Disposition of Same" (Ottawa: Government Printing Bureau, 1907), Reports and Maps.
57 Tarasoff, *Plakun Trava*, 65.

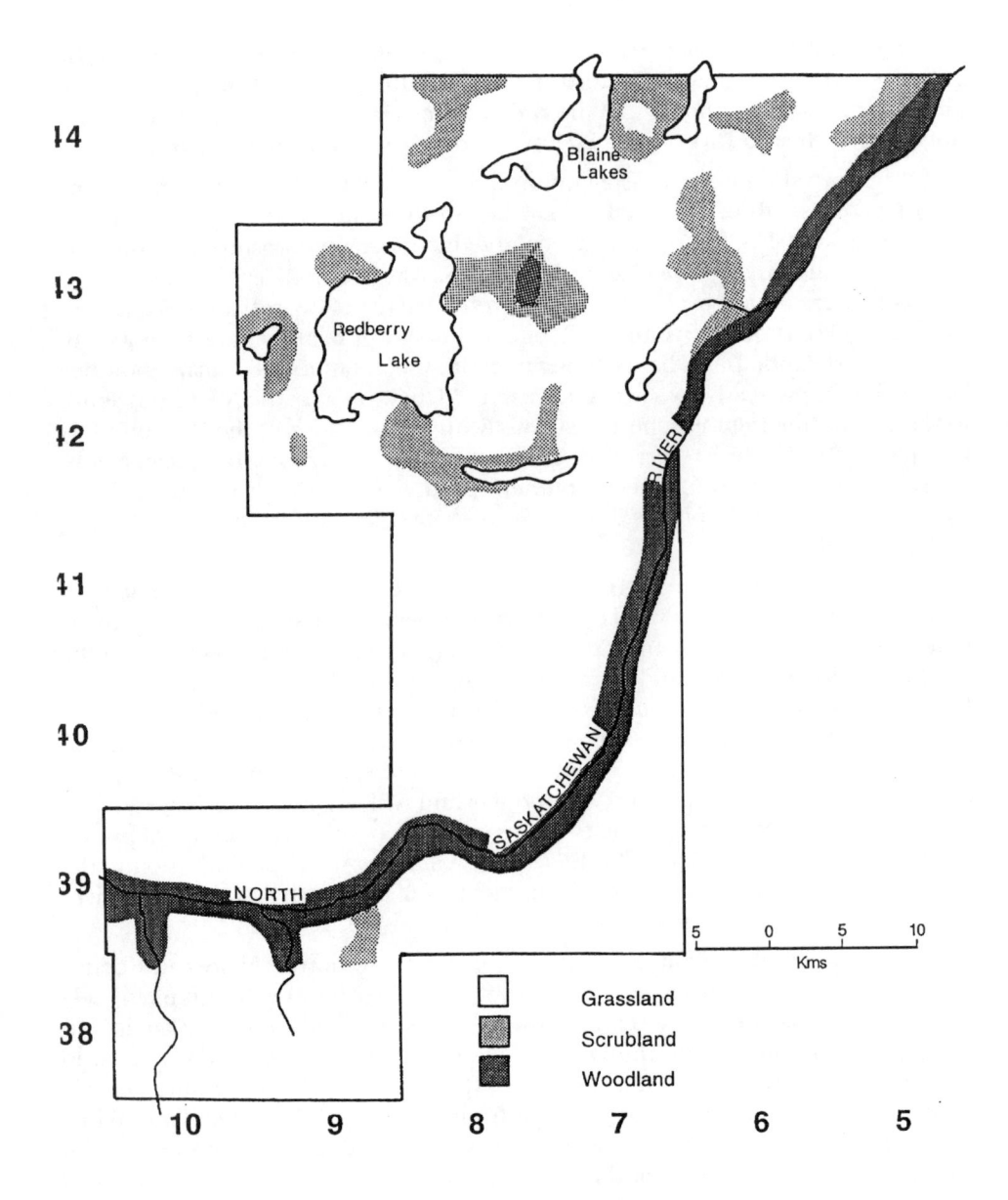

Map 4. Pre-settlement Vegetation, Saskatchewan Colony.

unknown in this region" and "the climate is good with no indications of summer frost."[58] His evaluation was confirmed by Mavor the next year. He included all but the northernmost tier of townships of the Saskatchewan Reserve as "areas in which wheat is a certain crop."[59] The only area assessed as unsuitable for agricultural purposes was the part of Township 39, Range 9 north of the North Saskatchewan River (too sandy), while the townships around Redberry Lake, although containing some good agricultural land, were evaluated as more suited to grazing.

Taking Up the Land

The first boatloads of immigrants arrived in midwinter and were housed at immigration halls and other facilities in Brandon, Yorkton and Selkirk until early spring when they moved out to blockhouses[60] in the North and South Reserves.

The first contingent of fifty settlers for the North Reserve moved out of the immigration sheds at Winnipeg under the direction of Leo Sulerzhitsky on 12 February 1899. They took the Manitoba and Northwestern Railway to the end of the line at Cowan, and from there tramped some fifty-four miles across the prairie and through the forest to the temporary residences which had been erected for them at the eastern edge of the reserve.[61] By early April, 500 Doukhobors occupied the blockhouses, which, by this time, apparently included additional houses built within the reserve on the site of Michaelovo and on an unnamed site about 2.5 miles southwest of Michaelovo (the first site of the village of Vosnisennie). Hubbell expected that new arrivals would bring the total to 1,450, a number easily accommodated since he had built sufficient houses for 2,000.[62]

---

58 Walter Beatty, Surveyor's Notebook #8457, 1903.

59 Mavor, *Report to the Board of Trade*, Map.

60 "Blockhouses" were constructed in advance of the Doukhobors' arrival by Canadians under the direction of the surveyors and the Commissioner. The plan was to have these ready for the Doukhobors so they would have a place to live until they could locate and build their own villages. They were designed to house 75-100 people per house in temporary quarters.

61 Sulerzhitsky, *To America With the Doukhobors*, 109, 143. Sulerzhitsky and his group arrived at the blockhouses built on Section 31, Township 34, Range 29 (McVey's camp) rather than at the site of Michaelovo (although the name as well as the site may have been transferred to the location within the reserve), as his description of the two blockhouses, one complete, the other unfinished and lacking a roof, agrees with Hubbell's statement that two blockhouses were built on Section 31, Range 29 before word was received that the townships in Range 29 were not to be included in the reserve. One hundred Doukhobors were still occupying these two blockhouses two months later (NA, RG15, V760 F502904, Hubbell to Smart, 10 April 1899).

62 NA, RG15, V760 F502904, Hubbell to Smart, 10 April, 1899. Hubbell's estimate is close to the figures given for the North Colony in the summer of 1899 by Archer (1369) (Fitzgibbon appendix) and by William Harvey (1,394) in November 1899 (NA, RG76, V184 F65101, Pt. 5). Sulerzhitsky himself gives a figure of 1,403 in July 1899 (*To America With the Doukhobors*, 172). His note that 2,140 "Cold Mountains" people settled the North Colony (ibid., 143) is either an error or must have included some of those who settled in the South Colony — some 1,000, according to "Doukhobor Statistics" (NA, RG76, V184 F65101, Pt. 5). Even by 1902, the population was only 1,643 according to Thomas Young's survey (NA, RG15, V754 F494483, Pt. 2). While the 1906 census gives a figure of 2,138, the 1905 figures included in the village files indicate a total of 2,364

In the South Colony, the move from the immigration sheds was hampered by the abnormally cold winter of 1898-99.[63] In early February, McCreary reported to Smart that the ten men he had sent to the "White Sand Colony" were "sadly hampered by cold weather" in getting out timber for the blockhouses being built on Sections 27 and 28 of Township 29, Range 1 (McMunn's Camp), although three houses 24' x 24' were completed.[64] Hubbell also reported activity on Section 30 of Township 29, Range 2, where he had located a timber camp and where houses were to be built.[65] By late March, 500 Doukhobors were reported at the South Colony with houses built for 2,000 more[66] and in April, thirty-eight houses had been built, capable of holding 1,700 to 1,800 people, with more houses being built in Township 31, Range 32, fronting on the Assiniboine River. By this time, 1,200 Doukhobors were located in the South Colony, with another 800 expected.[67] Sulerzhitsky's description of one of these temporary settlements (most likely that of the Kars and Elizavetpol people on Sections 28 and 29 of Township 29, Range 1) gives an impression of disorder and impermanence:

> Huge blockhouses could be seen from a distance, scattered about a cleared space in the poplar forest. Behind the village was a thick forest. These awkward buildings, without windows and with earth piled on the roofs, surrounded with glistening cut-off stumps, gave the impression of something primitive, strong and stubborn. Among the stumps lay many branches left from trees cut down for building logs. Here and there were two or three remaining birches. Behind the buildings there were holes from which clay was taken for sealing the cracks between the logs. Several wagons were scattered, here and there, among the buildings. On one of them a harness had been dropped. Everywhere there were girders, chips, different household articles. Here was an untidy pile of hay. Everywhere one felt a disorder, the absence of a master's hand, and the whole settlement appeared uncomfortable, scattered. Among the buildings, Doukhobor men and women wandered, children warmed themselves in the sun and elders, gathered here and there, conversed.[68]

It was from these temporary quarters that the Doukhobors set out to locate their

---

    people. The Commission lists 2,678 people in September 1906, although this includes the relocated families from the Saskatchewan Colony — 306 in the three villages built for these settlers.

63   There are constant references to the extreme cold of this winter in the correspondence between the surveyors and the Department, for example, Belleau to Deville, 8 March 1899 (NA, RG15, V760 F503047). McCreary noted that this was the coldest winter in the memory of the oldest inhabitants: "This morning, at nine o'clock, when I came down, the thermometer stood at forty four. Last night ... it stood about fifty one, and it has been running from thirty-five to forty-five, with a keen wind, for many weeks." (NA, RG15, V760 F503047, McCreary to Smart, 9 February, 1899).

64   Ibid.

65   NA, RG15, V760 F502904, Hubbell to Deville, 16 February 1899.

66   Ibid., Hubbell to Smart, 20 March 1899.

67   Ibid., Hubbell to Smart, 10 April 1899.

68   Sulerzhitsky, *To America With the Doukhobors*, 148-49.

villages in May 1899. The Cyprus people (the "Wet Mountains" people who came in late May and were waiting to see if they would be able to join their fellow villagers in the North Colony) moved out from the immigration sheds directly to the village sites which they had chosen in the southern part of the South Colony.

The last to locate their settlements were the 2,300 Doukhobors from the Kars region of Transcaucasia who arrived in Canada in early June and remained in the immigration shed at Selkirk until the choice of additional lands was finalized.[69] Delegates of this last contingent travelled to the North Saskatchewan to look over the land which had been selected for them in July,[70] and by early August, the main body of settlers left the immigration sheds, travelled to Saskatoon, and began the process of taking up their lands and building their villages.[71] The Saskatchewan Colony lands were more than sufficient for this group: they established three villages in the southernmost part of the reserve (the Langham area) and seven villages in the northernmost part (the Duck Lake area), leaving the area between essentially empty.

Summary

In June 1899, 7,400 Doukhobors set about as "nostalgic exiles seeking to reproduce home in the wilderness."[72] With a long cultural tradition to draw from and a recent recommitment to fundamental religious principles to sustain them, the Doukhobors appeared to be well equipped to survive and prosper. While the first full year in Canada tested the mettle of the Doukhobors and required the resources of sympathetic co-religionists and government alike for their survival, it also witnessed the building of fifty-seven Old World villages surrounded by scattered plots of tilled land and connected by rudimentary roads and trails. It was a beginning.

---

69 Canada, *Sessional Papers*, Department of the Interior Report, 1900, 112.

70 *Saskatchewan Herald*, 26 July 1899.

71 The manuscript "Doukhobor Statistics" records 1,472(NA, RG76, V184 F65101, Pt. 5) people in the Saskatchewan Colony. It is likely that some of the men were still away working at this time. Approximately 700 to 800 of the last boatload of Kars Doukhobors remained in the South Colony and established their villages there.

72 George Woodcock, "Views of Canadian Criticism," in his *Odysseus Ever Returning* (Toronto: McClelland and Stewart, 1971), 132. In this context, Woodcock is describing the tendency among first-generation colonists to carry their culture with them into the colonies.

Chapter 2
Beginning ~ 1899

By the summer of 1899, the Doukhobors had begun the task of recreating a familiar landscape from the new lands of their reserves. The first and most distinctive imprint on the 750,000 acres of reserved land was their villages and associated fields, replicating the familiar cultural landscape of their recently abandoned homeland. Fifty-seven villages, with plan and architecture as alien to the western Canadian landscape as their names, lined the banks of the Swan, Assiniboine, Whitesand and North Saskatchewan Rivers and dotted the uplands between.

A number of unfortunate circumstances resulted in locating some of the villages outside the confines of the reserved land. On the one hand, the rapid pace of negotiations with, and immigration of, the Doukhobors meant that the reserved lands had not been clearly outlined in time for their arrival. Confusion about the boundaries of the reserves,[1] adjustments of the reserved lands which had to be made in light of larger-than-expected numbers of Doukhobors, delays of surveys owing to a very severe winter, and the complications arising from personnel conflicts,[2] all delayed the clear demarcation of the lands set aside for the Doukhobors. For their part, the Doukhobors misunderstood the precise arrangements under which they were to take up the land, and they were not fully apprised of the reserved sections within the larger reserved blocks (school lands, Hudson's Bay Company lands)[3] all

---

[1] The discussion as to what lands comprised the North Reserve continued until at least March 1903 (NA, RG15, V754 F494483, Pt. 2, Keys to Obed Smith, 21 March 1903).

[2] A large file of correspondence concerning the delays and confusions occasioned by the work (or lack thereof) of one of the surveyors, E.W. Hubbell, attests to the extent to which the very basic task of surveying the Doukhobor lands complicated the process of settlement (NA, RG15, V760 F502904).

[3] The Department of the Interior had little difficulty in arranging for the exchange of railway lands, thus limiting the reserved sections to school and Hudson's Bay Company lands. The early optimism of doing the same with these latter reserves proved to be premature. "Hudson's Bay lands will probably be surrendered. I believe school lands could be had if badly wanted for a village" (NA, RG15, V760 F502904, Deville to Hubbell, 25 January 1899). Confusion over whether the odd-numbered sections in certain townships were to be included persisted until January 1903 (Archer to Moffat, 7 January 1903; Archer to Turriff, 10 January 190[3]).

of which contributed to the confusion over precisely where they could locate their villages.[4]

In a few cases, however, the Doukhobors appear to have located villages outside the reserve by deliberate choice:

> I think Mr. Cote will tell you that it would be almost impossible for me to prevent these people going where they wish. They are very strong-willed, and several villages have settled in districts where they were distinctly told they could not. Mr. Cote will tell you especially of two villages which settled on the edge of Good Spirit Lake, which will certainly have to be removed. The land is unfit for settlement, but notwithstanding all we could do, they were bound to locate there.[5]

In the final analysis, most of the villages were located inside the reserves, but seven villages at least were forced to relocate since they were located on non-reserve land.[6]

But setting aside these general problems, attempting to answer basic questions about how the village sites were chosen and what factors influenced the choices made reveals shifting responsibilities and tantalizingly sketchy information. The Topographical Surveys Branch of the Department of the Interior first assumed general responsibility for locating the villages. "The more I look into it [the problem of settling the Doukhobors in villages]," wrote Surveyor-General Deville to Hubbell, the surveyor initially charged with helping to settle the Doukhobors, "the more I feel that you must not go hap hazard [sic] in locating villages but that you must do so as nearly as possible in accordance with some preconceived plan."[7] Deville was prepared to be quite flexible in the arrangement of the homesteads around the villages, but his strong opinions about a regular and efficient arrangement of the villages reflected a surveyor's mind: "The line between two adjoining villages must

---

[4] One of the surveyors noted that the language problem prevented him from clarifying the reserve boundaries with the people of the three North Colony villages built outside the reserve. It is worth noting, however, that the Doukhobors had already erected about twenty-five houses by this time, so it seems that the clarification, even in the absence of language difficulties, would have been a bit tardy (NA, RG15, V760 F503047, Belleau to Deville, 16 August 1899). Smart gave some encouragement to the Doukhobors of this village a few months later by indicating "it is not at all likely that they will be troubled in their occupation" (NA, RG15, V174 F494483, Pt. 1, Smart to Konegaen, 23 December 1899). This, unfortunately, proved to be unduly optimistic; later the villages were forced to relocate inside the reserve.

[5] NA, RG15, V760 F502904, McCreary to Secretary, Department of the Interior, 16 November 1899.

[6] The North Colony villages of Bogdanofka, Teakomeernoe and Osvoborsdennie were either fully or partially outside the reserve and were subsequently moved, and Vosnisennie was moved from its original location on a Hudson's Bay Company section (a somewhat ironic situation in that the original location was chosen by the surveyor who was charged with overseeing the building of North Colony "blockhouses"). Moisayovo and Kyrillovo were relocated from sites outside the South Colony to the Good Spirit Lake Annex; in the South Colony, Voskrisennie had to be relocated from a school section. Two Saskatchewan Colony villages were located outside the reserve — Spasofka and Tonbofka — but neither was forced to move (although Tonbofka did relocate to the North Colony when Peter Verigin consolidated the Community Doukhobors).

[7] NA, RG15, V760 F502904, Deville to Hubbell, 20 January 1899.

run at 45 degrees from the Meridian" in order to provide for the minimum number of villages possible. Hubbell was instructed to choose "suitable" sites as close to the ideal distance (either four or eight miles) between villages as possible. Finally, he was to devise a system for dividing each quarter section (farms were initially assumed to be eighty acres each), and to draw boundaries between the village lands. Deville sent Hubbell four plans illustrating different village sizes, noting "the immense advantage" of having the villages connected by diagonal roads to the section corner nearest the village. Determining the "right size" of village lots was to be left to the Doukhobors, since likely "they will want a fair size garden, space for stables, barns, etc. There must be a few more village lots than there are farms within the boundaries of the village, so that the size of the village lot will determine the number of acres to be laid out into lots."[8]

Hubbell's response was that he would send out two teams of ten axemen and a foreman to erect buildings in two villages for each colony. When they had begun, he would take about eighty Doukhobors to each colony to be trained in getting out timbers:

> A committee of sixteen intended settlers are [sic] already selected to decide upon villages, hamlets and farm location, and plans of same. They will be instructed to consult with me upon this subject. I will then lay before them your communication of the 20th instant, explaining plans and ideas expressed by you.[9]

Deville revised his instructions when it was clear that the homesteads would be the regular size (160 acres) or larger, and sent along William van Horne's scheme for village settlement based on farms of 320 acres.[10] Deville sent two more settlement plans, expressing a preference for plan No. 6 with villages either 4.2 or 8.4 miles apart, and finally abandoned all specific directives for village location.[11] "All questions relating to the settlement are to be decided by the delegates, one for each village," he wrote the next day, still expressing the hope that the road connections between the villages might be "something like my plan No. 6." He went on to say:

> They propose to establish about twenty villages, say ten in each colony. That will be about one village per township. The villages are to be built along water courses, the lots to be about 4 1/2 acres so as to afford land for large gardens: the villages will therefore be several miles long. The farms are not to be in one block: each family is to have a plot of hay land, a plot of wheat land and so on.[12]

---

8   Ibid.
9   Ibid., Hubbell to Deville, 22 January 1899.
10 Ibid., Deville to Hubbell, 15 January 1899.
11 Ibid., Deville to Hubbell, 26 January 1899.
12 Ibid., Deville to Hubbell, 27 January 1899. The comments about the division of the various kinds of land suggest that Deville may have had in mind a cooperative arrangement similar to that by which the Mennonites had pooled land and redivided it among the families in their reserves. The full scope of the Doukhobors' communal commitment seems not to have been realized.

In the final analysis, the Doukhobors were left to decide the location of their villages without any outside direction, a process which was not begun until the summer of 1899.[13]

According to Maude, the able-bodied men left the immigration halls in early spring to find work, while the women and little children, the sick and the aged, removed to "huge barracks[14] that had been erected during the winter at convenient spots on the Doukhobor reserves," and from there "they selected suitable places for their future residence, and set to work energetically to build their villages. Almost all the villages were built by the Doukhobor women."[15] Tarasoff adds:

> the task of building the homes and cultivating the land [was left] to the women, children, and old men, under the guidance of one or two skilled carpenters in each village.[16]

As to the factors influencing the selection of village sites, Mavor notes that it was important "that the village sites should be carefully selected to have the villages located with due regard to proximity to cultivable land,"[17] a process which consumed much time, considering the area was great and the best judges of land were often old men. Tarasoff observes that the villages were spaced two to four miles apart, "and located so as to give ready access to the surrounding farm land."[18] Referring

---

13 The village sites were selected a month after seeding according to Brabazon, the surveyor who replaced Hubbell in the North Colony: "Doukhobors postponed selecting village sites a month till after seeding. What shall I do?" (NA, RG15, V760 F502904, Telegram, Brabazon to Deville, 27 April 1899). This is in agreement with the earliest list of the thirteen original North Colony villages in early July (Soulerjitzky to McCreary, 9 July 1899; NA, RG15, V754 F494483, Pt. 1) and with Sulerzhitsky's statement that the Doukhobors of the North Colony "began to move from their settlements to their own newly formed villages" in June 1899 (*To America With the Doukhobors*, 165).

14 See Chapter 1, note 60. In the North Colony, two blockhouses were built at what was known as McVey's Camp, along the Swan River just inside the Manitoba border (31-34-29-W1). When it was decided to keep the reserve entirely within the District of Saskatchewan, additional blockhouses were built just across the border on 36-34-30, on a plateau above the Swan River. This became the village of Michaelovo. Eight additional blockhouses were built on SW26-34-30-W1, although this village site had to be relocated as it was on Hudson's Bay Company lands [the original site of Vosnisennie — see Koozma Tarasoff, *A Pictorial History of the Doukhobors* (Saskatoon: Prairie Books, 1969), 69] (NA, RG15, V760 F502904, Hubbell to Smart, 9 March 1899). In the South Colony, three blockhouses had been built by early February under the direction of McMunn, foreman of the timber camp, on Sections 27 and 28, Township 29, Range 1 near a quantity of building timber along Kamsack Creek, but construction was hindered by cold weather (NA, RG76, V183 F65101, Pt. 3, McCreary to Smart, 9 February 1899). By April, thirty-eight houses had been completed on these sites, and more were in progress in another township [Township 31, Range 32] fronting on the Assiniboine River (NA, RG15, V760 F502904, Hubbell to Smart, 10 April 1899). These houses were designed for group accommodation, 75-100 per house, and were built of log. No blockhouses were built in the Saskatchewan Colony.

15 Maude, *A Peculiar People*, 180-81.

16 Tarasoff, *Plakun Trava*, 54-55.

17 Mavor, *My Windows*, 2:9.

18 Tarasoff, *Pictorial History*, 29.

to the South Colony in a subsequent work he adds, "Usually, respected elders walked the prairie and chose a location close to water and shelter."[19]

In all, fifty-seven villages were begun in the summer and fall of 1899: thirteen villages in the North Colony, twenty-four villages in the South Colony and another ten in the Annex, and ten in the Saskatchewan Colony (see Table 1).

The villages were laid out according to the instructions of their leader-in-exile, Peter "Lordly" Verigin, "whereby villages were constructed as they usually are i.e. the houses built in rows according to the lay of the land."[20] These *strassendorfer* (street-villages) were prompted by tradition and dictated by belief (see Figure 1). Not only were these the familiar plans of the *mir*, the settlements of generations of Doukhobors and other Russians, but the first-century Christian belief of having "all things in common" which Verigin had recently revived among the Doukhobors made a compact village plan a necessity. And the Canadian government was agreeable; these agricultural villages had been accommodated twenty-five years earlier when the Mennonites immigrated into southern Manitoba. The "Hamlet Clause," which was introduced to allow them to satisfy the residence requirements of the Dominion Lands Act by living in a village within three miles of the homestead quarter section, was reactivated for the Doukhobors.[21]

In the main, Doukhobor villages had houses facing each other across a wide central street, "so perfectly in line," according to one observer of the Canadian villages, "that we are sure the services of a Dominion land surveyor must have been available when the lines were laid," and in pairs "the mate of one being across the street, the same size to the fraction of an inch ... and not one of them in the smallest degree out of line with the other."[22] This exactitude was occasionally interrupted by topography (see Figure 2), or by other considerations (see Figure 3), and the earliest village descriptions reflect much more variety in both plan and placement than is indicated by Cormie's observation, but regularity and uniformity are quite striking features of individual village plans and architecture. It was also Verigin's "opinion"[23] that they plant trees along the wide central street — shrubbery for windbreaks and fruit trees if the climate would allow. All villages were built along these traditional

---

19 Tarasoff, *Plakun Trava*, 54.

20 P.V. Verigin to L.N. Tolstoy, in Andrew Donskov (ed.), *Leo Tolstoy-Peter Verigin Correspondence* (Ottawa: Legas, 1995), 43.

21 "If a number of homestead settlers, embracing at least twenty families, with a view of greater convenience in the establishment of schools and churches ... ask to be allowed to settle together in a hamlet or village, the Minister may, in his discretion, vary or dispense with the foregoing requirements as to residence, but not as to cultivation of each separate quarter section entered as a homestead" (Dominion Lands Act, 1903, Clause 37, 17).

22 J.A. Cormie, "Will the Doukhobor Survive?" *University Magazine* 10 (1911): 589.

23 As befitting the leader of a group which held the ideal of "no man better than another," Verigin modestly suggested, rather than commanded, knowing full well that these suggestions would be treated with the authority of a biblical edict.

Table 1
List of Doukhobor Villages - November 1899

SOUTH COLONY

Pozeryaevka - Cyprus (Pasariofka)	Efraimovka - Cyprus (Efromovo)
Voscreszenovka - Cyprus (Voskrisennie)	Radivsenovka - Cyprus (Riduonovo)
Vosoyania - Cyprus (Vosziennie)	Nicolaevka - Cyprus (Nickolaievka)
Kaminka - Cyprus	Petrovka - Cyprus (Petrovo)
Troozshdanie - Cyprus (Trusdennie)	Petrovka - Orlovsky (Petrovo)
Terpanie - Orlovsky (Terpennie)	Tambovka - Tambovsky (Tomboscoe)
Smirenovka - Tambovsky (Troodoloobevoe)	Pozeryaevka - Kars (Pasariofka)
Voznyshanie - Kars	Moisaievka - Kars* (Moisayovo)
Kireelovka - Kars* (Kyrillovo)	Blagoveshenka - Kars (Blagovishennie)
Smirenovka - Kars (Smyrennie)	Terpanie - Kars (Terpennie)
Pokrovka - Kars (Prokuratovo)	Spassovka - Kars (Spaskoe)
Verovka - Kars (Vernoe)	Blagodarenovka - Kars (Blagodarnoe)

GOOD SPIRIT LAKE ANNEX

Blagosclonovka (Blagosklonnoe)	Gorelovka (Gorilloe)
Novo-spassovka (Kalmakovo)	Ootyshanie (Ootishennie)
Novo-troitskoe (Nova-Troitzkoe)	Novo-gorelovka (New Gorilloe)
Besyaidovka** (Bisednoe)	Sovyaitovka** (Savetnoe)
Proterpevshe** (Poterpevshe; Otradnoe)	Slovyanka** (Slavyanka)

NORTH COLONY

Novotroitskoe	Bogdanovka (Bogdanofka)
Techomeerovka (Teakomeernoe)	Troitskoe (Troitzkoe)
Oospanie (Oospennie)	Lubomeerovka (Lubomeernoe)
Pokrovka (Procovscoe)	Spassovka (Hlebedarnoe)
Michailovka (Michaelovo)	Stradaevka (Old Libedevo)
Osvosbozshdanie (Osvoborsdennie)	Verovka (Vera)
Voznesenie (Vosnisennie)	

SASKATCHEWAN COLONY

Spasovka 1 (Troitzkaja ?)	Spasovka 2 (Pasariofka ?)
Spasovka 3 (Spasofka ?)	Terpanie (Terpennie)
Gorelovka (Large Horelofka)	Petrovka (Petrofka)
Oospanie (Oospennie)	Kirealovka - Neeshnya (Karilowa)
Kirealovka - Seredna (Bodenofka)	Kirealovka - Vyaknya (Pakrofka)

*Moisaievka (Moisayovo) and Kireelovka (Kyrillovo), originally located outside the reserve, were relocated later to the Good Spirit Lake Annex.
**These Elizavetpol villages were located in the South Colony proper.
Source: NA, RG76, V184 F65101, Pt. 5, "Doukhobor Statistics." Spelling as in the original. The most commonly used name is added in brackets.

lines. Trails — narrow cuts through the bush and twin tracks on the prairies — and later roads, connected the villages.

Modifications to the traditional settlement plan and buildings most often reflected Verigin's instructions regarding a communal way of life:

Figure 1. Plan of Simeonovo, North Colony, 1901 (C.C. Fairchild, D.L.S., Saskatchewan Archives Board (SAB), Saskatoon).

Figure 2. Plan of Spasofka, Saskatchewan Colony, 1909 (C.C. Fairchild, D.L.S., SAB, Saskatoon).

Figure 3. Plan of Michaelovo, North Colony, 1909 (C.C. Fairchild, D.L.S., SAB, Saskatoon).

> Your life in Canada should in my opinion, be on a communal foundation; that is, the absolute necessities like cattle, plows, and other implements as well as granaries and storehouses, grist mills, oil presses, blacksmithshops and woodworking shops, all these in the first years must be built by communal effort; every village commune must be equipped in this manner.[24]

Communalism marked a recent modification of the traditional village organization for the Doukhobors and it affected both plan and architecture. Those who revered Verigin as a "living Christ," took his opinions as divine directives and modified the traditional village plan to accommodate the communal barns and stables, and somewhat later, the community home or *dom*,[25] on larger plots of land, usually near the centre of the village. In building style, the traditional practice of building the house and barn together as one structure gave way to individual houses for the people and communal barns and stables for their animals. The Canadian villages of those Doukhobors, at least initially holding more to tradition (and individualism) than to divine pronouncements, reflected more faithfully their Russian models. They lacked the larger lots devoted to communal structures as well as the communal structures themselves (including the community home), and each farmstead maintained the traditional house-barn combination. The general distinction between the more individualistic Kars Doukhobors of the Saskatchewan Colony, and the communal settlements of the North and South Colonies, may explain some variations in building style within villages as well.[26]

The first buildings were constructed of local materials as the new settlers attempted to reproduce familiar architectural styles with the materials at hand. They were thoroughly foreign, neither borrowing nor modifying New World models. In their architecture, a contemporary traveller observed, "they are as yet absolutely insensitive to Western influences."[27] It is difficult to ascertain exactly what the earliest buildings looked like since most of the descriptions and photographs (and relict buildings) are from 1902 and later. It is also not clear which of the first buildings (and how many) were merely temporary "make-do" shelters and thus unlikely to reflect any particular architectural style, and which were substantial enough to be constructed according to traditional models. The "half dug-outs" noted in an early survey[28] seem clearly to be shelters constructed for temporary use (see Figure 4), but the log, log and sod, and perhaps many of the more substantial "sod" structures[29]

---

24 Quoted in J.F.C. Wright, *Slava Bohu* (New York: Farrar & Rinehart, 1940), 132.

25 See note 49, this chapter.

26 Carl J. Tracie, "Ethnicity and Settlement in Western Canada: Doukhobor Village Settlement in Saskatchewan," in B.M. Barr (ed.), *Western Canadian Research in Geography: The Lethbridge Papers* (Vancouver: Tantalus Research, 1975), 67-76. See the discussion on page 40 of Bernard's description of the traditional house-stable combination of Independent Ivan Ivin in the communal North Colony village of Michaelovo.

27 A.G. Bradley, *Canada in the Twentieth Century* (London: Constable, 1905), 298.

28 NA, RG76, V184 F65101, Pt. 5, "Doukhobor Statistics."

29 The term "sod" seems to have been used somewhat loosely and covered a range of building

Figure 4. Temporary earthen huts, winter 1899-1900 (British Columbia Provincial Archives (BCA) HP46958).

were of the latter type. Belleau's description of the twenty-five log houses (14' x 33') of Bogdanofka and Techomeerovka (Teakomeernoe) in August 1899 as "well plastered and comfortable and warm" suggests permanent, no doubt traditional, structures.[30] Even the "mud" or "willow and plaster" buildings of Kaminka in the South Colony were substantial enough to have reflected the Doukhobor building tradition. They were still being used three years later[31] and most likely were used until the village was abandoned about 1906. On the other hand, many of the smaller, initial structures were modified almost immediately. In his survey of the northern-most villages of Troitzkoe and Oospennie, Aylsworth described the early houses as "of a small size and rough character, each containing one, two, and three families,

---

materials. Some may have been actual sod houses, that is houses whose walls were built up with strips of sod or sod "bricks," including buildings described by others as "half dug-outs" — structures dug down three feet or so into the earth with sods heaped on a pole frame. These, according to early photographs, had no particular architectural style, although they did follow the long, narrow rectangular plan evident in the later, more permanent houses. In other cases, the term was used to describe houses which more discerning observers noted were built of poles and clay, or described as "willow and plaster." And, in some early photos of "sod" houses, the term was used to describe log structures whose roofs were layered with sods.

30   NA, RG15, V760 F503047, Belleau to Deville, 16 August 1899.
31   According to McCallum's 1902 survey, this village had twenty-seven houses of "poles and clay" (which would be analogous, I assume, to the "Doukhobor Statistics" description of "willow and plaster" as the building material). These were substantial houses: 14' x 40' (NA, RG15, V754 F494483, Pt. 2, N.G. McCallum Report).

but the Doukhobors are continually building, improving and enlarging their houses."[32]

Elina Thorsteinson was the first to attempt some sort of areal differentiation of Doukhobor architecture on the basis of building materials. She noted three basic kinds of houses distinguished by construction materials, each reflecting the environment in which the village was located. Houses of logs were built in wooded areas, while in prairie areas "they built wonderfully neat and compact houses of sod,"[33] adding a reference to "half dug-outs," perhaps describing the very earliest of the temporary houses some built.[34] A third type of house, in a village lacking both timber and sod, was

> made in a remarkably ingenious manner by the use of poplar sticks five or six inches in diameter. These poles were driven in to the ground one foot apart to form an enclosure thirty by twenty feet, and in and out of these, willow withes were tightly woven like baskets. The whole structure when completed was plastered inside and out by the women who used their hands as trowels in plastering the walls with a thick tenacious clayey mixture.[35]

This description would appear to fit the houses built in the South Colony village of Kaminka, described variously as constructed of "willow and plaster,"[36] of "mud,"[37] of "poles and clay,"[38] and of "willow and clay."[39]

Harvey's November 1899 schedule designates the building materials of most of the houses in three similar categories: log, log and sod (or sod and log), and sod, although it is not clear just exactly what he meant by "log and sod." The only departure from these categories is the "mud" houses of Kaminka.[40]

Lally Bernard observed four kinds of houses: log houses plastered inside and out with a "cold clay paste" made of water, clay and chopped grass; houses made of mud bricks with turf roofs;[41] houses built of "sods, neatly covered with plaster;" and willow

---

32 C.F. Aylsworth, Surveyor's Field Book #7397, 1900.

33 Elina Thorsteinson, "The Doukhobors in Canada," *Mississippi Valley Historical Review* 4 (June 1917): 30.

34 See Tarasoff, *Pictorial History*, 66.

35 Thorsteinson, "The Doukhobors in Canada," 30.

36 NA, RG76, V184 F65101, Pt. 5, "Doukhobor Statistics."

37 Ibid., William B. Harvey, "Schedule of Doukhobor Villages and Statistics."

38 In McCallum's more detailed report of 1902, six South Colony villages, with a total of 128 houses and twenty-six stables, used this building technique (NA, RG15, V754 F494483, Pt. 2).

39 Lally Bernard [May Fitzgibbon], *The Canadian Doukhobor Settlements* (Toronto: William Briggs, 1899), Appendix.

40 NA, RG76, V184 F65101, Pt. 5, Harvey, "Schedule."

41 A construction technique used in the Wet Mountains of the Transcaucasus and later by the Cyprus settlers (Woodcock and Avakumovic, *The Doukhobors*, 127).

Figure 5. Thatched roof house — Kalmakoff (Kalmakovo) (Good Spirit Lake Annex), c. 1907 (BCA HP86809).

Figure 6. Doukhobor house near Saskatoon, c. 1905 (Glenbow-Alberta Archives (GAA) PA-100-9).

Figure 7. Doukhobor house near Carlton, Saskatchewan, September 1902 (GAA NA-949-103).

Figure 8. Women and children placing turf [it is actually thatch] on pioneer Doukhobor house in village of Petrofka, ten miles south of present town of Kamsack, 1905 (BCA HP86812).

Figure 9. Doukhobor village in Saskatchewan (Vosnisennie, North Colony), c. 1901 (BCA HP46990).

Figure 10. Khristianovka (Moisayovo), near Buchanan, c. 1910 (SAB B-2113).

Figure 11. Doukhobor house near Carlton, Saskatchewan, 1902 (GAA NA-949-102).

and clay houses.[42] Some of the sod houses may have included the "half dug-outs" mentioned by "Doukhobor Statistics."

In a more recent survey of Doukhobor architecture, Mealing recognizes three distinct types of house, distinguished by style rather than materials: mud-plastered houses ("probably" of log) with perimeter porch, a full loft and a thatched roof; houses with "low, flat-ridged sod roof supported by purlins and supplemented by a side-length pent-roof"; and a third "essentially identical" to the second, but with a taller thatched roof.[43] The photo used to illustrate the third is similar to the Ukrainian houses built in western Canada, with a hipped rather than a gable roof.[44] Contemporary photos illustrating this type are rare; the first two types are the rule.[45]

The high-lofted structures appear to be the norm in the North and the South Colonies (see Figure 5), and the low-profile structures characteristic of the house-barn combinations of the Saskatchewan Colony (see Figure 6), although contemporary photos occasionally show departures from this generalization (see Figure 7). Simeonovo appears to be the only village in the North Colony where the low-profile house occurred, and even there, they were decidedly in the minority (see Figure 8). Bernard's description of Oospennie in 1899 as "this quaintly-built mass of chalet-like houses, built of mud bricks with turf roofs"[46] suggests the characteristic style of the North Colony, but also introduces confusion in the matter of materials. No other source suggests sods or mud bricks as building materials for the houses of Oospennie (see the discussion of Oospennie and Troitzkoe in Chapter 3). It might be argued that her description fits the earliest "half dug-outs" which housed some of the Doukhobors through the first winter and which were quickly replaced with more substantial log houses, but they were hardly "chalet-like," and these, it seems, were limited to the make-do shelters of late summer in the Saskatchewan Colony. Bernard does go on to say that the houses were coated with a clay plaster and gives a detailed description of the clay-making and clay-plastering process used on the log houses.[47]

Taking into account both style and materials, the evidence in the North Colony points to full-lofted, clay-plastered log houses (Mealing's first category) without attached barns, having roofs with overhanging and often boxed gables and eaves

---

42   Bernard, *The Canadian Doukhobor Settlements*, 15, 30, 60, 64-65.

43   Mark Mealing, "Doukhobor Architecture," *Canadian Ethnic Studies* 16 (1984): 73-88.

44   Ibid., 75, 78.

45   The only contemporary evidence I have seen of similar roof types is the thatched, hipped roofs used in the temporary half dug-outs constructed in a few localities, and the roof of a partially-visible structure fronting the central street in an unnamed village (British Columbia Archives, Catalogue #HP86725, Negative E-7286; see Figure 30, chapter 4). An unlocated and undated photograph captioned "Typical Doukhobor farm" also shows a house and a stable (?) in this style (Saskatchewan Archives Board, photograph #A7459).

46   Bernard, *The Canadian Doukhobor Settlements*, 15.

47   Ibid., 16, 64-65.

ornamented with dadoes and extending out to full-perimeter or half-perimeter porches in many houses. In some villages, these houses were as uniform and ordered as those noted by Cormie (see Figure 9).[48]

In the South Colony, the photographic evidence indicates a somewhat more mixed architectural style, although the full-lofted log houses appear to be more common than the low, double-purlin houses (see Figure 10). Despite the appearance of isolated examples of the full-lofted houses in the Saskatchewan Colony, the original villages appear to have been uniformly of the low-profile type (see Figure 11).

The community homes[49] built in the North and South Colonies were similar in external appearance to the high-lofted houses, differing from them more in size and ornamentation than in style. These community gathering places tended to be larger than most houses, brick-clad in most cases, and ornamented with metal filigree in the upper gables and along the roof ridge. They usually featured a small balcony in the boxed gable, built to allow their leader to address an open-air gathering of the villagers. (Some of the homes also had similar balconies.) A few such structures remain to the present: Gromovoe's community home (North Colony) was moved to the National Doukhobor Heritage Village at Veregin and restored there; the community homes of Vosnisennie, Oospennie, and Procovskoe (North Colony), Vosziennie and Voskrisennie (South Colony) remain on the sites of their respective villages. Each adheres to a common plan (see Figures 12 and 13).[50] No community homes were built as part of the villages in the Saskatchewan Colony.[51]

The basic distinction between the individual houses and the house-barn combinations briefly noted above reflects differences in the method of agricultural production. The more individualistic settlers in the Saskatchewan Colony, in the main, built the traditional Russian house-barn combination, since the livestock and

---

48   Cormie, "Will the Doukhobor Survive?," 589.

49   The term "community home" or *dom* is used to refer to the building used for religious and community meetings of the villagers. In their wholesale rejection of the trappings of institutionalized religion, the Doukhobors avoided the idea of a church as a specialized structure for religious worship, which they regarded as opposed to spiritual individualism. Although some used the term "prayer home" to identify these multipurpose meeting places, most preferred the more neutral designation "community home" to avoid any connotation of a specifically religious structure. The officials who collected information about the early villages used a variety of terms for these structures, club houses, council houses, and meeting houses being the most common. Extant community homes range from eighteen to twenty-four feet wide and from fifty-six to fifty-eight feet long (field notes 1973, 1974, 1992). According to the village files, the community homes were built beginning in 1905.

50   Although only half the community home of Vosnisennie remains and the *dom* at Procovskoe is of sawn lumber without any evidence of the brick cladding characteristically added to many community homes, all are built to a common plan. Contemporary photos of community homes at Libedevo and Lubomeernoe, and photos from South Colony villages, as well as the recently dismantled community home at Spaskoe, provide additional corroboration of this statement.

51   Two prayer homes were built in the Horelowka (Horelofka) area but were not a part of either of the villages of Large or Small Horelofka (Blaine Lake School, "Our Historical Blaine Lake," mimeographed typescript, 1957), 27.

Figure 12. Community home, Gromovoe, North Colony (SAB).

Figure 13. Community home, Oospennie, North Colony, 1975. Log, mud-plastered house in the background (author's photo).

the produce were owned individually. The communally minded settlers of the other two reserves, however, modified the traditional form by eliminating the barn section of the house in favour of communally built and shared barns.[52] However, the situation in the North Colony may not have been so straightforward. Bernard describes Ivan Ivin's house in Michaelovo as "the best house in the village, three rooms and a stable" and then later describes another North Colony village where "all were busily engaged in building their log houses, in many cases putting the stable at the end of the house, with a door communicating with the main building."[53] The explanation may lie in the fact that some of the North Colony villagers were of an independent turn of mind, especially in the earliest period of settlement. Herbert Archer, the Quaker teacher living in the North Colony village of Vera wrote in August 1900: "Among the Swan River villages there are three really communistic and likely to remain so; one is avowedly individualistic, and in the rest is war: individualists versus communists."[54] In Michaelovo, home of Ivan Ivin, the war was particularly sharp:

> There is a disposition amongst the people to move the village, the only discoverable reason being that they might be removed from the Independents. They have the foundation of [the] Club House building [community home] erected but are removing it as the house of an independent is opposite.[55]

It is also possible that Bernard's description of the "other" North Colony village was of Troitzkoe, a village of independent Doukhobors who left the communal structure of nearby Oospennie.

Generally, then, single or double houses with communal barns and other storage structures were the norm for the North and South Colony villages, while the traditional house-barn combination was the standard structure in the Saskatchewan Colony villages; departures from this generalization are indicated but they appear to be relatively rare.[56]

The collective effect of transplanted plan and architecture was to produce villages which "looked as if they had been carried over from Russia to Canada in one piece"[57] and, of course, which bore a striking family resemblance to each other.

---

52 Tarasoff, *Pictorial History*, 75; Tracie, "Ethnicity and Settlement in Western Canada," 72.
53 Bernard, *The Canadian Doukhobor Settlements*, 27, 32.
54 Quoted in Maude, *A Peculiar People*, 253.
55 NA, RG15, V1167 F5412457, 1905 schedule, Michaelovo village file. At least two incidents reveal Ivin's hard-nosed independent tendencies (Maude, *A Peculiar People*, 64; NA, RG76, V184 F65101, Pt. 5, Anonymous typescript).
56 Saskatchewan Archives Board (Saskatoon), Doukhobor Village Plans.
57 Peter Maloff, "The Christian Community of Universal Brotherhood" (unpublished typescript, 1948), Peter Maloff Papers, University of British Columbia Special Collections, 6. Dr. J.I. Perevereseff, born in the village of Goreloye (Horelofka) near Blaine Lake, expresses the same sentiment: "I clearly remember a typical Russian village of log buildings with sod roofs, exact replicas of the homes that they so recently abandoned in Russian Transcaucasia. It seems as if some giant had

The fields which accompanied these early villages ranged from little more than garden-size patches in the nearest natural openings for the poorest villages to small, scattered fields totalling five to ten acres for some of the more "prosperous" villages.

It is tempting to suggest a general association between field pattern and agricultural system: small, scattered fields of the individualists contrasting with the larger, more cohesive, communally worked fields surrounding the villages of those adhering to the communal way of life. The evidence seems to indicate otherwise, at least as it relates to the communal villages. Herbert Archer noted that the seventy-two acres cultivated by the village of Vosnisennie were comprised of fourteen different parcels,[58] and Thomas Young, in his 1902 survey of the North Colony villages, noted, "Broken areas are in small detached pieces" in the village of Pakrovka (Procovskoe).[59] John Seale, a homestead inspector, commented on the difficulty of determining the amount of cultivated land on the Doukhobor holdings in late 1905: "As to measuring the land it will necessarily be slow as their plowed land has been broken or plowed in many small patches and in all manner of shapes and forms so it will require careful measuring to get a correct estimate of the cultivated lands."[60]

At least in the early cultural landscapes, the picture of large, communally cultivated fields immediately adjacent to the village communes, based on the logic that a communal system of agriculture would produce larger and more concentrated fields than would an individualistic system, is at least unrepresentative and may be largely false.[61] Instead, a group of people, poorly provisioned and inadequately equipped, faced with the immediate challenge of growing enough staples to survive the first winter, chose scattered patches of the most easily tilled land as a focus for their energies. They had neither time nor resources for the niceties of tidily squared fields or large clearing operations. In 1899, this was survival agriculture. Even in the South Colony, where open, scrubby grassland comprised fairly large sections of the natural landscape, the fields tended to be small and scattered.[62] Also, any

---

    bodily lifted them off their native soil, transported them across the ocean and set them down gently, without disturbing anything, on the Saskatchewan prairie." Interview with Dr. J.I. Pereverseff," *Mir* 2, nos. 1 and 2 (May 1974): 12.

58 NA, RG76, V184 F65101, Pt. 5, Herbert Archer to McCreary, 15 June 1900.

59 NA, RG15, V757 F494483, Pt. 2, Thomas Young, "Report."

60 NA, RG15, V755 F494483, Pt. 4, John Seale to P.G. Keyes, 17 October 1905.

61 I have contributed to this misrepresentation in an earlier article. See C.J. Tracie, "Ethnicity and the Prairie Environment: Patterns of Old Colony Mennonite and Doukhobor Settlement," in R. Allen (ed.), *Man and Nature on the Prairies* (Regina: Canadian Plains Research Center, 1976), 50.

62 For example, in McCallum's report of 1902, smaller villages such as Old Voskrisennie and Nickolaievka had fields of two to twenty-five acres on three and four quarter sections of land respectively, while the larger villages did have larger, but also more widely scattered, fields; Old Kaminka, fields of five to sixty acres on eight quarter sections; and Najersda, fields of five to 100 acres on nine quarter sections. It must be noted that the "fields" are total acreages on a particular quarter, and may have been divided into several parcels within the quarter. The 100 acres cultivated on the village quarter of Najersda would be the closest approximation to the "ideal" picture, but

generalization about field patterns and agricultural organization must take into account the fluctuation between individual and communal organization that marked the life of most villages, especially in the first three or four years of settlement.

Villages, fields, trails — these were the components of the incipient cultural landscape of the Doukhobors. In the case of the village-and-field component of the settlement landscape, variations in beliefs and environmental realities modified traditional plans and systems, architecture, and building materials. The interplay among these factors and the initial cultural landscapes produced in each of the three reserves is the subject of the next three chapters.

Summary: Doukhobor Houses

The "houses" first built in several Doukhobor villages were large log structures built as temporary shelters for the group in a few central locations in the North and South Reserves. Canadian axemen put together these "blockhouses" as quickly and efficiently as possible with no concern for style or ornamental detail, and they were quickly abandoned and dismantled after the Doukhobors began constructing their own villages. In the Saskatchewan Colony, some of the Kars people lived in "dug-out" homes the first winter. A few were reported to be dug into the banks of the North Saskatchewan River, and some were no doubt temporary sod houses with floors dug below the surface about three feet and low turf walls and roof rafters covered with sod completing the "half dug-outs." These crude buildings were mere shelters, not homes, and included few reminders of peasant Russian architecture.

As the Doukhobors left the temporary shelters to establish permanent dwellings in their villages, they brought with them the architectural heritage of their homeland. Village plan and building design replicated homeland settlements, although differing religious perspectives introduced some modifications of traditional structures. The first permanent buildings were constructed of locally-available materials as the new settlers attempted to reproduce familiar architectural styles with the materials at hand. According to contemporary observers, the houses were thoroughly foreign, neither borrowing nor modifying New World models.

Two styles of houses dominated the villages. The "high-lofted" house, as the term suggests, had a second floor under the steeply pitched gable roof. The roof projected out over the gable ends giving a chalet-like appearance to the dwelling. The street-facing gable end was often boxed in, or occasionally had a door opening out onto a small balcony. The eaves were ornamented with dadoes and extended out over an open verandah supported by a row of pillars which ran along one or two sides of the house, or, in a few houses, right around the house. These houses were constructed of log or an ingenious combination of small logs and sod. In both, the structures were plastered inside and out with a chopped-straw and clay paste which dried to a hard, smooth surface. A coating of whitewash and some blue trim completed the finish. Originally thatched with slough grass streaked with mud, the roofs were later covered with shingles. These were imposing structures, twelve to fourteen feet wide and thirty to forty feet long. The high-lofted style was characteristic of the Community villages of the North and South Colonies where houses were built as separate structures and rarely attached to the barn as was the traditional practice. In the Community villages, barns and stables were built and used communally; the houses were occupied

---

this was three years after the initial cultivation pattern I have been describing. Even here, one adjacent quarter (SW24) had only twenty acres cultivated while another quarter (SE13) more than a mile away, had sixty acres cultivated (NA, RG15, V757 F494483, Pt. 2, "Report").

by individual families, although these were often extended families with two or three generations represented.

The second prevailing style was the "low-lofted" house. The projecting gable roof and open, pillared verandahs around the house were similar in form to the high-lofted type, however the profile was quite different. These were one-storey houses with low-pitched gable roofs. Gables were rarely boxed and a small window was the only indication that the upper portion of some of the houses might be used for storage. Beyond variations in dimension, the only structural distinction among these houses was between the single-purlin and double-purlin roof construction. In single-purlin houses, one timber was used as support for the roof rafters, while in a double-purlin house, two timbers were used, resulting in a flat, rather than a peaked, roof ridge. Houses were constructed of log or of sod (the latter with walls nearly three feet thick) and were plastered inside and out. The low-pitched gable roofs were often covered with sod as well, although thatch was sometimes used.

The houses were of similar dimensions to the high-lofted type, but since they were usually constructed in the traditional manner of connecting the house to the barn or stable, the plan of the full structure was much more elongated. Some of the larger house-barn combinations were fourteen feet wide and 100 or more feet long. This second type of house dominated the villages of the Saskatchewan Colony. Although the general association of the high-lofted type with the North and South Colonies, and the traditional low-lofted house-barn combination with the more independently minded Saskatchewan Colony is supported by contemporary evidence, there were exceptions as well. A few isolated examples of the high-lofted style appear in early photographs of the Saskatchewan Colony settlements (see Figure 7). Several low-lofted structures are evident in the North and South Colony villages, but some of these appear to be stables rather than houses.

The community homes built in the North and South Colonies were similar in external appearance to the high-lofted houses, differing from them more in size and ornamentation than in style. They had the overhanging gable roof which was flattened in a "bellcast"[63] on the sides to encompass a perimeter verandah, and the traditional side entrance. These community gathering places tended to be larger than most houses — eighteen to twenty-four feet wide and fifty-six to fifty-eight feet long — and were clad in locally made brick in most cases, and ornamented with metal filigree in the upper gables and along the roof ridge. They usually featured a small balcony in the boxed gable, built to allow their leader a visible platform from which to address an open-air gathering of the villagers. It appears that no community homes were built in the original villages in the Saskatchewan Colony, although at least two were constructed near villages in the succeeding years.

---

63   "Bellcast" is an architectural term describing the practice of flattening the roof just at the eaves to produce a bell-like roof profile.

Chapter 3
The North Colony ~ 1899

The North Colony was the most compact of the three colonies, and in many respects the most cohesive in the outlook and practice of its people. Approximately 1,400 of the Wet Mountains people (the *Kholodenskie* or "banished"[1]) from the high plateau region north of Tiflis who came on the first boat began to move there in stages beginning in February 1899. A thousand more of the Wet Mountains people from the ill-fated Cyprus colony were to join them in May, but there was insufficient agricultural land to accommodate them (although one "Cyprus" village, Kaminka, did relocate from the South Colony to the North Colony some five years later). All but one of the thirteen villages established in early summer were communal — Troitzkoe was built by individualistic Doukhobors who left the neighbouring village of Oospennie[2] — although Michaelovo and Vosnisennie each had a few individualistic families.[3]

Village Location

In view of general statements made about what the Doukhobors were looking for in choosing their lands and locating their villages — wood, water, proximity to

---

1   So named since they were banished from their high plateau villages north of Tiflis to take up lands in four valleys in the vicinity of Batoum, Georgia after the burning of the arms in 1895 (Woodcock and Avakumovic, *The Doukhobors*, 104-5).

2   Tarasoff, *Plakun Trava*, 64.

3   The whole matter of designating villages according to organization is anything but straightforward. Bonch-Breuvitch distinguished between villages which were "collectivist" (agricultural produce and equipment shared but profits divided among all) and "true communists" (profits placed in a village fund and the means of production held in common); see Kathlyn R.M. Szalasznyj, "The Doukhobor Homestead Crisis" (M.A. thesis, University of Saskatchewan, 1977), 75. Ashworth's report of May 1901 uses four categories: communistic (production and distribution), communistic (divided into more than one commune), partly communistic and partly individualistic, and individualistic. In his assessment, ten of the North Colony villages are indicated as communistic, two partly communistic and partly individualistic, and one individualistic; see C.A. Dawson, *Group Settlement* (Toronto: Macmillan, 1936), 13. The manuscript "Doukhobor Statistics" (NA, RG76, V184 F65101, Pt. 5) compiled in the fall of 1899 indicated all thirteen villages as communistic.

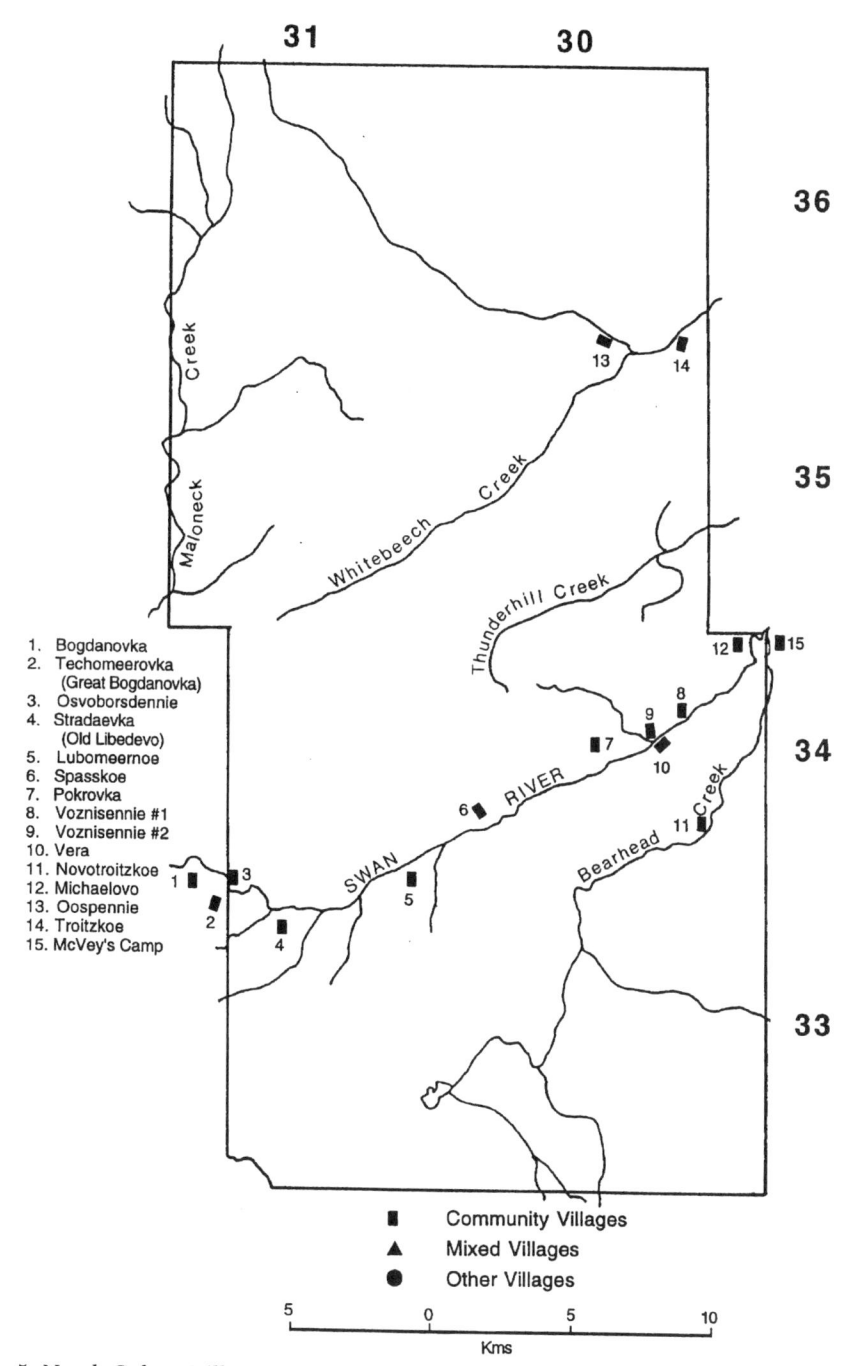

1. Bogdanovka
2. Techomeerovka
   (Great Bogdanovka)
3. Osvoborsdennie
4. Stradaevka
   (Old Libedevo)
5. Lubomeernoe
6. Spasskoe
7. Pokrovka
8. Voznisennie #1
9. Voznisennie #2
10. Vera
11. Novotroitzkoe
12. Michaelovo
13. Oospennie
14. Troitzkoe
15. McVey's Camp

■ Community Villages
▲ Mixed Villages
● Other Villages

Map 5. North Colony Villages — 1899.

agricultural land and to railroads, adequate spacing between villages — it is worth examining the sites actually chosen to see how these factors were practically assessed. An evaluation of these sites is particularly fruitful since their choice initially was made without any of the restricting regularities of individual homestead entries, or concerns for already occupied land. In a very real sense, the Doukhobors built their villages where they wished. The sites, then, should reflect accurately their locational priorities at the time.

Surface water, particularly streams, clearly influenced the siting of the original villages of the North Colony (see Map 5). Deville had indicated as early as January 1899 that the Doukhobors wanted to locate their villages along water courses[4] and all thirteen of the original village sites were in close proximity either to the Swan River (ten villages), its tributary, Bearshead Creek (one village), or Whitebeech Creek, a tributary of the Woody River (two villages).

Three of the five villages built in subsequent years were sited along streams: Kaminka on Bearshead Creek (relocated from the South Colony); Perehodnoe and Archangelskoe on a branch of Maloneck Creek, a tributary of the Swan River. Streams also figured prominently in the sites chosen for villages which, for one reason or another, moved from their original location. There were at least eight[5] of these relocations; in five, the new sites were adjacent to streams. The old village of Bogdanofka, originally located outside the reserved land and forced to move to a site within the reserve, initially chose a non-stream site, but soon moved again to a location along Whitebeech Creek; this third incarnation was named Boghumdanoe. Bogdanofka's sister village outside the reserve, Tichomeerofka or Teakomeernoe (also sometimes identified as Great Bogdanofka), moved to a location along Bearshead Creek. The village of Osvoborsdennie moved from a site straddling the reserve boundary to a site a little more than a mile east and a few hundred yards farther from the Swan River, but near a small lake.[6] Stradaevka (or Old Libedevo as it is called in the village files) moved from its original location adjacent to the Swan River to a non-stream site, but within a few hundred yards of a small lake; it was renamed Libedevo. The transplanted South Colony village of Kaminka moved again to a non-stream location some ten miles west (New Kaminka), Procovskoe moved almost two miles due south across the Swan River to a site along Bearshead Creek, and Lubomeernoe moved back from the Swan River to a site on a small,

---

4   NA, RG15, V760 F502904, Deville to Hubbell, 27 January 1899.

5   The probable relocation of Michaelovo from a site right on the Swan River to a location overlooking the river, and of Spasskoe (Hlebedarnoe) within the same quarter section are not included.

6   Herbert Archer mentions three villages outside the reserve in Townships 33 and 34, Range 32 (NA, RG15, V754 F494483, Pt. 1, Archer to McCreary, 26 May 1900), although in subsequently supporting a petition to allow them to remain where they are, only two villages — Bogdanofka and Techomeerovka (Teakomeernoe) — are mentioned (NA, RG15, V754 F494483, Pt. 2, Archer to McCreary, 12 June 1900); it appears the third may well have been Osvoborsdennie (see note 17, this chapter).

unnamed tributary creek. Of the twenty-six original or subsequent village sites chosen, then, twenty-one appear to have been influenced by the presence of streams.

The role of cultivable or suitable agricultural land is less clearly influential than surface water in village location in the North Colony. If it is assumed that a relationship exists between the "best" agricultural land and certain vegetation characteristics, the description of the vegetation cover supplied by surveyors as they ran the survey lines provides the detail necessary to assess this relationship (see Map 2, Chapter 1). Based on the further assumption that the most desirable land for agricultural purposes would be prairie or parkland — combining the advantages of minimal clearing and good soils — what is striking about the relationship of village location to a detailed reconstruction of vegetation based on the surveyors' notes is the apparent disregard for good agricultural land. Only one of the original villages located in what is described as "prairie," and three others located in what might be designated as "scrubby prairie." The other nine villages located in areas where the notes describe a more closed cover of smaller trees, together with *brûlé*, indicating a second-growth cover following a fire.[7] If the village locations are assessed in the context of the vegetation cover of the available land in the whole reserve, it is apparent that large parcels of open or scrubby prairie were passed by, apparently in order to be close to a water supply.

Of the five villages built after 1899, only Perehodnoe located in prairie. Archangelskoe located in heavy timber while the other villages located in areas of vegetation similar to the original sites. There was even some indication that previously occupied prairie land might be abandoned for more timbered land. The Doukhobors were very "emphatic in their desire to retain" Township 36, Ranges 30 and 31, a matter of some concern "especially in view of the fact that they are desirous of moving some of those who are now living on the open prairie into country which is more wooded."[8]

Another way of assessing the importance of this variable is to use the summary assessment made by the surveyors of the agricultural capability of the townships they surveyed. According to these assessments, the Doukhobors were being attracted by something more important than agricultural capability. The surveyors described as most favourable the lands of Township 33, Range 30, a township completely avoided by the original villagers and subsequently occupied by only two villages — Kaminka and Teakomeernoe. In fact, Kaminka was subsequently moved to a neighbouring

---

7   The original thirteen villages were located as follows with respect to vegetation cover: Oospennie — scattered poplar scrub; Troitzkoe — prairie; Michaelovo — willow scrub, dry and green; Vera — thick willow, dry and green; Vosnisennie — scrub willow and alder, thick; Procovskoe — thick poplar, willow and alder with windfall; Novo Troitzkoe (Simeonovo) — willow and alder scrub with windfall; Spasskoe (Hlebedarnoe) — open willow scrub; Lubomeernoe — willow scrub with poplar and spruce *brûlé*; Stradaevka (Old Libedevo) — light *brûlé* and scattered poplar; Osvoborsdennie — light scrub and *brûlé*; Teakomeernoe — light scrub; Bogdanofka — light scrub and *brûlé*.

8   NA, RG15, V754 F494483, Pt. 3, Obed Smith to Secretary, Department of the Interior, 9 March 1903.

township, leaving only Teakomeernoe in this township which the surveyor Aylsworth ranked as "the best of any of the Township[s] I have surveyed."[9]

There was, of course, a tension between choosing good farmland (assumed to be the more open prairie areas) and the need for timber for building. The Doukhobors had rejected one of the blocks of potential reserved land because it lacked building timber, and they continued to put a high premium on treed locations, as Smith's memo above confirms. The Wet Mountains people from the treeless plateau in the Transcausus especially, knew well the hardships of life without timber for building and heating. It was true that the more open land could be brought into production more quickly and the soils were usually of better quality (and, in fact, the villagers gave their attention to the small prairie patches where they existed for the first cultivation), but a village location central to this kind of land meant that timber supplies were likely to be distant.

Bernard commented on the difficulties imposed by such a location by noting that occasionally houses were put together near a bluff of trees, and then taken apart and reconstructed on the village site. The labour saved in moving only those materials which would actually be used apparently outweighed the labour involved in erecting, dismantling, and re-erecting the structure.[10] A village site close to building timber conserved this energy, particularly crucial where the task of building the villages, including hauling the logs, was usually left to the old men, women and children while the men were away at work. People often substituted for draught animals owing to the scarcity of horses and oxen, and this made a dauntingly difficult task even more demanding. Sulerzhitsky gives a moving account of meeting a sad trio, "a no-longer-young, bowed woman" together with a "brown old man on bent legs, and a youth as long as a pole" hauling a pine log on a crude cart for a barn they were building at their village of Osvobozhdenie (Osvoborsdennie). He observed that their slow, painful struggle was exacerbated by poor and insufficient food.[11] Especially in the central and southern sections of the North Colony, the land along the streams also contained, in many cases, the largest trees. The combined advantages of water and building timber at streamside locations apparently outweighed the long-term advantage of good soil.

One final factor thought to influence village location was the allocation of sufficient farmland to each village.[12] The pattern of the original villages shows little concern for the kind of efficient spacing which Deville originally envisioned. Far from his ideal of uniformly spaced villages, diagonally distanced at 4.2 miles or 8.4 miles apart,[13] the striking feature of the initial village placement is the tight grouping

---

9 C.F. Aylsworth, Surveyor's Notebook #7395, 1900.
10 Bernard, *The Canadian Doukhobor Settlements* 33.
11 Sulerzhitsky, *To America With the Doukhobors*, 193-94.
12 Tarasoff, *Pictorial History*, 29; Mavor, *My Windows*, 9.
13 NA, RG15, V760 F502904, Deville to Hubbell, 26 January 1899.

of several "clusters" of villages. On the western edge of the reserve, one cluster of three villages located within one-half mile of each other with another village barely a mile away. One of these villages was by far the largest of all the North Colony villages, and the other three larger than the average. Another cluster of three villages bunched together within 1.2 miles of each other towards the eastern edge of the reserve. Five villages were spaced out more generously along the line of the Swan River between these two clusters, while a third "cluster" of two villages about one mile apart stood in splendid isolation some eight to ten miles north of the nearest villages, separated from them by the rough lands of Thunder Hill. Subsequent additions and relocations dispersed the pattern somewhat, but even at the peak of settlement, the concentration along the rivers and streams of Township 34 in Ranges 30 and 31 is still apparent.

As to other site characteristics, a general preference for an elevated site seems apparent. Michaelovo's original site near the edge of the Swan River was abandoned for a location "on a lovely plateau overlooking the old site."[14] All but two of the eighteen sites surveyed by Fairchild in 1909 reflect a similar preference for elevated plateaus or ridges: Vera and Vosnisennie were located on bottom land near the river.[15] There is no indication that rail lines, either actual or proposed, had any influence on the siting of the villages.

In sum, the sources suggest that the major factors considered in choosing the village sites were water, shelter, centrality to cultivable land, and an appropriate distribution so as to give each village adequate land while maximizing proximity. The sites actually chosen, however, indicate that access to water was by far the most important consideration. In most cases this provided the village with the twin advantages of water and building timber. Eleven of the thirteen original villages relied on streams or springs as a water source,[16] and all were stream-oriented. At this initial and subsistence stage of settlement, access to good agricultural land appears to have been much less important. There appears to be little indication that the Doukhobors were concerned about an even spacing of villages. They were apparently satisfied that the surrounding land should be sufficient to support each cluster of villages rather than each individual village. With a communal system of agriculture, situated in what appeared to be a huge endowment of land where they had the freedom to occupy whatever part of it they chose, this seems a reasonable attitude.

Three of the original villages were located either wholly (Bogdanofka and Teakomeernoe) or partly (Osvoborsdennie)[17] outside the reserve on the eastern

---

14   Bernard, *The Canadian Doukhobor Settlements*, 35.

15   The "wanderers" section of Hlebedarnoe, isolated from the main village, was on the lower slopes of the Swan River as well.

16   NA, RG76, V184 F65101, Pt. 5, Harvey, "Schedule."

17   It would appear that the original site of Osvoborsdennie was at least partly on NE1-34-32, outside the reserve. Henry Vanin showed me basement pits on the eastern edge of that quarter (field trip

margin of Township 34, Range 32, and one (Michaelovo) was located just outside the reserve in Township 34, Range 29. These "errors" in location were hardly surprising. Dividing the land up in this "artificial" and arbitrary manner was considered by the Doukhobors as not only meaningless, but directly opposed to the idea that the land was God's gift and under His control. And they were not above removing the evidence of this unchristian practice.[18] It has been noted (see Chapter 2) that the reserve boundaries themselves were unclear owing to delays in surveying and to changes in the land comprising the reserves. As late as August, Sulerzhitsky was asking for clarification as to the conditions under which the people could take up land:

> I do not know who is responsible that the people on Thunder Hill have not yet been told about the conditions on which they can occupy land, but the fact of the matter is that they do not know yet anything about it. In the mean time, they are building in the direction of Swan River (11 villages - 1,214 men) and in the N.W. of Thunder Hill (2 villages - 188 men).[19]

He expressed concern that the labour which had been expended in building the villages might be lost "only for the reason that no one told them at the right time anything about the rules necessary before occupying land."

The "blockhouse" village of Vosnisennie was also located on unreserved (Hudson's Bay Company) land. This seems to have been an error prompted by the overly optimistic expectation that the Hudson's Bay Company, like the railroads, would exchange the land it owned within the Doukhobor reserves for land elsewhere. It did not and Vosnisennie, too, had to be relocated.

The Villages

The villages in the North Colony, like the villages in the other reserves, were built on the traditional *strassendorf* plan (see Chapter 1). Aylsworth provides the most detailed depictions of the initial layout of these villages in his survey of Oospennie and Troitzkoe in July and August 1900, approximately one year after they were begun (see Figures 14 and 15).[20] Houses and other structures face each other across a wide central street, faithfully reproducing in this new environment, the traditional Russian *mir*. There is no indication, in plan or building size, of the communal organization evident in the larger central lots and oversize buildings of Fairchild's 1909 plans; however, both villages have only one barn — suggesting a departure

---

June 1991) and Thomas Young's schedule identifies Ozvobozshdanie on NE1-34-32 and NW6-34-31 (NA, RG15, V754 F494483, Pt. 2). Whether this village moved once or twice is not clear. The move from NW6 to NE5-34-31 was made either in 1907 or 1908 (NA, RG15, V1167 F5412455, Osvoborsdennie Village Files).

18 The surveyors' communications occasionally suggest that the Doukhobors systematically removed the survey markers before the section corners could be mounded (NA, RG15, V760 F502904, Belleau to Deville, 25 June 1899).

19 NA, RG15, V754 F494483, Pt. 1, Copy attached to McCreary to Pedley, 12 August 1899.

20 C.F. Aylsworth, Surveyor's Notebook #7397, 1900.

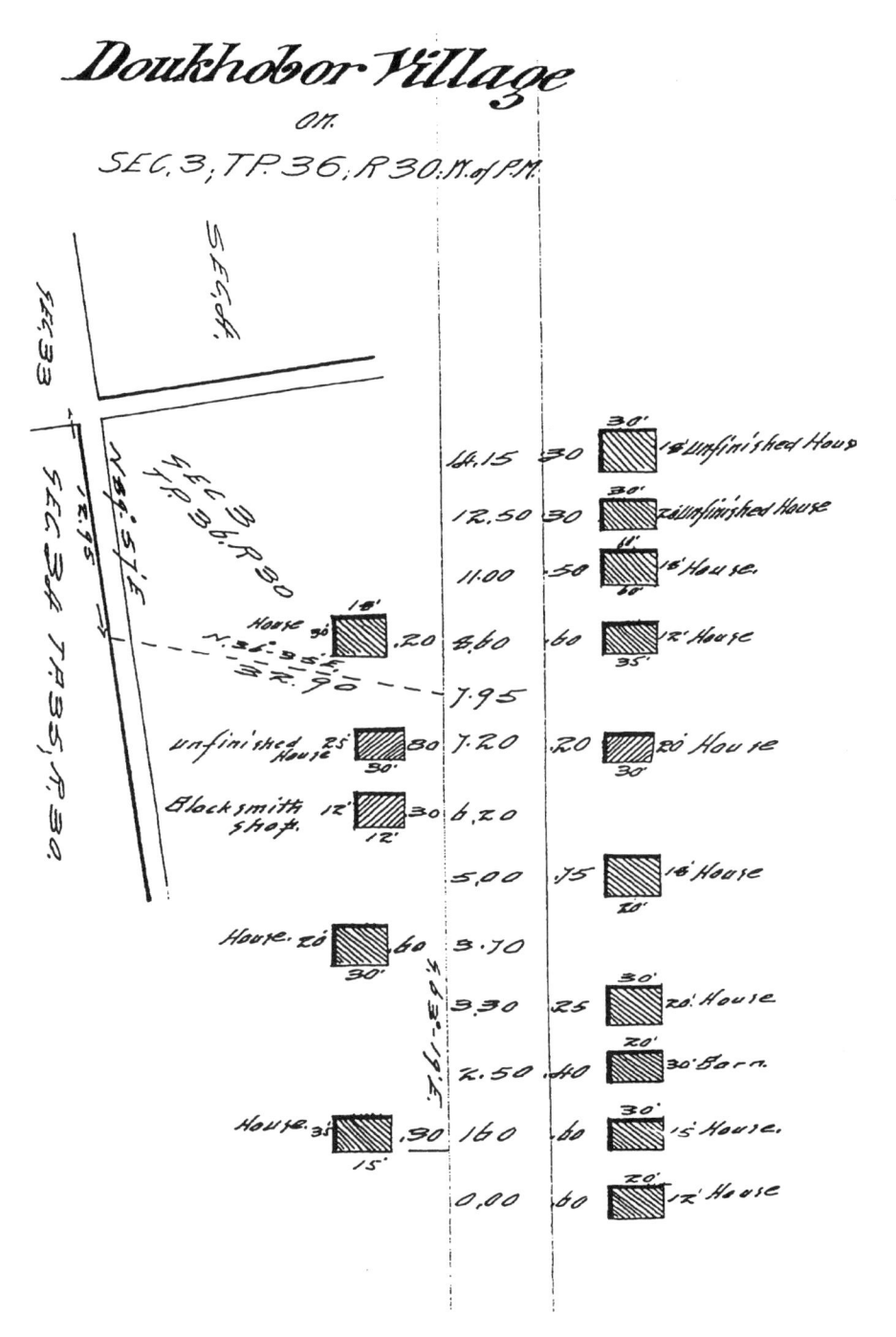

Figure 14. Plan of Oospennie, North Colony, 1900 (C.F. Aylsworth, Jr., D.L.S., Field Book #7397).

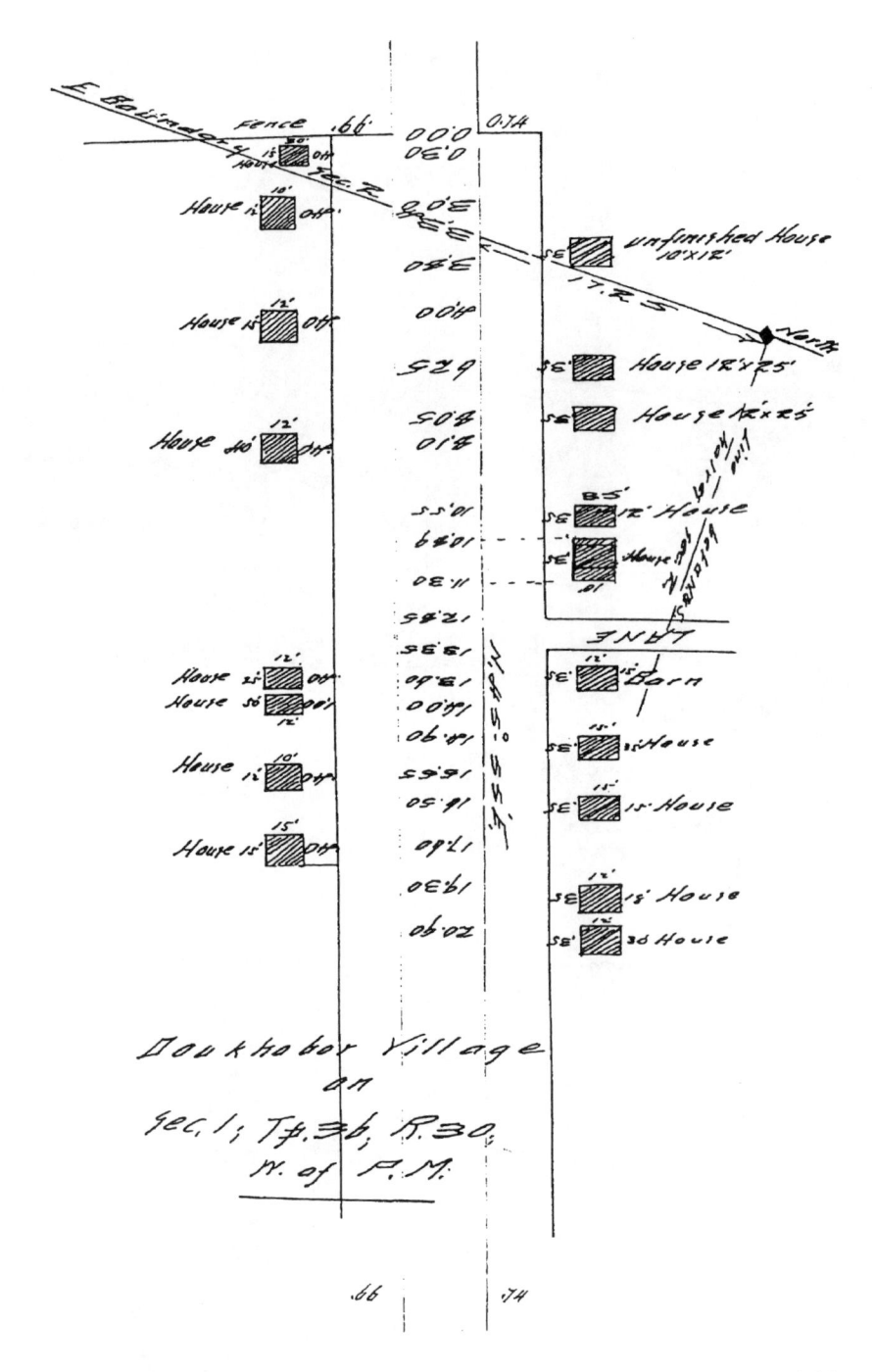

Figure 15. Plan of Troitzkoe, North Colony, 1900 (C.F. Aylsworth, Jr., D.L.S., Field Book #7397).

from the traditional house-barn structure characteristic of private ownership. Presumably at this early stage of development, the distinction between individually occupied houses and communally shared stables and workshops did not influence the overall village plan. Until the larger structures of a later time dictated larger lots, it is likely that modifications to traditional lot size and spacing were minor.

The buildings were arranged somewhat more irregularly in Oospennie than in Troitzkoe with houses, barn and blacksmith shop set back from fourteen to fifty feet from the centre of the street. Troitzkoe's layout was much more suggestive of the surveyor-like accuracy portrayed in later descriptions and photos, with all the buildings on either side of the street lined up at a set distance (twenty-six feet and twenty-three feet) from the centre of the street. The only departure from this regularity was the largest house which is set back sixty-six feet.

Detailed descriptions were also given for two of the villages built just outside the western perimeter of the reserve. In the fall of 1899, Bogdanofka and Teakomeernoe had 228 people in twenty log houses;[21] in June 1900, there were 225 people in twenty-two "well-built" log houses, with stables, granary, forge and other buildings. Fences were being put up, trails improved, and two bridges across the Swan River were built.[22] The descriptions indicate that these were fully functioning, permanent villages from the outset; indeed Archer's report was intended to convince the authorities that to force relocation on such well-established villages would work unjustifiable hardship on the villagers.

Buildings

Since building timber was readily available along the watercourses and in clumps near swamps and other upland areas, almost all the houses, stables, barns and other buildings of the North Colony villages were built of log and then neatly plastered inside and out with clay. The manuscript schedule prepared by McCreary and Ashworth[23] lists 141 log and ten sod houses. As noted above, the villages were still

---

21   NA, RG76, V184 F65101, Pt. 5, "Doukhobor Statistics."
22   NA, RG15, V754 F494483, Pt. 2, Archer to Sifton, 21 June 1900.
23   It is not clear which of the several manuscript sets of village statistics was prepared by whom. A covering letter (NA, RG76, V184 F65101, Pt. 5, Bellows to Pedley, 12 December 1899) accompanying the most detailed and complete (as well as the most readable) schedule thanks Pedley for the enclosures from McCreary and John Ashworth, "both of which convey valuable information on the conditions of the Doukhobors in their respective colonies." The "Doukhobor Statistics" was likely compiled by McCreary from material gathered by Ashworth on his tour through the villages, (apparently an earlier visit than his 15 May 1901 trip which was the basis of Dawson's table (13)). I have been unable to ascertain whether this schedule made use of material collected by Vladimir Bonch-Breuvitch [V. Olhovsky]. The published schedule prepared by William B. Harvey from his visit in November 1899 (NA, RG76, V184 F65101, Pt. 5, "Schedule of Doukhobor Villages and Statistics") is very similar to the manuscript schedule, although it is less detailed in the matter of building materials and provides no statistics for one of the Saskatchewan villages. The table reproduced in Bernard's appendix (*The Canadian Doukhobor Settlements*, 69) differs from both the above schedules, although the number of homesteads is the same as that given in the "Doukhobor Statistics" schedule.

incomplete at this time, and these early schedules only described a stage in the developing village structure. Houses and other structures were being added; existing structures were being improved and enlarged. As an indication of the pace of expansion compare the northernmost villages of Oospennie and Troitzkoe in the fall of 1899 with a year later. Oospennie had seven log houses in 1899 and Troitzkoe had thirteen sod houses.[24] A year later Oospennie had thirteen houses (three unfinished), a barn, and a blacksmith shop; Troitzkoe had seventeen houses (one unfinished) and a barn.[25] If we assume that the structures Aylsworth found in Oospennie and Troitzkoe in the late summer of 1900 were typical of the buildings initially built in the other villages, houses were much more diversified than some later accounts would suggest. The smaller houses were ten to fifteen feet wide and twelve to thirty feet long; larger houses were fifteen to twenty feet wide and up to sixty feet long. Between the smallest house (10' x 12') and the largest house (18' x 60'), almost every variation in dimension can be found in these thirty houses. In Troitzkoe, the houses were somewhat smaller and many were square or nearly so — structures that would be appropriate to the sod construction indicated by the "Doukhobor Statistics" schedule.[26]

Jackson's description of houses in one of the North Colony villages (either Stradaevka or Lubomeernoe), which in 1903 had twenty houses and a population of 121, could stand for most of the North Colony houses in their finished state:[27]

> Their houses are all built in a uniform shape of logs, about 24 x 36, with a roof projecting about 4 feet all round, and supported with posts. This forms a verandah all around the house. ... They have an oven in the corner of the house built of sun-dried bricks, in which they do their baking. You cannot see the logs in these houses, either inside or out, as they have been plastered with a mortar made of yellowish clay. They have roofs thatched with grass and clay, and which perfectly shed the water.[28]

---

24 The table indicates sod as the construction material although it is written over the ditto marks that would indicate log as the material ("Doukhobor Statistics," December 1899). Troitzkoe was situated in a prairie area with only poplar and willow scrub for several miles around (C.F. Aylsworth, Surveyors' Note Book #7397, 1900), so houses built of sod would be understandable. One additional note: while the numbers of houses given in the detailed listing and the summary listing is the same (151), the detailed listing breaks this down as 138 log and thirteen sod, but the summary notes 141 log and ten sod.

25 "The houses [of Oospennie and Troitzkoe] are of a small size and rough character, each containing one, two, and three families, but the Doukhobors are continually building, improving and enlarging their houses" (C.F. Aylsworth, Surveyor's Note Book #7397, 1900).

26 However, Bernard's description of "the quaintly built mass of chalet-like houses, built of mud bricks with turf roofs" was for the village of Oospennie in September 1899 (*The Canadian Doukhobor Settlements*, 15). The one house still standing in 1973 fits the description as "chalet-like" but it, like most of the houses in the North Colony, was built of log and plastered inside and out. This house has since collapsed (field notes, 1973, 1989).

27 Thomas Young noted that the houses "are of a uniform design either single or double, a single house being about 18.24 and a double 18.40" (NA, RG15, V754 F494483, Pt. 2, Young to Commissioner of Dominion Lands, 28 October 1902).

28 S.J. Jackson, "Report," Appendix 19 to the Report of the Surveyor General, *Sessional Papers*, 74-75.

Figure 16. House, Oospennie, North Colony, 1975 (author's photo).

Figure 17. House, Osvoborsdennie, North Colony, 1992 (author's photo).

Bradley adds that houses were painted white and ornamented with yellow dados.[29]

The few remaining structures on or near the village sites support these generalizations, although it is not clear whether they were built as early as 1899. A house stands on each of the sites of Michaelovo and Osvoborsdennie #1 (see Figure 17); two others stand near the sites of Osvoborsdennie #2 and Pavlovo. With the exception of the house at Michaelovo, all are of fine, squared-log construction with dovetailed corners in the characteristic high-lofted style. A similar but somewhat shortened version of this type of house on the site of Oospennie (see Figure 16) has recently succumbed to time and gravity; the logs have given way and the roof now rests on the ground. The log house at Michaelovo is an exception, unlike any of the Doukhobor structures with a steep gable roof, and with a plan and window placement unlike other contemporary Doukhobor structures. This may be either one of the early blockhouses built by Canadian carpenters — thirty-three were built on the site of Michaelovo, and presumably not all were the large, barracks-like structures — or a later addition after the village had disbanded.

Agricultural Organization

As a group, the North Colony villages were perhaps the most faithful to the principles of communal living. General meetings in July and August 1899 confirmed the communal way of life, first on a Colony-wide basis, and then as individual village communes,[30] and, while observers differed in the way in which they classified the agricultural organization of the villages,[31] all thirteen villages were reported as communistic in organization in late 1899.[32] To some extent, as Woodcock and Avakumovic have pointed out, a communal way of life was a practical necessity in the early years of settlement, even for those who were anxious to farm independently.[33] The funds, stock, and materials provided to them were provided to the group, not to individuals. Also, the scarcity of ploughs and oxen meant that some sort of communal cultivation and harvest was essential to survival. For others, group disapproval kept individualistic tendencies in check:

> Even those families which were rich or strong (in numbers of men available for work), who could begin independent life, did not venture to raise this question before its time. It would be too apparent that they were simply running away from the poor so as to save their own money and their strength for themselves.[34]

Nonetheless, there appears to have been an individualistic bent among some of the individuals, even in the North Colony. Ivan Ivin, in the village of Michaelovo,

---

29 Bradley, *Canada in the Twentieth Century*, 298.
30 Sulerzhitsky, *To America With the Doukhobors*, 176, 189.
31 See note 3, this chapter.
32 NA, RG76, V184 F65101, Pt. 5, "Doukhobor Statistics."
33 Woodcock and Avakumovic, *The Doukhobors*, 152-57.
34 Sulerzhitsky, *To America With the Doukhobors*, 166.

for example, was known for his self-interest, even before settlement in Canada, and his house-stable combination in the village was several cuts above the dwelling of the average communal Doukhobor, described by Bernard as "the best in the village, three rooms and a stable" and having "several well-glazed windows" and "stout wooden shutters."[35] The "restrained dissatisfaction" by which Sulerzhitsky characterized the scarcely concealed tension between individualists and communalists[36] broke out into sharp conflict here, perhaps because of Ivin's individualism. As noted earlier, the open hostility apparently provoked Michaelovo's villagers to move the foundation of their proposed prayer home because it was located across the street from the dwelling of an Independent.[37] Troitzkoe was begun as an individualistic village by a splinter group of people from nearby Oospennie unsatisfied with its communal organization,[38] but this departure from the communal arrangement seems to have been temporary; by 1905, the population had reverted to communalism.[39]

Herbert Archer summed up the situation in August 1900: "Among the Swan River villages there are three really communistic and likely to remain so; one is avowedly individualistic, and in the rest is war: individualists versus communists."[40] The seeds of this dissention were present in the initial settlements of 1899.[41]

As noted, the scarcity of stock and agricultural implements inhibited any inclination to individual farming. Bonch-Breuvitch, in August 1899, underlined this limitation, reporting only one plough per 130 North colonists, one horse per sixty-eight persons, one ox per fifty-eight persons, and one cow per seventy-four persons.[42] Other surveys indicate a slightly more favourable situation: Harvey lists fifteen ploughs, fifty horses, twenty-nine oxen, and six cows for the Colony;[43] and Bernard lists sixteen ploughs, fifty-four horses, twenty-five oxen, and twenty-four cows, figures identical to the unrevised totals of "Doukhobor Statistics."[44] In any case, with 428 potential homesteaders in the Colony,[45] there were far too few draught animals and implements to engage in individual farming. There were, of course, too few even for communal cultivation what with the other demands on the draught animals. They were needed for skidding logs for new buildings, for hauling provisions from the nearest railhead (more than fifty miles distant that first year), as well as for ploughing:

---

35 Bernard, *The Canadian Doukhobor Settlements*, 27, 38.
36 Sulerzhitsky, *To America With the Doukhobors*, 166.
37 NA, RG15, V1167 F5412457, Michaelovo Village File, 1905 Schedule.
38 Tarasoff, *Plakun Trava*, 64.
39 NA, RG15, V1165 F5404672, Troitzkoe Village File, 1905 Schedule.
40 Quoted in Maude, *A Peculiar People*, 253.
41 Sulerzhitsky, *To America With the Doukhobors*, 166..
42 Cited in Szalasznyj, "The Doukhobor Homestead Crisis," 70.
43 NA, RG76, V184, F65101, Pt. 5, Harvey, "Schedule."
44 Bernard, *The Canadian Doukhobor Settlements*, "Appendix," 60. The information in Table 3, Chapter 5 reflects the revised totals of the "Doukhobor Statistics."
45 NA, RG76, V184, F65101, Pt. 5, "Doukhobor Statistics."

> Let us take for example the village of Laybomirovka [Lubomeernoe] (North Settlement), where for one hundred and fifteen persons there was not a single horse, and only one cow and a pair of oxen, of which one has fallen sick. And the people there must build, and skid logs from the woods, and plough, and more important, haul provisions for sixty or seventy versts [thirty-eight or forty-four miles] or further. It went without saying that the Laybomirovka villagers did not go without bread. Other villages helped them load their bags, but how much could they help one another when for all thirteen villages, with 1403 inhabitants, there were in all eighteen teams of livestock, even less, because some of them were always sick.[46]

Life was difficult in the first year for these settlers. With the able-bodied men away earning cash by working on railway construction (Sulerzhitsky comments on the initial reluctance to engage in nonagricultural pursuits, and then, once the North Colony villages decided how necessary this work was to their agricultural survival, their energetic, if somewhat uneven, participation),[47] the work of establishing the villages and cultivating the land was left, in the main, to the women, children, and old men who often took on the work normally done by draught animals. Near the village of Osvoborsdennie, Sulerzhitsky observed this scene:

> A no-longer-young, bowed woman, with wrinkles on her hands and with a brown, dried-up face, together with a brown old man on bent legs, and a youth as long as a pole, with rope harnesses over their shoulders were silently pulling a home-made wagon on which lay a large, fresh pine log. They were so absorbed in this work that they did not notice me. Barely moving one foot past the other, all ragged and dusty they slowly moved down the road. The ropes cut deeply into their thin shoulders but they did not change position and continued to walk without stopping, looking at the ground with pale tired faces, on which streamed shining stripes of abundantly flowing perspiration. And with each turn of the crooked wheels the home-made wagon squealed sadly, as if it too were in pain.[48]

But it was especially the widely publicized accounts of women pulling ploughs to cultivate the land which provoked the most negative comments from outsiders. Sulerzhitsky captures the melancholy stoicism of one such group of women:

> Pair after pair of these women passed me as in a dream; then came the last pair with faces apathetic from weariness, with distracted eyes looking straight ahead. The plough rustled, turning over the furrow from under which the tops of partly-covered field flowers waved sadly — and the ploughers passed by as in a dream. From a distance I heard their song. It was a song of weeping; it was more a groan escaping at last from chests exhausted and over-strained by long suffering, the groan of reproach, the wail calling for righteousness, for all that is human in man distinguishing him from animals.[49]

---

46 Sulerzhitsky, *To America With the Doukhobors*, 172.
47 Ibid., 185ff.
48 Ibid., 193-94.
49 Ibid., 154.

Figure 18. Working the land by hand and by oxen power at South Colony, forty-five miles from Yorkton, 1899 (BCA HP86677).

Far from being a single, symbolic act, nor yet a widespread brutalization of women, this was willing involvement in an essential task. Sulerzhitsky's sombre description notwithstanding, Doukhobors today look back on these labours as heroic, rather than tragic, and Tarasoff estimates that over 100 acres in the North Colony was ploughed in this manner.[50]

With such restrictions on their agricultural endeavours, the settlers cultivated only small patches of the most easily worked land. Figure 18 portrays the variety of ways in which this initial cultivation was undertaken. A riding plough drawn by a team of oxen is breaking the sod of a prairie patch in the background, while a group of villagers are adding their effort with picks and spades. Just how much land was cultivated in total in the North Colony that first season is uncertain; estimates vary quite considerably, reflecting, no doubt, both difficulties in estimating the areas owing to the irregular shapes and scattered locations of the fields, and the differing times of survey. Sulerzhitsky estimated 121 acres sown in July 1899; this no doubt includes all the land broken at that date as the colonists needed every bit of land in crop.[51] It is possible that additional land was broken after this time, although Harvey's estimate is only 113 acres broken by November.[52] The "Doukhobor Statistics" schedule gives a much more generous figure of 238 acres;[53] Bernard's "Appendix" figure is the same.[54] Bonch-Breuvitch's calculation of 1,215 acres broken this first year in the North Colony is the anomaly among the estimates, especially mystifying since he spent considerable time among these people. Perhaps a decimal point is missing (or has been missed).[55]

As might be expected, the acreage cultivated by each village differs considerably owing to variations in village size and access to draught animals.[56] Verovka (Vera), the smallest of the North Colony villages with forty-one people, recorded only 7.5 acres while Procovskoe, the second largest village with 150 people, had ploughed thirty acres. Interestingly, Osvoborsdennie, the largest village with 205 people, reported only sixteen acres ploughed. It is possible that some of their cultivation was inaccurately ascribed to the adjoining villages of Bogdanofka and Teakomeernoe. On this cultivated acreage, the Doukhobors grew a wide range of crops. About 60 percent of the seeded land was devoted to rye, barley, and oats, while the remaining 40 percent was seeded to a borsch mixture of vegetables: potatoes, cabbage, carrots, tomatoes, beans, onions, watermelons, radish, beetroot, cucumbers,

---

50   Koozma Tarasoff, "In Search of Brotherhood," 3 volumes mimeographed (Vancouver: UBC Special Collections, 1963), 216.
51   NA, RG15, V754 F494483, Pt. 1, Soulerjitsky, copy attached to McCreary to Pedley, 12 August 1899.
52   NA, RG76, V184 F65101, Pt. 5, Harvey, "Schedule."
53   Ibid., "Doukhobor Statistics."
54   Bernard, *The Canadian Doukhobor Settlements*, "Appendix," 60.
55   Cited in Szalsznyj, "The Doukhobor Homestead Crisis," 71.
56   I have used the "Doukhobor Statistics" manuscript schedule as the most detailed and comprehensive source for cultivated acreage.

turnips and pumpkin (noted in order according to the acreage planted).[57] The Doukhobors had recently committed themselves to vegetarianism, so the range of vegetables not only reflects traditional taste, but a more necessary reliance on garden produce. Some villagers, however, had decided that fish was an acceptable supplement to a meatless diet; long strings of fish hung out to dry in the passages between the neat and orderly buildings of Vosnisennie gave it the appearance of a fishing village according to one observer.[58]

Michaelovo in 1899

The village of Michaelovo, although hardly typical of other North Colony villages, suggests the industry and cooperation which rapidly initiated a distinctive cultural landscape in 1899. Considering that building the villages did not really get underway until halfway through the year, and keeping in mind that the energies of the people were divided among breaking the land and working off the reserve on railway construction, as well as village building, the creation of thirteen well-established villages by the fall of 1899 is remarkable.

Michaelovo was the first village built in the North Colony, and along with Vosnisennie, served as the location of the temporary blockhouses which sheltered the Doukhobors until their own villages could be located and built. A group of builders sent out to the Thunder Hill area under the foremanship of McVey began building the blockhouses along the Swan River just inside the Manitoba boundary (McVey's timber camp). In February, Sulerzhitsky brought to the two blockhouses — one ready to be occupied, the other still lacking the roof — the first contingent of fifty North Colony Doukhobors. A few weeks later the second blockhouse was finished, but by then Department of the Interior officials had decided that the North Reserve should be wholly in the District of Saskatchewan. The camp was relocated west just across the border to a plateau overlooking the river and renamed Michaelovo.[59] Here they built additional houses and other structures for the stream of Doukhobors who were moving from the immigration sheds to the North Colony. Michaelovo became a base of operations as groups of Doukhobors moved out into the surrounding reserve lands to choose village sites and to begin construction.

By May 1899 Michaelovo was a bustling village of twenty-eight houses, three tents, six baggage houses, a stable, a large barn, and a blacksmith shop, as well as a "large vapour bathroom" and six outdoor ovens dug into the banks of the Swan River and roofed over to protect them from the rain.[60] Many of the houses bore little resemblance to the traditional structures built in the other villages. The "Canadian" builders were concerned with erecting the buildings quickly and simply. They were

---

57 NA, RG15, V754 F494483, Pt. 1,Soulerjitsky, copy attached to McCreary to Pedley, 12 August 1899.
58 Sulerzhitsky, *To America With the Doukhobors*, 151.
59 I am assuming that the move described by Bernard (*The Canadian Doukhobor Settlements*, 35) is coincident with this short move; it is unlikely that the village moved three times in the space of a few months.
60 Argue to Harley, 16 May 1899, NA, RG76, V183 F65101, Pt. 4.

Figure 19. South Colony houses, Doukhobor Reserves, Assiniboia, 1899. These are most likely the temporary houses built in one of three locations in the South Colony (BCA HP86660).

built for mass accommodation (two of the houses were vacant and it was noted that they could accommodate 200 people)[61] without the niceties of finished detail or complicated plan. The blockhouses at Vosnisennie were likely similar to those built at Michaelovo (see Figure 19). The earliest village layout, surveyed by Fairchild in 1909 (see Figure 3, Chapter 2), shows a radial arrangement of three central streets which may reflect an earlier attempt to impose something of the *strassendorf* tradition on the large number of buildings initially erected on a somewhat limited site. In the course of dismantling the larger structures for their logs and erecting their own houses, this compact plan either evolved or later structures merely followed the initial pattern. The later schedules of Harvey (November 1899) and of McCreary and Ashworth (December 1899) list only twelve log houses at Michaelovo, so it is likely that most of the blockhouses had been dismantled by this time.[62]

In July, Sulerzhitsky reported ninety-one people in Michaelovo (representing thirty-five homesteads) with two horses, a cow, a wagon and a plough, somewhat above the average complement of implements and animals by North Colony standards.[63] By October most of the blockhouses had been abandoned, many torn apart for the logs, and new "huts" built to replace them. One blockhouse had been repaired and served as the hospital, clinic and pharmacy from which Dr. Vera Velichkina, aided by Nurse A.A. "Sacha" Satz, dispensed medical aid, and one "lower" blockhouse was the home of Dr. Velichkina.[64] Sulerzhitsky described the "new appearance" of Michaelovo in October:

> The villagers have built clean new log huts; barns have been built for livestock. Among the buildings rise large cones of logs, wood reserves for the winter are in sheltered corners. Among the barns and huts, stacks of hay are hidden. No one lives in the blockhouses any more; the elders divided them among the villages, and a large number have been taken apart for new buildings."[65]

By December, eighty-five people occupied the twelve log houses. Now the villagers had five horses, two cows, two wagons, and a plough; they had brought twenty acres of the scrubby prairie near the village under cultivation, and it had produced ninety bushels of potatoes and twenty-five bushels of carrots, but no cereal crops of any kind.[66] For Sulerzhitsky, Michaelovo and Vosnisennie epitomized the "more integrated and more comfortable" settlements of the North Colony as compared to those of the South Colony.[67]

---

61   Ibid.
62   NA, RG76, V184 F65101, Pt. 5, Harvey, "Schedule"; ibid., "Doukhobor Statistics." See also Sulerzhitsky, *To America With the Doukhobors*, 205.
63   NA, RG15, V754 F4944483, Pt. 1, Soulerjitzky, "Report," attached to McCreary to Pedley, 12 August 1899.
64   Sulerzhitsky, *To America With the Doukhobors*, 205.
65   Ibid.
66   NA, RG76, V184 F65101, Pt. 5, "Doukhobor Statistics."NA, RG76, V184 F65101, Pt. 5,
67   Sulerzhitsky, *To America With the Doukhobors*, 115.

Chapter 4
The South Colony and Annex ~ 1899

The South Colony, including the Good Spirit Lake Annex, was the largest and most diverse of the three colonies. Nearly 4,500 people in thirty-four villages[1] here divided up some 310,000 acres of reserved land including extensive open and scrubby prairies, low-lying marshy and swampy areas, light sandy areas, and broken, often heavily wooded areas adjacent to the major streams and their tributaries (see Map 3, Chapter 1). The origin, outlook, and material prosperity of these settlers were no less diverse than the lands they inhabited.

The Elizavetpol people and the approximately 700 Kars Doukhobors who accompanied them, together with about 700 of the *Mokryje Gory* (Wet Mountains) Doukhobors from the Orlov and Tambov areas, settled here. The Wet Mountaineers who had been temporarily relocated in Cyprus[2] and another 700 Kars Doukhobors who came on the second voyage of the SS *Lake Superior* also joined them in this area. These settlers built thirty-four villages in the South Colony and Annex; each of the five groups represented tended to settle together in a particular section of the reserved land (see Map 6).

The Cyprus contingent, still in Yorkton in late May 1899, was beginning to move out very slowly onto its land.[3] They settled along the watercourses in the southernmost section of the reserve, joining the Tombovsky and Orlovsky people, also from

---

[1] Harvey's schedule of November 1899 identifies only thirty-two villages, twenty-two in the South Colony proper and ten in the Good Spirit Lake Annex (NA, RG76, V184 F65101, Pt. 5). "Doukhobor Statistics" lists thirty-four villages, but erroneously refers to all fourteen Elizavetpol villages as belonging to the Good Spirit Lake Annex, and all eleven Kars villages as belonging to the South Colony (NA, RG76, V184 F65101, Pt. 5). In fact, four of the Elizavetpol villages were South Colony villages, and three Kars villages were Annex villages. The remaining nine villages were either Cyprus or Wet Mountains villages (see Table 1, Chapter 2).

[2] The Wet Mountains Doukhobors wished to settle in one group, but the North Colony could only accommodate the first group of them. The nearly 1,700 Wet Mountaineers from Cyprus who came later remained in the South Colony.

[3] Sulerzhitsky, *To America With the Doukhobors*, 148.

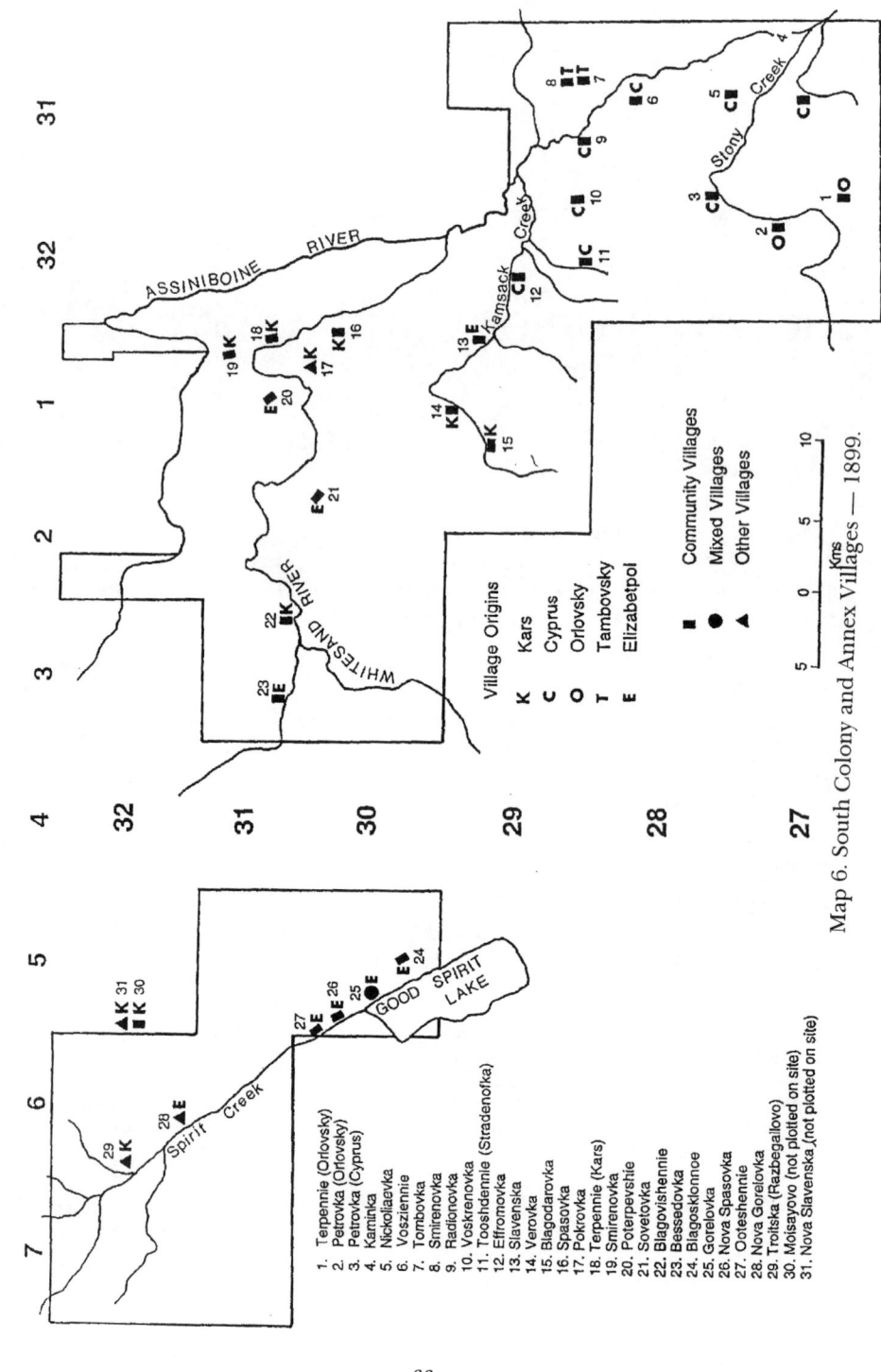

Map 6. South Colony and Annex Villages — 1899.

Village Origins
- K Kars
- C Cyprus
- O Orlovsky
- T Tambovsky
- E Elizabetpol

- ■ Community Villages
- ● Mixed Villages
- ▲ Other Villages

1. Terpennie (Orlovsky)
2. Petrovka (Orlovsky)
3. Petrovka (Cyprus)
4. Kaminka
5. Nickoliaevka
6. Vosziennie
7. Tombovka
8. Smirenovka
9. Radionovka
10. Voskrenovka
11. Tooshdennie (Stradenofka)
12. Effromovka
13. Slavenska
14. Verovka
15. Blagodarovka
16. Spasovka
17. Pokrovka
18. Terpennie (Kars)
19. Smirenovka
20. Poterpevshie
21. Sovetovka
22. Blagovishennie
23. Bessedovka
24. Blagoskionnoe
25. Gorelovka
26. Nova Spasovka
27. Ooteshennie
28. Nova Gorelovka
29. Troitska (Razbegallovo)
30. Moisayovo (not plotted on site)
31. Nova Slavenska (not plotted on site)

the Wet Mountains area, who had established two pairs of villages somewhat earlier, being drawn to this area, according to Sulerzhitsky, because "they preferred the land there." This southern section was connected to Yorkton, a distance of about sixteen miles, by a good, all-weather road.[4]

The Kars and Elizavetpol villages were somewhat intermixed in the central area of the South Colony proper and in the Annex. Six Elizavetpol villages in the Good Spirit Lake Annex were strung out along Spirit Creek like beads on a string. In the South Colony proper, seven Kars villages and four Elizavetpol villages located along the Assiniboine and Whitesand Rivers (the one Elizavetpol village initially located on the Whitesand River eventually joined the other three along the Assiniboine River). Two Kars villages which had initially located beyond the confines of the reserved land joined the Elizavetpol villages along Spirit Creek sometime later.[5]

It is tempting to see in this areal concentration a grouping not only conditioned by previous village and regional ties in the Caucasus, but by relative prosperity. The poorest groups — the Wet Mountains Doukhobors — located on the marginal land, both in location and in agricultural capability, in the southern periphery, and the wealthiest — the Kars and Elizavetpol Doukhobors — occupying the core areas of better agricultural land. Sulerzhitsky offers some substantiation for such a view by noting that the well-to-do Kars Doukhobors avoided settling close to the poor Wet Mountains Doukhobors because if they did, "they would have to use their money to help them."[6] There were exceptions; a few of the Kars and Elizavetpol villages were as poor as the Wet Mountaineers. More probably, the placement of the people reflected the natural tendency of village and family groupings to stay together and the timing of their arrival in the reserved lands. The Cyprus people, arriving later than the bulk of the Elizavetpol and Kars people, were left with the empty, marginal lands. While some of the well-to-do Kars did arrive after the Cyprus contingent, they were attracted to the central area of the reserve, where Kars settlers had preceded them.

Village Location

As in the North Colony, the Doukhobors were able to choose village sites with a minimum of restrictions over most of the South Colony lands, particularly in the central area and the Annex where railway lands had been exchanged, and only the Hudson's Bay Company lands and school lands remained unavailable. In only seven townships, representing perhaps 25 percent of the reserved land, were the available lands restricted to the even-numbered sections.

---

4   Ibid., 143.

5   I could not determine the locations of three villages: Voznyshanie (Kars) and Pozeryaevka (Kars) in the Good Spirit Annex, and Pozeryaevka (Cyprus) in the South Colony. It is quite possible that this last village is one located (but not named) near the Cyprus village of Nickolaievka in McCallum's 1902 survey of South Colony villages (NA, RG15, V754 F494483, Pt. 2, McCallum to Dominion Lands Office, 25 October1902).

6   Sulerzhitsky, *To America With the Doukhobors*, 167.

Sulerzhitsky described the general process of locating the South Colony villages:

> The elders wandered whole days over the Southern District picking places for villages, trying to locate them so that it would be convenient for each village to get to its land. They considered how many villages the Kars people should break up into, and the same for the Elizabetpol people and the Cyprus people. They also considered how many should be in each village, etc.[7]

These general concerns provide the rationale for village distribution, but a consideration of the original locations of the thirty-four villages built in the South Colony and Annex underlines again the importance of streams in determining specific village sites (see Map 6). Thirty-one of the thirty-two villages for which original locations could be determined chose sites adjacent to streams or to Good Spirit Lake.[8] Thirteen villages relied on rivers, creeks, lakes or springs to supplement wells as a source of water, and two relied on them as the sole source; the other nineteen villages relied on wells for water.[9] Since the larger trees were found almost exclusively along streams and around lakes and swamps,[10] these locations also promised a better supply of building materials (although not consistently, as the sod structures of the streamside villages of Vosoyanie (Vosziennie) and Petrovo in the southern portion of the reserve indicate).

As in the North Colony, it would appear that the necessity for water and building timber outweighed the desire for good, open agricultural land. The five townships that had the greatest proportion of well-drained prairie — Township 28 in Ranges 2 and 3, and Township 30 in Ranges 32, 1, and 2 — were almost completely avoided by the earliest settlements (see Map 3, Chapter 1). Two villages chose locations on the eastern edge of the prairie portion of Township 28, Range 31 near the Assiniboine River, and three villages built on the eastern margin of the prairie which ran west of the Assiniboine River in Ranges 30, 31 and 1. Only two of the four villages in the townships for which vegetation notes are available chose sites within the prairie. In sum, only twelve of the villages in the South Colony and Annex located on sites with prairie or scattered scrub cover.

The appeal of surface water and shelter over good agricultural land was not quite as evident in the siting of relocated villages, yet only four of some eleven village relocations were to non-stream sites characterized by open land. Since these relocations took place after Verigin's consolidation of the Doukhobor Community,

---

7   Ibid., 150.
8   The Kars village of Spaskoe was the exception. I have included in the stream-oriented villages the assumed location of Pozeryaevka (Pasariofka) (Cyprus) along a tributary of Stony Creek. I have excluded the two unlocated Kars villages of Pozeryaevka (Pasariofka) and Voznyshanie.
9   This information is available for all thirty-four villages. NA, RG76, V184 F65101, Pt. 5, "Doukhobor Statistics."
10 The major exception was the building timber located on the slopes of Duck Mountain along the eastern edge of the reserve.

it seems reasonable that the early necessities of wood and water were giving way to a concern for a more commercial agriculture.

The villages were fairly evenly distributed over the South Colony and Annex, perhaps in response to the concern for arranging the villages so as to provide adequate agricultural land for each that Sulerzhitsky noted.[11] The linear pattern of settlement with villages strung out along streams was similar to that of the North Colony, but the villages were much less clustered. Two exceptions to this general pattern were the twin Tambovsky villages of Tomboscoe and Smirenovka (Troodoloobevoe), located on adjoining quarters, and the Cyprus villages of Nickolaievka and Pasariofka with less than a mile between them.[12]

In general, then, the sites chosen for the South Colony and Annex villages reflected the same priorities shown in the choice of North Colony sites: water and wood. Although proximity to good agricultural land seems to have been relatively unimportant in determining village sites, the more even spacing of the villages, as compared with the North Colony, suggests a greater concern for the equitable distribution of agricultural land. This may also reflect a more commercial bent on the part of the Elizavetpol and Kars people, although the Wet Mountains villages of the southern portion of the reserve were quite dispersed also.

As in the North Colony, a few villages chose sites outside the limits of the reserved land. Moisayovo and Kirilowa located well beyond the northern boundary of the South Colony but both moved to sites within the Annex by 1902. Novo Slavyanka chose a site initially outside the reserve, but the partial township in which it was located was later added to the South Colony.[13]

The Villages

The earliest plan of any of the South Colony-Annex villages is that of Novo Troitzkoe (Good Spirit Lake Annex) surveyed 31 October to 3 November 1905 by C.F. Aylsworth, Jr.[14] Nine villages were surveyed by W.J. Deans in September and October 1907 — seven Annex villages, including a resurvey of Novo Troitzkoe, and two South Colony villages.[15] The remaining plans are those of Fairchild's 1909 surveys.

Aylsworth surveyed the outlines of Novo Troitzkoe in 1905, measured the buildings and their relationship to the central street, sketched out the fences along the central street and around the garden plots, and identified the individual structures with an unscaled portrayal of their orientation and relationship to each

---

11 Sulerzhitsky, *To America With the Doukhobors*, 160.
12 Again assuming the unnamed village adjacent to Nickolaievka is Pasariofka (NA, RG15, V754 F494483, Pt. 2, McCallum to Dominion Lands Office, 25 October 1902).
13 NA, RG15, V754 F494483, Pt. 2, J.S. Crerar to J.S. Turriff, 31 May 1902 (Map).
14 C. F. Aylsworth, Surveyor's Note Book #8707, 1905.
15 W.J. Deans, Surveyor's Note Book #10583, 1907.

Figure 20. Plan of Novo Troitzkoe, Good Spirit Lake Annex, 1905 (C.F. Aylsworth, Jr., D.L.S.).

other (see Figure 20). He did not survey lot lines, for as yet there was no need to formalize the internal structure of village landholding (see Chapter 11). As with the early plans of the North Colony, the plan of Novo Troitzkoe reflects the traditional *strassendorf* layout, but fails to show a rigid template of orientation and building placement. There is no indication of special areas reserved for communal buildings; conversely, the granaries, storehouses and stables are scattered throughout the village, a reflection, perhaps, of the individualistic tendencies that marked some of the Annex villages.[16] The plan does indicate a clear attempt to orient the buildings in a somewhat uniform fashion toward the central street (most of the buildings are set back .15 *chains* — about ten feet), but there are many departures, with some structures built flush with the fence at the edge of the street (the street is about 100 feet wide), and other buildings set back as much as 132 feet. Several buildings are oriented with the long side of the structure paralleling the street, rather than the more common practice of orienting them at right angles to the street. Again, there is little of the strict regimentation of buildings noted in early popular accounts, but nonetheless a definite adherence to a familiar model. Although this plan reflects conditions a few years after Novo Troitzkoe was established, and the buildings portrayed were log structures which had rapidly replaced the earlier ones of sod, there is little reason to suspect that the village layout of 1899 was much different in plan or regularity.[17]

These early village layouts reflect attempts to follow Verigin's dictates of communal organization under conditions which were not only novel, but where there was no centralized leadership — village elders provided leadership in each village, but there was no overall authority which would formalize the activity of construction and farming — and where the survival of the group for the coming winter was still a matter of grave concern. The uncertainty about just exactly how the villages would be organized both in terms of activity and plan was exacerbated by individual and group differences in attitudes toward property and community. As a result, the initial villages built in the South Colony and Annex did not include communal barns and warehouses, even though these structures were needed badly.[18] In short, the early villages reflected some of the confusion and uncertainty between traditional ways and the new way, a confusion which was eased, but not eliminated, when Verigin joined his followers in late 1902. The later village plans with large communal

---

16 One of the Elizavetpol villages of the Annex was identified as an Independent village (Old Gorilloe) and three communistic villages had independent members, Novo Troitzkoe being one of these (NA, RG76, V184 F65101, Pt. 5, "Doukhobor Statistics"; Sulerzhitsky, *To America With the Doukhobors*, 182-83; NA, RG15, V1168 F5412973, Novo Troitzkoe Village File).

17 Photos of Blagodarnoe (Saskatchewan Archives Board B2131) and Voskrisennie (see Figure 24) in 1900 show permanent houses and a regular plan. Although McCallum's 1902 survey notes log as the construction material for this village, whereas the earlier schedules (Harvey, November 1899 and "Doukhobor Statistics," Fall 1899) identify sod as the building material, the early schedules might have identified the building materials based on the heavy sod roofs of the Novo Troitzkoe structures (see Figure 21).

18 Sulerzhitsky, *To America With the Doukhobors*, 212.

Figure 21. A well sweep, Novo Troitzkoe, Good Spirit Lake Annex, early 1900s (BCA HP86790).

Figure 22. Doukhobor farmyard near Canora, Saskatchewan, c. 1906 (GAA NA-303-170).

Figure 23. Early Doukhobor village south of Kamsack (Kaminka), before 1905 (BCA HP47260).

Figure 24. Doukhobor village of Voskrisennie, near Kamsack, c. 1900 (SAB B-2111).

Figure 25. Model Doukhobor village of Terpennie (probably Terpennie Kars), 1902 (GAA NA-2878).

Figure 26. Early Doukhobor home near Veregin, Saskatchewan (BCA HP47326).

Figure 27. A Doukhobor house near Canora, Saskatchewan, c. 1906 (GAA NA-2878).

Figure 28. Village of Kalmakovo, Good Spirit Lake Annex, just under construction, early 1900s (BCA HP86811).

Figure 29. Stable under construction in Doukhobor village of Terpennie, c. 1906 (BCA HP86808).

Figure 30. "Up-to-date" Doukhobor village on the Canadian Prairies, 1899 (BCA HP86725).

structures on large central lots, reflect the impress of reasserted central authority and a more formal communal organization.

Prairie and scrubby poplar and willow covered much of the reserve so the scarcity of building timber in the South Colony was a problem from the beginning. Even before the Doukhobors began to erect their own villages, the building of blockhouses in early 1899 was hindered by the lack of suitable timber. McCreary, anticipating problems in the construction of the villages, felt that at first, at least, the buildings would have to be erected where timber could be found, and then moved to the appropriate locations later.[19] Whether this was done or not is uncertain, but it is worth noting that the blockhouse sites appear to have been abandoned in favour of villages which were erected nearby. The Doukhobors had their own solution to this dilemma, so structures of "sod" were nearly as common as log structures (see note 29, Chapter 2). By the fall of 1899, a total of 491 houses had been built in the thirty-four villages of the South Colony and Annex — 255 of log and 236 of sod.[20] It would appear that most of the latter were not true sod houses, but were made of poles and clay in the ingenious manner described by Thorsteinson.[21] This would corroborate her assessment that where neither open prairie nor building timber was found, this "wattle and daub" method of construction was employed, utilizing the immature poplar and abundant willow which covered much of the area.

The villages of the "Cyprus" Doukhobors tended to be smaller and more uniform than the Kars and Elizavetpol villages. The villages were constructed almost exclusively of sod[22] and varied in size from Troozshdanie (Trusdennie, also called Stradenofka) with seventy-one people occupying ten houses, to Kaminka (see Figure 23) with 143 people in twenty-four houses. The other six villages were close to the average size of 111 people and fifteen houses. The Orlovsky and Tambovsky villages were much larger — more like the larger Kars and Elizavetpol villages. The Orlovsky village of Terpennie (not to be confused with the Kars "model" village of the same name) was the largest with 191 people in thirteen log houses. The smallest of the four was Tambovka (Tomboscoe) with 155 people in twenty smaller sod houses.

The Kars villages were larger on average, but much less uniform, both in size and building materials. Pasariofka had only thirty-nine people in ten "log & sod" houses while the "model" village of Terpennie (later called Najersda or Nadjesda)

---

19   NA, RG15, V760 F503047, McCreary to Smart, 9 February 1899.

20   NA, RG76, V184 F65101, Pt. 5, "Doukhobor Statistics."

21   Thorsteinson, "The Doukhobors in Canada," 30. The 1902 schedule of McCallum either identifies these houses as constructed of log (in which case either the "sod" houses were in fact made of sod, and they had been replaced by more permanent log structures, or the early schedules reflected an analysis based on roof material; see note 17) or of poles and clay, which is likely a more accurate description of many of these "sod" houses (NA, RG15, V754 F494483, Pt. 2, McCallum to Dominion Lands Office, 25 October 1902).

22   Only twelve of 153 houses in the Cyprus villages were built of log (NA, RG76, V184 F65101, Pt. 5, "Doukhobor Statistics").

had a population of 254 crowded into seven log houses. Blagodarenovka (Blagodarnoe) had even more crowded quarters with 200 people in five log houses.[23] The ten Elizavetpol villages with an average population of 135 people occupying fourteen log or sod houses were somewhat more uniform than the Kars settlements: the smallest, Gorelovka (Old Gorilloe), had seventy-two people in eight log houses, and the largest, Novo Troitzkoe, had 200 people in twenty-one sod houses. Again, the living space in the houses in some villages was quite restricted — Poterpevshe's (later renamed Otradnoe) 189 people were crowded into ten log houses — while other villages enjoyed more spacious accommodations: Ootishennie's population of 180 occupied twenty-five log houses.

It is almost impossible to generalize about the appearance of these villages, or to attempt to make distinctions among the structures built by the three groups. Photographic evidence is selective and vague in terms of date and location, verbal descriptions are similarly selective for this early period of settlement, and the general categories of construction materials in the manuscript sources give no sense of the nature and character of the structures they tabulate. That the villages and the structures within them were diverse, there is no doubt. The limited photographic evidence at this early date attests to that diversity, despite the frustrating lack of detailed identification. Figures 22 to 25 show the great variety of plans, structures, and building materials of a few of the South Colony and Annex villages near the beginning of settlement. What can be seen of the village plan in Figure 20 shows a somewhat disordered arrangement of buildings, with none of the regimented regularity of the Cyprus villages of Kaminka (see Figure 23) and Voskrisennie (see Figure 24), or the model Kars village of Terpennie (see Figure 25). While it is true that the photographs of Kaminka and Terpennie might reflect a later stage of organization — the photograph of Kaminka is undated (although it was taken before 1905 when the village was relocated to the North Colony), and that of Terpennie is dated 1902 — the 1899 photograph of Voskrisennie indicates that such a regular layout was characteristic of at least some villages right from the beginning of settlement.

Similarly, the structures pictured show a good deal of variation within the basic architectural categories suggested in Chapter 2. The high-lofted, boxed-gabled houses which I have suggested were the norm for the North and South Colonies are the dominant structures in each of the photographs. Some present the "cookie-cutter" uniformity which Cormie described[24] while others show minor variations: some gables are entirely boxed, others partially, leaving a "walk-out" opening, and others are completely open (these last appear on houses which are not quite as high-lofted and on which the eave extensions are not as wide). There are, however,

---

23   With the first blockhouses built just over a mile away, it is possible that some were moved to this village and used for the first few years, or that some families continued to live in the nearby blockhouse while the village was being completed.

24   Cormie, "Will the Doukhobor Survive?," 589.

some representatives of the double-purlin type as well (see Figure 27) with much lower roof pitches, and eaves which protrude only slightly over the walls; others include a full-length eave extension (see Figure 26). Some houses bear little similarity to these styles, and were probably uncommon.

It is almost impossible to determine the construction materials from the photographs, but the houses of Voskrisennie (see Figure 24), Kalmakovo (see Figure 28), and some of the structures in Terpennie (see Figure 25) are clearly of log.[25] The fine houses of Kaminka (see Figure 23) were built in the same style, but the early schedules agree that the buildings were of "sod" or "poles and clay."[26]

A final variation in the complexity of these villages is the orientation of buildings to the central street. While almost all of the houses were oriented with the gable end toward the street, several structures are oriented parallel to the street. In many cases, they appear to be stables, but in Terpennie (see Figure 29) and in the "up-to-date" village (see Figure 30), an occasional house is also oriented in this manner.

As to village plans and architecture, it is possible to make some generalizations about the settlements of the South Colony and Annex Doukhobors: they built their villages on the traditional *strassendorf* plan with houses oriented to, and facing each other across, a wide central street; and they built houses of the high-lofted gable type, whether using log or poles-and-clay construction. But they also occasionally built houses of different styles, oriented them parallel to the street, and set structures back from the street at varying distances. In a word, even within the characteristic village pattern and architectural style, there was a good deal of variation.

Agricultural Organization

As long as the Doukhobors remained in the immigrant sheds or in the blockhouse villages, the "Southern Settlement" constituted one large communal group, bound together by the "bonus fund"[27] and an underlying sense of community which most felt to be essential for genuine Christians. When they separated from these larger groupings to take up life on a village basis, they were faced immediately with the question of how to organize their village communities. Even before the move to the villages began, there were differences between those favouring family organization

---

25 "Doukhobor Statistics" identified houses of sod in both of these villages (NA, RG76, V184 F65101, Pt. 5), but McCallum (1902) noted log as the building material. Since the photograph of Voskrisennie is dated 1899, I assume McCallum's schedule is more accurate; perhaps the manuscript used the term in a distinctive way. On the other hand, some of the structures of Novo Troitzkoe appear to be of poles-and-clay construction, the term which McCallum used where the manuscript used "sod" in those villages where the two sources agree more closely.

26 NA, RG76, V184 F65101, Pt. 5, "Doukhobor Statistics"; NA, RG15, V754 F494483, Pt. 2, McCallum to Dominion Lands Office, 25 October 1902.

27 A bonus of $5 per person usually paid to agents for attracting settlers to Canada, was in the Doukhobors' case paid into a fund to assist them in their settlement and was administered on behalf of the whole community (Woodcock and Avakumovic, *The Doukhobors*, 133; Sulerzhitsky, *To America With the Doukhobors*, 166-67).

and those favouring a larger, communal organization; later, within those villages which chose a communal system, the nature of communal life varied from village to village.[28] The Wet Mountains villages were set up on a communal basis, while those of the Elizavetpol and Kars people were set up on a cooperative basis, with livestock and equipment being shared personal property, but each family having its own "treasury."[29]

The McCreary and Ashworth manuscript "Doukhobor Statistics" classifies all Wet Mountains villages ("Cyprus," Orlovsky and Tambovsky villages) and seven of the eleven Kars villages in the South Colony as communal. Curiously, nine of the Elizavetpol villages, the most independent of the three groups according to Sulerzhitsky, are also classified as communal although a note indicates that three of the communal villages have individualist members. Four Kars villages are identified as "individualist" along with one Elizavetpol village. It is likely that there were at least some incipient individualists in other communal villages as well.

The distinction between those who were relatively prosperous[30] and those who were completely impoverished may also have affected village organization. The Elizavetpol and Kars villages were characteristically, although not uniformly, the most "prosperous" villages; those of the Cyprus exiles were the most impoverished. Differences in financial resources and material goods created quite different attitudes toward the kind of agricultural organization each village favoured. The more prosperous villages tended to favour an individualistic approach at the outset, although this tendency in many cases was suppressed in order not to appear selfish nor to oppose the idea of community life, which "every Doukhobor in the depth of his soul, even the most ardent supporter of private property, considered ... essential for genuine Christians."[31] Even where this independent spirit was strongest (among some of the more prosperous Kars and Elizavetpol people), at first the people "had to harden their hearts and support at meetings the proposal to live a community life" lest "it would be too apparent that they were simply running away from the poor so as to save their own money and their strength for themselves."[32] The poorer villages, having little in the way of either finances or equipment to support individual agriculture, had little choice but to opt for the communal system no matter what their individual feelings were. I have noted that in Michaelovo, of the North Colony, these differences surfaced in the same village. In the South Colony, Sulerzhitsky singles out the Good Spirit Lake village of Novo Troitskoe as an example of the "disgraceful things" which happened in a village split over material goods. Here, the ninety rich members of the village were not only taking advantage of the ninety

---

28 Ibid., 150, 166.
29 Ibid., 167.
30 If, as Woodcock and Avakumovic point out, one can use the term prosperity to convey gradations of poverty (*The Doukhobors*, 148).
31 Sulerzhitsky, *To America With the Doukhobors*, 166.
32 Ibid.

Table 2
Prosperity and Efficiency — South Colony and Annex, 1899

Group/Population	Horses	Oxen	Cows	Ploughs	Wagons	Cult. Ac.*
Kars 1,442	90 1:16	11 1:131	37 1:39	27 1:53	37 1:39	185 1.8/dr. an.
Cyprus 1,000	21 1:48	20 1:50	18 1:56	11 1:91	15 1:67	142 3.5/dr. an.
Elizavetpol 1,345	54 1:25	34 1:40	19 1:71	27 1:50	27 1:50	164 1.9/dr. an.
Tambovsky 320	7 1:46	4 1:80	3 1:107	2 1:160	4 1:80	33 3.0/dr. an
Orlovsky 372	9 1:41	6 1:62	4 1:93	2 1:181	4 1:93	38 2.5/dr. an.

*Ratios following cultivated acreages refer to acreage per draught animal.

Source: NA, RG76, V184 F65101, Pt. 5, "Doukhobor Statistics."

poor members, but were threatening their very livelihood.[33] But the association between "prosperity" and individualism is only a generalization; some Kars and Elizavetpol villages were neither well-off nor individualistic. The Kars villages of Terpennie and Verovka, for example, were both regarded as model communal villages, although the former was relatively prosperous and the latter poor.[34]

A comparison of the villages by origin provides some additional insights as to the variations in "prosperity," as well as efficiency. The Kars and the Elizavetpol villages were certainly better off by most standards than the other three groups. In the per capita proportion of draught animals, cows, ploughs, and wagons, these villages were much better supplied than those of the Cyprus, Orlovsky, and Tambovsky Doukhobors (see Table 2). However, in terms of cultivation, relating ploughed acreage either to the number of villagers or to the number of draught animals, these "more prosperous" groups lagged behind the Cyprus villages. Even considering cultivated acreage on a village-by-village basis, they were only slightly better off than these poorer villages. In terms of utilization of ploughs, the poorest villages (the Tambovsky and Orlovsky villages) outperformed all others, and were second only to the Cyprus villages in the proportion of cultivated acreage per draught animal. The Kars and the Elizavetpol villages were the best supplied for agricultural pursuits, but they did not transform that potential into productive acreage as efficiently as the "poorer" villages. Perhaps those committed to personal advancement considered communal cultivation to be wasted effort whereas those of the poorest villages, who were committed to the communal life, bent every effort to advance the community good, knowing their individual welfare depended on community progress.

---

33   Ibid., 182-83.
34   Ibid., 150-51.

Table 3
Regional Prosperity and Efficiency — South Colony and Annex, 1899

Area	Horses/ ind.	Oxen/ ind.	Cows/ ind.	Ploughs/ ind.	Wagons/ ind.	Ac/ ind.	Ac/ vill.	Ac/ dr.an.	Ac/ plough
Core (Population 1,746)									
Kars	20	133	54	70	50	.12	21.3	2.2	8.8
Elizavet.	39	69	138	55	69	.17	23.5	4.3	9.4
Total	23	100	65	53	53	.14	22.1	2.7	9.0
Good Spirit Lake (Population 1,041)									
Kars	8	124	17	25	19	.10	6.5	0.8	2.6
Elizavet.	21	31	53	47	42	.09	11.7	1.9	3.7
Total	16	37	35	39	33	.09	9.6	1.0	3.6
South (Population 1,692)									
Cyprus	48	50	56	91	67	.14	15.8	3.5	12.9
Orlovsky	41	62	93	181	93	.10	19.0	2.5	19.0
Tambov.	46	80	107	160	80	.10	16.5	3.0	16.5
Total	46	56	68	113	74	.13	16.4	3.2	14.2

Source: NA, RG76, V184 F65101, Pt. 5, "Doukhobor Statistics."

During the first months of settlement in the temporary blockhouses, the problems caused by the shortage of draught animals were especially acute. In the attempt to cultivate as much land as possible with the few horses and oxen available, the animals were often quite literally worked to death. This, of course, was not intentional. Since no one wanted to be a driver for long, and the number of draught animals was limited, the teams of horses and oxen frequently passed from one driver to another. The new drivers were not always informed as to how much the horses had been worked previously, or when they had been fed, consequently underfeeding and overworking the animals was common. Horses were especially vulnerable to such conditions.

It might be assumed that agricultural progress might be related more closely to variations in the natural landscape than to variations among the people. A comparison among the three more or less discrete areas in the South Colony — the Good Spirit Lake settlements (six Elizavetpol and four Kars villages), the "core" area of the upper Assiniboine and Whitesand Rivers (seven Kars and four Elizavetpol villages), and the lower Assiniboine River (eight Cyprus, two Tambovsky, and two Orlovsky villages) — reveals some regional variation, suggesting that the villages in the "core" area progressed somewhat more rapidly than the other areas (see Table 3). Table 4 provides a broader comparison on the basis of the three colonies.

Using proportions of cultivated acreage as the basis for assessing progress makes the comparison among villages or regions somewhat flawed, however. The Annex settlers, for example, appear to have progressed less rapidly, but in keeping with the environmental conditions of the area around Good Spirit Lake, they focussed their efforts more on stock raising than on crop agriculture. They had relatively large numbers of horses and cows but a more limited amount of cultivated acreage.

Table 4
Prosperity and Cultivation Efficiency — Regional Comparison

	Population	Village	Houses	Horses	Oxen	Cows	Ploughs	Cult.
North Colony	1,404	13	151	49	24	30	17	238ac (3.25/animal)*
South Colony	4,479	34	491	181	75	81	69	562ac (2.2/animal)
Saskatchewan Colony	1,472	11	153	119	73	73	44	277ac (1.44/animal)

* There are several problems with using ratios of draught animals to cultivated land to estimate relative progress. The numbers of draught animals in the fall of 1899 were not necessarily present throughout the spring and summer; those that were, were used for many things other than ploughing. The poor showing of the Saskatchewan Colony in the regional comparison probably reflects their late arrival on their reserve (July 1899) — at least a three-month delay in cultivation as compared with the other colonies. Also, as has been noted with reference to the South Colony, some of the villages preferred to put their energies into stock raising rather than into cultivation.

Source: NA, RG76, V184 F65101, Pt. 5, "Doukhobor Statistics."

In any case, while the "core" area had the greatest amount of cultivated acreage, the poorer Wet Mountains villages of the southern periphery were still the most efficient in using their limited resources of draught animals and ploughs.

Diversity characterized the cultural landscape of the South Colony and Annex in 1899 — diversity in the cultural landscape and diversity in social and economic organization. This was to be expected where peoples having quite different assessments of essential values and possessed of quite different material means, settled a natural landscape of quite varied physical endowments. Yet this diversity was thrown into relief against the background of common characteristics: villages were laid out to a common plan and dwellings were built which, despite variations in local building materials, were remarkably similar (compare the contemporary photographs from the two colonies) and which reflected a similar departure from the traditional house-barn arrangement. The fields around the villages were perhaps somewhat larger and less scattered than those of the North Colony, but they contained the same crops — oats, barley and rye — and the large garden plots were planted to the usual vegetable crops. And while the concept of communalism predominated, that commitment soon lapsed in many of the villages.

Chapter 5
The Saskatchewan Colony - 1899

The largest contingent of Doukhobors, about 2,300 from the Kars region, came on the second voyage of the SS *Lake Huron*, the last of the four sailings. The North and South Reserves were not large enough to accommodate this number of settlers, so nearly 1,500 were sent some 300 miles northwest to the Saskatchewan Reserve.[1] These settlers were among the most prosperous of the Doukhobors and settled in two fairly concentrated groups at the southern and northern extremes of the initial twelve-township reserve: the Saskatoon settlement (three villages along the south bank of the North Saskatchewan River), and the Duck Lake settlement (seven villages south and west of Duck Lake across the North Saskatchewan River). Only the villages of Karilowa and Bodenofka, in the southwest corner of the reserve, located within the original reserve.[2] Pakrofka (Usachefka), the other village in this southern area, settled west beyond the reserve boundary, while the seven villages of the Duck Lake settlement were all located north and east of the northern boundary (see Map 7). Later additions brought all but the northernmost village, Spasofka, within the confines of the reserved land. Whether owing to their relative prosperity or to their isolation from the rest of the Doukhobors, or both (see the earlier discussion in Chapter 4), most of these settlers exhibited an individualistic bent from the beginning.

Village Location
Not much is known about how the Doukhobors chose their village sites in the Saskatchewan Reserve. Commenting on the coming of the Doukhobors to the Saskatoon district, the *Saskatchewan Herald* merely noted that Doukhobor delegates "are out inspecting the lands assigned to them between here and Saskatoon,"[3] and

---

1   Sulerzhitsky's estimate of 100 is either a misprint or an error (*To America With the Doukhobors*, 143).
2   NA, RG76, V184 F65101, Pt. 9, Map, May 1900.
3   *Saskatchewan Herald*, 26 July 1899.

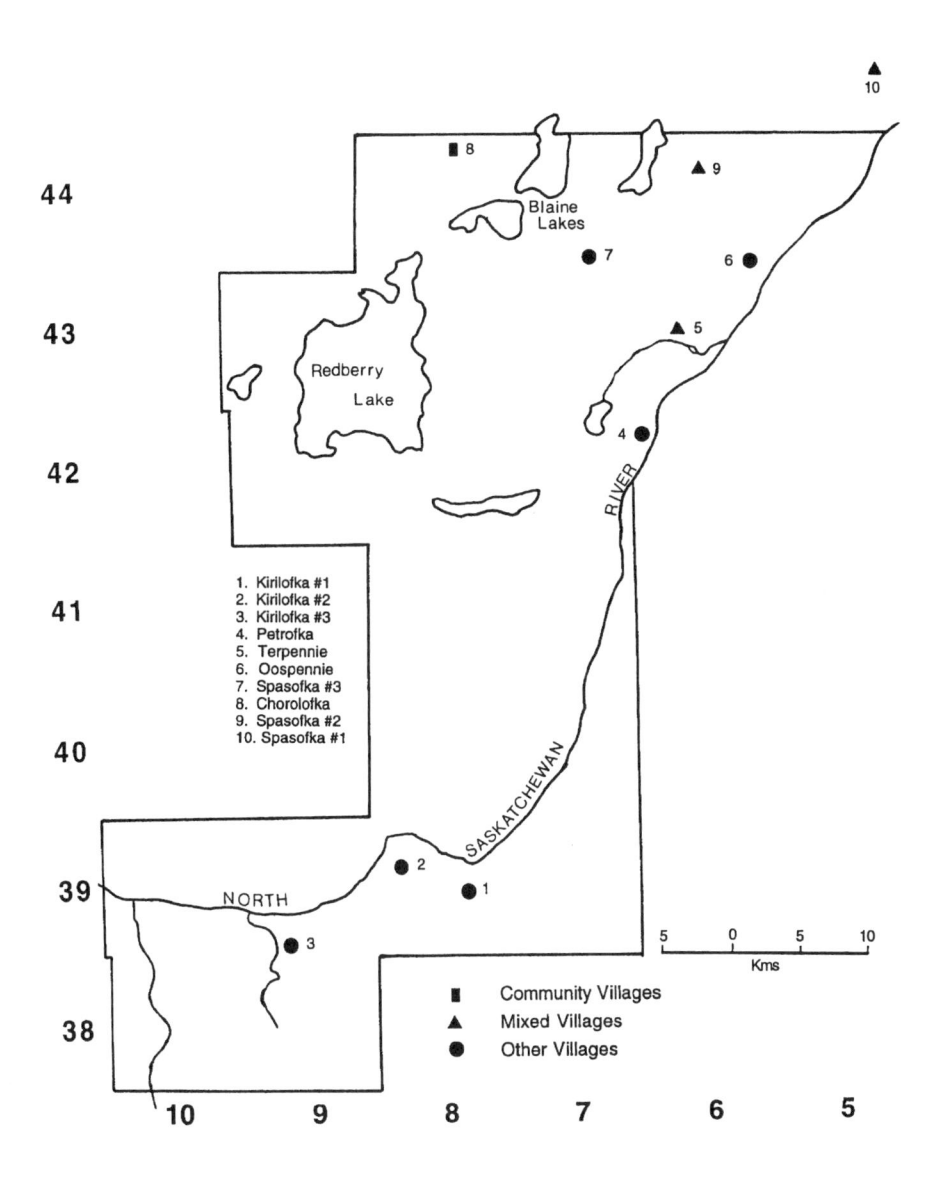

1. Kirilofka #1
2. Kirilofka #2
3. Kirilofka #3
4. Petrofka
5. Terpennie
6. Oospennie
7. Spasofka #3
8. Chorolofka
9. Spasofka #2
10. Spasofka #1

■ Community Villages
▲ Mixed Villages
● Other Villages

Map 7. Saskatchewan Colony Villages — 1899.

that they subsequently selected lands "between Saskatoon and the Elbow and will locate in the neighborhood of Redberry Lake on the north side of the Saskatchewan."[4] About 600 had settled there by the middle of August. Meanwhile, an "advance guard" of the Doukhobors who were to occupy the southern section of the reserve was expected daily to begin building houses between Saskatoon and Henrietta.[5] The next issue of the paper reported that "a large number" of Doukhobors had gone out to their land and would use timber from a well-wooded township on the east side of Eagle Creek for their houses.[6] Three villages, with a combined population of 309, were eventually established east of Saskatoon along the south bank of the North Saskatchewan River.[7] Since they were located near the main Saskatoon-Battleford trail, their activities tended to be reported more frequently than those of the Duck Lake settlement.

The first 700 Doukhobors of a contingent which would eventually number nearly 1,200, destined for the northern part of the reserve, detrained at Duck Lake in August after a long and tiresome train trip from Selkirk. They had difficulty in crossing the North Saskatchewan River because of high water,[8] but eventually they got their belongings across and began the process of selecting village sites. They chose four sites along the west bank of the river — Spasofka, Oospennie, Terpennie, and Petrofka — and three widely separated sites on the upland to the west — Pasariofka, Horelofka and Troitskaja. Nostalgia seems to have been the guiding force in choosing at least one village site. The Petrofka village group "arrived at their destination and nostalgically were looking for rolling hills, grass, water and warm sandy soil."[9] They found a favourable place for their headquarters, but were not fully satisfied. They wanted a spot "more reminiscent of home," so they backtracked toward the river and found a location with "a strong spring of clear water, trees, rolling hills" and began to build their village.[10] It appears that this site, like the original site of Oospennie village,[11] might have been originally located among the brakes of the North Saskatchewan River, and relocated later to a more level, upland site. Certainly, "rolling hills" is not a particularly apt description of the surveyed site of Petrofka on NW30-42-6, and there is some evidence of bankside half dug-outs a mile northwest of this site which might mark the location of an earlier village site.[12]

---

4   Ibid., 9 August 1899.
5   Ibid., 16 August 1899.
6   Ibid., 23 August 1899.
7   NA, RG76, V184 F65101, Pt. 5, "Doukhobor Statistics."
8   NA, RG76, V183 F65101, Pt. 3, McCreary to Pedley, 1 September 1899.
9   Peter J. Serhienko, "Settlement of the Petrofka Village," in *Bridging the Years, Era of Blaine Lake and District, 1790-1980* (Blaine Lake, SK: Town of Blaine Lake and Rural Municipality of Blaine Lake #434, 1984), 25.
10 Ibid.
11 John I. Bondereff, "Oospennia 'Dug-Out Hut' Village, 1899-1904," in *Bridging the Years*, 22.
12 Personal communication, Donald Stewart, July 1989; field trip notes, June 1992.

Whether it evoked some nostalgic remembrance of the homeland or it promised the more "practical" fulfillment of immediate needs, some combination of wood, water and shelter appears to have guided the choices of at least seven of the ten initial village sites. Rivers, creeks or springs provided water for six of the villages, supplemented in two villages by wells. All ten villages were located on what the surveyors described as prairie, but in most sites this was semi-open prairie with scattered clumps of poplar and willow, and in seven villages, the sites were adjacent to the well-wooded slopes of creeks or ravines tributary to the North Saskatchewan River. Nonetheless, perhaps because of their late arrival, the Doukhobors turned to the prairie turf for materials for their first buildings: in all but the three villages south of the river, the initial structures were built of sod.[13] These were replaced quite quickly by more substantial structures of log in the years immediately following the initial settlement. In the village of Terpennie, forty-foot logs were being hauled by oxen from the ravines running into the North Saskatchewan River in February 1900,[14] and Oospennie villagers used logs for building when they moved from the "dug-out" village to the level land above the river in 1902.[15]

The Villages

No plans exist for these villages in 1899. The only sources for reconstructing the early villages are contemporary observations, early photos, and Fairchild's surveys in 1909 (again assuming that the survey of the lot lines merely formalized a plan which had been evident from the beginning of the village). A sketch of the village of Oospennie by Sam Kalesnikoff portrays a very regular arrangement and orientation of structures, but it reflects the plan of the village about 1901 or 1902 after it relocated to level ground from the "dug-out" village carved into the west bank of the North Saskatchewan River.[16]

Jonathan Rhoads, a Quaker visitor to the Saskatchewan Colony in February 1900,[17] provides a detailed description of the village of Terpennie:

> The village consisted of but one long street. It ran in a straight line, and was about a hundred and fifty feet in breadth. It was neatly fenced with rails on either side, and the buildings were all arranged with their gable end to the road. All were built on the same general plan as that of Iwachin's — with a middle entry, the dwelling portion nearest the road, and the stable in the other end of the building. Occasionally a pole fence could be seen running back from the road to the depth of the lot, but in general there was no division between the communal properties. At the rear of

---

13 NA, RG76, V184 F65101, Pt. 5, "Doukhobor Statistics."

14 Jonathan Rhoads, *A Day With the Doukohobors* [sic] (Philadelphia: Wm H. Pile and Sons, 1900), 6-7. The bibliographic reference indicates that this booklet was published in 1900, but internal evidence indicates a later date.

15 *Bridging the Years*, photograph, 108.

16 Ibid., 22-24.

17 Rhoads, *A Day With the Doukohobors*, 24.

Figure 31. Doukhobor village of Petrofka, Saskatchewan Colony, early 1900s. This photograph is incorrectly identified as Novo Troizkoe, South Colony, in the British Columbia Archives collection (BCA HP86787).

Figure 32. A group of Doukhobors in the village of Gorelovka (Horelofka), c. 1907 (BCA HP92943).

every stable were one or more fine stacks of well cured hay, some of the villagers having as much as fifty tons. ... In every yard was a building used as a granary. Its construction was in every case as careful as that of the dwelling house, the walls having well built "footings" and being carefully plastered and neatly whitewashed. Built against the granary in almost every instance was a lean-to implement shed, well stock [sic] with binders — a McCormick in every instance — harness, plows, mowers, rakes and every necessary agricultural implement. Out in the yard were to be seen wagons and sleighs. The hay-racks were carefully put on platforms ready to be put on. About the whole village was an air of method, of care, of cleanliness and of order that would compare favorably with that of many a Canadian homestead.[18]

I have been unable to find photographic evidence relating to the Saskatchewan Colony villages at this initial stage of settlement. Photographs of Pakrofka, Petrofka, Oospennie, Slavyanka, Troitskaja, and Tonbofka[19] exist, but, with the exception of the 1899 photograph of a "dug-out" village whose location is unidentified (see Figure 4, Chapter 2), the earliest of these photographs is from 1902. These photographs depict the regular *strassendorf* village plan, with a good deal of variation in the structures which front the central street. Petrofka village (see Figure 31) had examples of the double-purlined, low-profile house-barns (which dominate this village, and probably most other villages), the higher-profiled structures of the same general plan, but more protruding eaves, particularly along one long side (see Figure 32) and one or two structures of a decidedly western style (see also Figure 33). I have been unable to determine whether the structures first built were of the same variety.

The plans of Fairchild (1909) confirm the regularity of Oospennie and Terpennie (and all other Saskatchewan Colony villages), but of course these later plans reflect the mature villages after a decade of settlement. Only Spasofka village deviated from this plan; its irregular central street may have been an accommodation to the uneven topography of the site, and may have been influenced also by a shift in the village centre between its origin and 1909.[20]

The buildings erected by the more independent Doukhobors of the Saskatchewan Colony were almost entirely traditional in general plan, although, as I have noted above, there was considerable variation in elevation and orientation:

> The gable end of each building — they are from fifty to sixty feet long — is divided into almost equal parts by a door admitting into an inner porch. Doors at opposite ends of this admit, the one towards the road to the

---

18 Ibid., 21-22.

19 If the deserted village is, in fact, the Tonbofka of the Saskatchewan Colony, the caption seems to be in error as no Tonbofka was built in the North Colony. The long, low structures pictured, and the date of the photograph (c. 1906; Tonbofka was deserted about this time as its residents moved to the North Colony) point to such a conclusion (British Columbia Archives, Cat. #HP86798, Neg. #E-959).

20 Saskatchewan Archives Board (Saskatoon), Spasofka Village Plan; field trip notes, 1973, 1992.

Figure 33. Doukhobor village of Pakrofka, southwest of Langham, Saskatchewan, 1902 (BCA HP47243).

dwelling house, and the one remote from it to the stable. The buildings are all one story high, though a small window in the gable showed that the upper portion is used, presumably for purposes of storage. The walls of all the buildings are of immense thickness, and have a pleasing chrome tint. They have almost as smooth and finished an appearance as the best plaster work of a Canadian artisan. The sod roofs are laid with the care, and almost the regularity, of shingles.[21]

Rhoads also noted that some of the roofs were thatched. Corporal Lindsay of the Henrietta detachment of the North-West Mounted Police noted that the houses were built of both sods and logs, with most having a stable attached; the houses were "warm and clean, but very dark."[22]

Of the 153 traditional dwellings built by the Doukhobors of the Saskatchewan Reserve, 109 were sod including fifty-six indicated as "1/2 dug out sod," presumably referring to the *semlin*, a structure where the floor was dug down about three feet so the walls would only have to be built up three feet or so (see Figure 4, Chapter 2).[23] The twenty-four houses of Bodenofka and Pakrofka, located near the more substantial stands of timber along Eagle Creek and another creek tributary to the North Saskatchewan, were built of "wood." Whether this means hand-sawn logs or sawn lumber is not indicated; "hand-sawn logs" were used in the ceiling of at least one house in Pakrofka in 1903[24] and a 1902 photograph of Pakrofka shows at least one building of sawn lumber (see Figure 33). Finally, the northern village of Gorelovka (Horelofka) had twenty houses of "various" construction materials, a reference either to buildings constructed of both log and sod or, more likely, to some combination of sod buildings and log buildings in the village.[25]

Jonathan Rhoads gave a detailed description of the interior of these traditional structures, noting that the stable portion had walls of turf, thirty inches thick, plastered within and without, making "the warmest of stables."[26] He then described the living area:

> The room was about fourteen broad and twenty feet in length. Its floor was of earth, packed smooth and hard as though made of boards. The walls were smoothly plastered and neatly whitewashed. Two windows, each about three feet square, supplied the apartment with light. The sashes,

---

21 Rhoads, *A Day With the Doukohobors*, 7-8. The beginning of this citation may seem to indicate that the door is in the gable end of the house; however, the description following makes it clear that it was in the long side of the house. A gable entrance was unknown in the traditional architecture.

22 Corporal Lindsay, "NWMP Report," *Sessional Papers*, 1900, 75-76.

23 NA, RG76, V184 F65101, Pt. 5, "Doukhobor Statistics." It is possible that the term might also have included the "bank" houses which were dug into the river slopes and had extensions of sod-covered porches (Bondereff, "Settlement of the Petrofka Village," 22).

24 Saskatchewan Archives Board (Saskatoon), Koozma J. Tarasoff, "Pioneer Housing," Saskatchewan Archives Pioneer Questionnaire #9. Sawn logs were also used further north in the village of Petrofka (Serhienko, "Oospennia 'Dug-Out Hut' Village," 25).

25 NA, RG76, V184 F65101, Pt. 5, "Doukhobor Statistics."

26 Rhoads, *A Day With the Doukohobors*, 8.

being set almost flush with the outside of the thick turf wall, gave window ledges fully two feet in breadth on the inside. ... The principal object in the room was the large stove and oven, built in the corner at the right of the entrance. It was about seven feet square, made, as was the building, of plaster. ... Around three sides of the room ran a bench. On the sides opposite the stove and the entrance it was of thick planed plank, supported by stout legs, and scrubbed to a spotless cleanliness. But on the other side the bench was continued flush with the front of the stove, and completely filled the broad space between it and the opposite end of the room. It thus formed a broad shelf, from twelve to fourteen feet in length, and more than six feet in width, the boards were polished a dark brown by constant use. This shelf was the family sleeping place.[27]

Rhoads also described a small apartment (about six by nine feet) for the "headman's" married son.[28]

Each villager had a granary — usually a separate structure — beside the house, often with a shed attached to the back. In some instances, the granary and shed were positioned between the house and stable, making for a very long (as much as 100 feet), narrow structure (see Figure 34).[29] Steam baths (bath-houses) were an early feature of the villages as well; some note that the sauna was among the first structures built, as cleanliness was of highest importance to the Doukhobors. Other structures — mill houses, blacksmith shops, and the like — were also added quite early. The size, elevation, and orientation (usually oriented parallel to the street) often distinguished these structures from the houses.

Agriculture and Organization

The more prosperous Kars Doukhobors who settled this area were of an individualistic bent, yet the earliest schedules reveal a strong communal component within the group. In the fall of 1899, four of the ten villages were communal in organization, although even of these, three had individualist members.[30] Gerhard Ens' survey of 1900 confirms that Horelofka, Terpennie, Pasariofka, and Spasofka, representing nearly 45 percent of the Saskatchewan Doukhobors, cultivated the land and harvested the crops communally, and had "everything united and divided equally to number of souls."[31] In commenting on the Duck Lake villages, the *Prince Albert Advocate* noted that the Doukhobors "live chiefly on the community plan" and that while "the rights of personal property is [sic] observed, their chiefs are commissioned to do the principal purchasing for the community."[32] This would suggest the

---

27   Ibid., 9-10. Corporal Lindsay notes that the ovens were made of sun-dried bricks (Lindsay, "NWMP Report," 75-76).

28   Ibid.

29   Bondereff, "Oospennia 'Dug-Out Hut' Village," 22.

30   NA, RG76, V184 F65101, Pt. 5, "Doukhobor Statistics."

31   Ibid., Gerhard Ens, "Crop Report Saskatoon Villages, 1900."

32   *Prince Albert Advocate*, 25 December 1899.

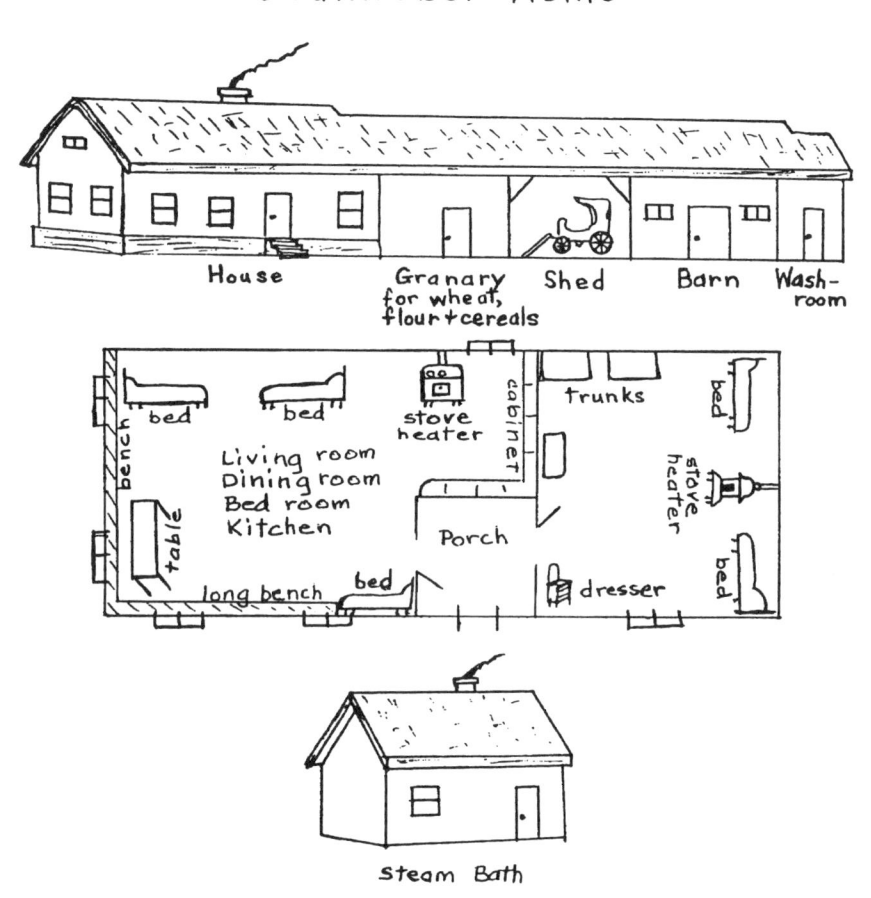

Figure 34. Sketch of a Doukhobor home, Saskatchewan Colony (Sam Kalesnikoff, *Bridging the Years*, 22).

more traditional village organization which retained individualism within a general cooperative structure.

By fall 1899, the ten villages had cultivated a total of 277 acres, an average of nearly twenty-eight acres per village. The four communal villages cultivated 121 acres that first summer (an average of thirty acres per village), while the six "independent" villages cultivated 156 acres (an average of twenty-six acres per village). The three villages west of Saskatoon were hindered in their first year's efforts by fewer ploughs and draught animals, and were able to cultivate an average of just over fifteen acres per village. The dramatic increase in cultivated acreage the next year was in large part accounted for by the four communal villages; more than half of the total of 2,243 acres ready for crop in the Saskatchewan Reserve belonged to these villages.[33] The village of Horelofka alone had nearly 25 percent of the total.

The cultural impress stamped on the landscape of the Saskatchewan Reserve was perhaps the most traditional of any of the colonies. Where recent religious commitments to a communal way of life had somewhat modified the traditional built landscape in the North and South Colonies, these Kars settlers maintained, almost unchanged, the traditional cultural landscape of farm and field. Distance, as well as a different perspective on community and community leadership, no doubt were factors. While early difficulties created by their late arrival on their lands forced at least one village (Oospennie) to abandon traditional architecture and village layout, the earliest sources portray carefully planned *strassendorf* composed of traditional house-barn farmsteads on lands which were cultivated, in most instances, cooperatively.

Summary — The Doukhobor Colonies in 1899

Considering the timing of the Doukhobors' arrival in the winter and early spring of 1899, the severity of the winter and the lateness of the spring break-up, the lack of a leader, the great shortage of implements and draught animals, and the absence of a large segment of the workers who were away employed on railway construction, the state of Doukhobor settlement in the fall of 1899 is quite remarkable. They had established fifty-seven Old World villages, ranging in size from thirty-nine to 254 people, with an average size of 129 people, throughout more than 750,000 acres of western Canadian prairie and parkland. They had constructed nearly 800 houses of various materials — from a village of five half dug-out sod houses to one of twenty-five log houses — as well as granaries, bath-houses, stables, sheds, shops, and root-cellars. In the short time available to them, they had broken nearly 1,100 acres, perhaps 10 percent of which was accomplished by women pulling the ploughs or digging with spades and hoes. In addition, they hacked trails through the bush and built crude ferries to provide contact between their villages and to connect with the supply centres along the rail lines.

The environmental and social factors which combined to influence farmstead or village location were evaluated somewhat differently by the Doukhobors than by the individual homesteader. While individual settlers may have put more stress on the ease by which land could be transformed to cash-producing viability, or on nearness to markets via the railway, the Doukhobors evaluated the land in terms of cultural rather than commercial requirements. Preservation of the group and group values took precedence over the more commercial factors related to agricultural viability. As well, the environmental essentials of shelter and a water supply assumed heightened significance. A water supply for a single family, or wood for a single house and barn, could be had much more easily in these areas than water or wood for twenty or forty families. It is not surprising that streamside locations which provided both these essential elements, figured as dominant factors in the choice of village sites in all three reserves.

In a few short months, a distinctive group of people was slowly changing the natural landscape of each of the reserves into a cultural landscape reminiscent of their homeland. They built villages that in their nostalgic familiarity recreated the security so necessary in a foreign land. Their villages, in plan and architecture foreign and exotic to the local populace, reestablished culture and community with comfortably familiar plans and buildings. And if, at first, they were forced to construct make-do shelters of roofed-over pits or log huts, they quickly replaced or modified them to repeat the familiar styles of their homeland. If their communal way of life was somewhat new, their reliance on community within the agricultural village was ancient. And if the replicas were not yet exact images of the originals, from the outset there was much to suggest the form and structure which these villages would ultimately take.

---

33   NA, RG76, V184 F65101, Pt. 5, Ens, "Crop Report."

Chapter 6
Flux ~ 1899~1905

The period between 1899 and 1905 brought into sharp contrast the differences between the attitudes and practices of the Doukhobors and the regulations and expectations of the Canadian government. The changing nature of the settlement environment, of agricultural enterprise in the West, and of national goals, brought the full glare of public opinion to bear on just how "fully satisfied" the Doukhobors and the government were with each other. Conflict was almost inevitable: the Doukhobors were communal, mystical and parochial; Canadian society represented by government and business was individualistic, pragmatic and nationalistic.[1]

Waves of new settlers were now swirling around the reserves set aside for the Doukhobors. Once either beyond, or at the margins of, agricultural settlement, Doukhobor lands were now in the midst of a horde of land-hungry settlers. Significant sections of the reserves, particularly conspicuous in areas where both the odd and even sections were reserved for the Doukhobors, were soon observed to be "idle" (Tables 5, 6, and 7 indicate the status of the North and South Colonies at this time). These lands were not being cultivated, the public and its press pointed out. Why were they being kept from settlers who were eagerly seeking homesteads? The questions became more pointed and insistent when it was found that these lands were being held for the Doukhobors under special conditions with respect to the residence and cultivation requirements of homestead law. Who were these people, these "foreigners," that they should be given special concessions unavailable to "our own people," good "white" Anglo-Saxon stock from Ontario, the British Isles, and the United States? A clear message should be sent to the Doukhobors. No special concessions. Use the lands or lose them.

---

1 Adrian Kershaw identifies the conflict in slightly different terms. He characterizes the Doukhobor ideology as collectivistic, antimaterialistic and pacifistic in contrast to the dominant ideology in Canada which was one of "laissez-faire uniformitarianism" which stressed capitalism, materialism and individualism. See "Ideological Conflict, Assimilation, and the Cultural Landscape: A Case Study of the Doukhobors in Canada," in Nigel M. Waters (ed.), *Aspects of Human Geography: The Kelowna Papers, 1981* (Vancouver: Tantalus Research Ltd., 1982), 10.

Table 5
North Colony, Autumn 1902

Village	Population	Houses	Stables	Granaries	Other	Cult.*	Horses	Cattle
Bogdanovka	115	19	2	1	5 root 1 bath	120 (3)	0	0
Lubomeernoe	128	30	4	2	1 bath 2 wksp	150 (4)	10	47
Michaelovo	122	18	6	1	1 bath	132 (6)	5	18
Novotroitskoe	140	20	14	3	10 root	109 (6)	6	59
Oospennie	110	14	2	1	1 mill	105 (4)	0	0
Osvoborsdennie	226	27	3	1	1 wksp 1 root	160 (5)	9	0
Pakrovka	170	24	3	1	1 blk-shop	95 (6)	2	15
Spassovka (Hlebedarnoe)	131	23	5	2	2 root 1 bath	122 (6)	4	6
Stradaevka	87	11	4	1	1 bath	77 (5)	4	17
Techomeernoe	124	24	4	1	1 root 1 bath 2 wksp	140 (5)	3	4
Trotizkoe	112	18	5	1	—	150 (5)	15	34
Vera	61	11	3	3	2 bath	60 (3)	6	32
Vosnisennie	117	13	5	2	2 root mill**	100 (5)	2	12
Totals	1,643	252	60	20		1,520 (63)	66	244

* in acres; bracketed figures refer to the number of quarter sections on which cultivation was done.
** in the course of erection.
wksp = workshop.
Source: NA, RG15, V754 F494483, Pt. 2, Thomas Young, "Report," October 1902.

The attitudes and actions of the Doukhobors themselves did not help to win public sympathy. Pressures from without and tensions within not only fragmented and weakened the group, but encouraged the government in its belief that most of the Doukhobors would eventually become good, independent farmers like all the other settlers coming to the West. Those Doukhobors who refused to acknowledge individual ownership of land were thought to be a minority and were lumped together with those clearly unbalanced protesters who turned their animals loose and wandered over the prairie in search of their "Messiah." There was little to be gained in listening to their complaints or attempting to negotiate with them.

The government was wrong on both counts. It clearly underestimated the resolve of the majority of the group to adhere to its communal beliefs, and it underestimated, as did Verigin, the impact and persistence of the radicalism of the dissidents who refused to countenance either the actions of the government or of their own leader.

The pivotal year of this period of flux was 1902. Three events lay at the heart of the ferment of this period and provided the seeds of even greater change in the period following 1905: the "mania" which reflected the discontent and frustration

Table 6
South Colony, 1902

Village*	Houses	Size (feet)	Stables	Size (feet)	Cult.**	Fenced	Const.
Bisednoe	12	14x40	6	15x35	120 (6)	60	Log
Blagodarnoe	26	14x30	6	15x25	105 (4)	10	Log
Kaminka	27	14x40	4	15x30	235 (8)	50	PC***
Lubovnoe	21	14x30	5	14x5	63 (2)	60	PC
Najersda	35	14x35	10	15x40	275 (9)	25	Log
Nikolaevka	24	14x25 14x30	8	15x30	27 (4)	37	PC
Old Petrovo	26	14x30	6	20x30	120 (6)	10	PC
Otradnoe	24	14x30	4	14x30	80 (3)	10	PC
Petrovo	20	14x22	3	14x20	20 (1)	25	PC
Prokuratovo	24	14x35	4	14x30	120 (3)	10	Log
Riduonovo	22	14x22	1	14x25	50 (2)	20	PC
Slavyanka (Kapustina)	11	14x25	3	14x20	45 (3)	10	PC
Smyrennie	32	14x35	10	14x30	340 (10)	40	Log
Spaskoe	15	14x25	3	14x30	150 (3)	5	Log
Terpennie	29	14x30	1	20x60	105 (4)	10	PC
Trusdennie	2	14x25	4	14x20	40 (2)	35	PC
Vernoe	25	14x25	4	15x25	65 (4)	10	Log
Voskrisennie	20	14x25	3	14x30	47 (3)	20	Log
Vosziennie	26	14x30	5	14x30	84 (3)	84	Log
Kamsack‡	13	14x25	1	14x25	65 (3)	55	PC

* village names are taken from the locations of known villages.
** in acres; bracketed figures refer to the number of quarter sections on which cultivation was done.
*** poles and clay.
‡ this village is identified on Crerar's 1902 map as "Kamsack Village" (NA, RG15, V754 F494483, Pt. 2).

Source: NA, RG15, V754 F494483, Pt. 2, N.G. McCallum, "Report," October 1902.

of a group attempting to make religious sense of the demands of a government they did not trust, without benefit of their leader; the "cultivation concession," which some viewed as a token concession to encourage compromise on the central issue of communal land ownership but which others saw as a softening of government insistence on the individualistic nature of the homestead regulations and thus a step on the way to final communal ownership and organization; and the coming of Peter Verigin, which brought both a measure of stability for the majority and a sharper schism for a few.

The issue of land and land ownership was at the heart of Doukhobor difficulties in Canada. Reporting vital statistics and solemnization of marriages were other contentious issues which kept alive fears about the intentions of government in Canada, but the key issue was land. The Doukhobors were "sons of the soil." Working the land was vital to, even synonymous with, the Doukhobor way of life:

Table 7
Good Spirit Lake Annex, 1902

Village	Houses	Size (feet)	Stables	Size (feet)	Cult.*	Fenced	Const.
Blagosklonnoe	19	14x30	8	15x35	115 (3)	115	Log
Kalmakovo	14	14x35	6	14x30	92 (3)	70	Log
New Gorilloe	11	14x40	4	14x30	101 (6)	12	Log
Novotroitzkoe	26	13x40	5	14x30	145 (3)	145	Log
Old Gorilloe	7	14x20	2	14x25	35 (2)	15	Log
Ootishennie	22	12x28 13x30	5	14x30	213 (8)	118	Log

* in acres; bracketed figures refer to the number of quarter sections on which cultivation was done.

Source: NA, RG15, V754 F494483, Pt. 2, N.G. McCallum, "Report," October 1902.

> Moreover we declare sincerely to the Government and the people of Canada, that we are agriculturalists and that we prefer this work as being the most regular, the most honest, the most lawful and most fundamental in our life and that we have always tried and will always endeavor, with all our strength to work in cultivating the soil.[2]

In the Doukhobor slogan, "Toil and Peaceful Life," toil was understood to be toil on the land. Work away from the villages was sometimes necessary, but only to ensure the survival of life on the land. The Doukhobors were attached to the soil, but by use rather than ownership. They belonged to the land, but not to any particular piece of land. The idea of each Doukhobor owning a plot of land individually was antagonistic to their belief in communal ownership of property; in fact, it opposed the rightful rule of God who alone owned the land. God gave the land for the benefit of all; it was like the air, available without division, common property:

> the earth is God's creation, created for the benefit of the human race and for all that live on it ... the earth is our common mother who feeds us, protects us, rejoices us and warms us with love from the moment of our birth ... and mankind has not yet come to understand by their reasoning that one can live and utilize the soil without any survey and division.[3]

This, of course, was an attitude similar to that of the aboriginal inhabitants of the Prairies who believed that the land was given to them by the Great Spirit to be used and passed on, undiminished, to their children.[4] This essential distinction of use rather than ownership characterized the understanding of the Doukhobors; it is not surprising that one of the early requests the Doukhobors made of the government

---

2   NA, RG15, V756 F494483, Pt. 3, "Petition to the Minister of the Interior and All People in Canada from the Christian Community of the Universal Brotherhood, the Doukhobors in Canada"; Sulerzhitsky, *To America With the Doukhobors*, 193. This deep attachment to the "rightness" of farming at first prevented many from taking work on the railway.
3   Ibid.
4   James R. Miller, *Skyscrapers Hide the Heavens* (Toronto: University of Toronto Press, 1991), 165.

was to grant them land under the same conditions that it granted land to the Indians, that is, a reserve system where the land would be granted "in one round section, and without dividing to whom personally which belongs."[5]

When the Doukhobors learned that the large reserves they had been given were to be seen, not as the common property of the whole Doukhobor community, but as individual plots of land which had to be assigned to each eligible Doukhobor, they refused to legitimize that sacrilege by signing individually for their homesteads. Had the government been fully prepared to register their homesteads immediately, the problem might have been averted, however. Aylmer Maude suggests that the delay in the survey which occasioned the mistakes in village location was also responsible for the Doukhobors' resistance to land registration. Arthur St. John, a Toronto Quaker who had accompanied the ill-fated Cyprus contingent and had followed them to Canada, had a list of those who wanted to take up land and a plan of the land wanted. Had the land been surveyed, according to Maude, the "whole matter" would have been settled. Instead, by spring of 1900, the Doukhobors "had begun to change their minds"; they were increasingly suspicious of government actions which they construed as reversing formerly agreed-upon conditions. In this state, they were vulnerable to the blandishments and rabble-rousing tactics of Alexander Bodyansky, a non-Doukhobor Russian agitator, who appeared to champion their cause.[6]

Sulerzhitsky also suggested that initial delays in registering the homestead lands caused a hardening of the Doukhobors' resolve on the matter. He had discussed with the Doukhobors the process of taking up the land individually, and, although they were not happy with the idea, they seemed to have come to terms with it in their own minds. Sulerzhitsky and Herbert Archer, an English Quaker who took Aylmer Maude's place as negotiator for the Doukhobors, drew up the maps showing the distribution of lands; all that was left was for the surveyor and officer to list in a special book the names of the individuals together with the land being registered to them:

> the surveyor and the officer delayed their arrival, and, by the time they came, the Doukhobors sharply changed their views on this matter, with the result that a long struggle developed between the Doukhobors and the government.[7]

The Doukhobors' refusal to sign for individual homesteads baffled the authorities. Had they not done all in their power to help the Doukhobors settle in the village groups they requested by putting aside blocks of land? Did they not realize, as Sifton would remind them later, that once the land became theirs, they could do anything they wanted with it — even give it to trustees in the name of the Community if they

---

5   "Journals of the House of Commons," Petition of May 12, 1900, The Immigration and Colonization of 1900, Appendix No. 1, Edward VII, 1901, 330.

6   Maude, *A Peculiar People*, 200-201.

7   Sulerzhitsky, *To America With the Doukhobors*, 214.

wished?[8] And surely, in the final analysis, the prospect of losing the lands on which their eventual prosperity would depend would force them to accept individual registration. But the reasoning of the authorities fell on ears attuned to different values. The Doukhobors would not acknowledge individual ownership of land. Even the threat of losing their lands could not deter them. Only the arrival of their leader, Peter Verigin, resolved this problem, and his intervention, as time would prove, was more a temporary compromise than a capitulation.

After a meeting with the North Colony villagers in February 1902, Sifton made a final appeal in which he reiterated the concession respecting residence — they could live in their own villages rather than on their homesteads — but added that he would be satisfied (implying that the *regulations* would be satisfied, since, as the Minister of the Interior, he was in charge of administering the Homestead Act) if the Doukhobors cultivated *altogether around the village* [my emphasis] an acreage equal to the total required by the number of homesteads in that village. To ensure that the thrust of the concession would not be misunderstood, Sifton gave a specific example:

> If, for instance, a village wants fifty homesteads around the village, I will be satisfied if the amount of improvements required on each quarter-section is done around the village, only for the whole fifty.[9]

For some Doukhobors, this concession was viewed with suspicion. It had the look of a suggested compromise designed only to persuade them to register for their land as individual property, and thus to abandon their belief in the communal ownership of land. It was one step down the slippery slope leading to individualism. For others, however, the concession was seen as an indication that the government was recognizing their way of life by allowing communal cultivation, and was taken at face value. Unfortunately, the local land agents were not informed of this concession; the directives either were not sent or went missing. Throughout the correspondence of 1904 and 1905, especially when applications for cancellations of Doukhobor homesteads became common, the Dominion Lands agents assumed that cultivation had to be done individually, and could not be done in community. For their part, the Doukhobors were equally certain that the provisions expressed in Sifton's letters were the "new articles" in the "new agreement."[10] For example, in February 1905, P.G. Keyes, Secretary of the Department of Interior, notified the lands agent at Prince Albert that there was "no way" the individual cultivation duties could be waived.[11] James Peaker, Dominion Lands agent at Yorkton, was apparently taken by surprise when the issue of communal cultivation was raised. He said "no instructions" relating to communal cultivation were sent to his office, therefore the

---

8   NA, RG15, V755 F494483, Pt. 6, Clifford Sifton to Thunder Hill Settlement, 15 February 1902.
9   Ibid.
10 See the petition and dialogue with Frank Oliver in Canada, *Papers Relating to the Holding of Homestead Entries by Members of the Doukhobor Community* (Ottawa: Government Printing Bureau, 1907).
11 NA, RG15, V755 F494483, Pt. 4, Keyes to Thomas Young, 11 October 1905.

cancellations "must be carried out."[12] Speers also referred to the matter as if it were another delaying ploy of the Doukhobors,[13] but J. Obed Smith, the Commissioner of Immigration, confirmed that the matter of communal cultivation was in force, and sent copies of Sifton's letter to the Deputy Minister of the Interior, W.W. Cory.[14] FitzRoy Dixon, of the Secretary's Office, Department of the Interior, apparently still did not accept that this concession was to be applied to the Doukhobors as late as July 1905.[15] The instructions of October 1905 clearly indicate that the community cultivation provision was in force, and that the detailed inspection of 1905 was to provide the base for determining whether this communal cultivation had been sufficiently done.[16] Speers, too, confirmed the provisions of the Hamlet Clause, both in residence and in cultivation *en bloc*, in October.[17]

Beyond this, miscommunication between lands agents in the three agencies and the Department of the Interior raised other problems. In carrying out their normal duties (including instituting cancellation proceedings against those homesteads on which residence or cultivation requirements were delinquent), the agents failed to advise the Department which of the cancelled homesteads belonged to Doukhobors. "Had attention been drawn to the location of these homesteads," said Dixon, "we should certainly have stopped proceedings, and this action I may say was taken in a few cases where the actual facts came to my knowledge."[18] The attached list of homesteads cancelled in the Doukhobor reserves indicate that this oversight involved nearly 100 homesteads: seven in the North Colony, sixty-three in the South Colony and Annex (two of which were not Doukhobors, and a third arguably a non-Doukhobor), and twenty-eight in the Saskatchewan Colony, for a total of ninety-eight homesteads.

The confusion about the provisions or concessions was exacerbated by conflicts within the Doukhobor Community as well. Peter Verigin had joined his followers in December 1902 and, at a general meeting in February 1903, had persuaded them to view the registration of homestead lands as a trivial formality rather than a serious departure from their beliefs. As a consequence, some 1,926 entries were made by a committee comprised of Peter Verigin and two others, on behalf of the individual Doukhobors.[19] Despite the strong affirmation of solidarity at this meeting, some Doukhobors began leaving the Community (Speers estimated about twenty-five families by 1905) and their entries were apparently being cancelled without their

---

12   Ibid., Peaker to Secretary, Department of the Interior, 13 March 1905.
13   NA, RG76, V184 F65101, Pt. 7, Speers to Cory, 15 March 1905.
14   NA, RG15, V755 F494483, Pt. 4, Smith to Cory, 4 April 1905.
15   Ibid., Dixon to Greenway, 6 July 1905.
16   Ibid., Keyes to White, 11 October 1905.
17   Ibid., Speers to Department of the Interior, 16 October 1905.
18   Ibid., Dixon to Greenway, 14 December 1904.
19   NA, RG15, V756 F494483, Pt. 8, Harley to J. Obed Smith, 14 February 1903. Later entries, also by proxy, brought the total to 2,383 (ibid., Pt. 4, Speers to Oliver, 7 September 1905).

knowledge. Since Verigin was the recipient of all correspondence respecting land, the notice to show cause was never delivered to the individual Doukhobors; therefore, there was no protest against the cancellation.[20] In fact, Verigin was apparently instituting cancellation proceedings against the homesteads of some who left the Community. Several families contacted Justice of the Peace E.C. Clark at Fort Pelly to put their case before Sifton. Their complaint was that as soon as they left the Community

> Peter Veregan [sic] applies to have their Homesteads cancelled and they never get the notice. They say it is sent to Peter Veregan consequently at the expiration of the two months they loose [sic] there [sic] lands.[21]

Notwithstanding his difficulties in written expression, Clark had no trouble grasping the double-edged problem that such departures raised. If the homestead in question had improvements done by the Community, the Community was upset; if the homestead had no improvements, the individual was upset, having shared in the Community cultivation of other lands but receiving no benefit to himself on his own homestead. In fact, he was in danger of cancellation, since now he could not claim the common improvements which would make his homestead viable under the special provisions of the cultivation concession. Despite the pacifist principles of the Doukhobors, this mutual dissatisfaction often erupted into conflicts of a more violent nature. Clark reported eight cases of assault in ten days, "on account of disagreement with regard to houses in village — goods — & land."[22]

From the Department's point of view, even the actual number of homestead entries was suspect. Many more entries were recorded than appeared justified. According to Verigin, there were forty-four villages and forty homesteaders per village, or 1,760 entries (the Saskatchewan Colony villages had already gone their own way by this time). But by 1905, 2,383 entries had been made. Even if one allows some latitude for a combination of underage reporting (for fear of the government using this data for conscription records) and the coming of age of 15- and 16-year-old males in the intervening three years, it would appear that the number was inflated by 150-200 entries.[23] Since the entries were made by proxy (that is, the list of eligible homesteaders for each village was made by the "Committee of Three" — Peter Verigin, Simeon Reiben and Pavel Planidin), the Department had difficulty

---

20 "They [agents at Yorkton, Prince Albert and Regina] are also being informed that it has been represented to the Department that the notices to show cause fell into the hands of Peter Veregan [sic], and failed to reach the defendants, who were, consequently, unaware of the cancellation of their entries" (NA, RG15, V755 F494483, Pt. 4, FitzRoy Dixon to Greenway, 14 December 1904).

21 Ibid., Clark to Sifton, 26 November 1904.

22 Ibid.

23 NA, RG76, V184 F65101, Pt. 5, "Doukhobor Statistics," shows 1,869 eligible homesteads in the North and South Colonies. At the meeting of 10 February 1903, it was determined that there were at least 1,926 eligible homesteads in the North and South Colonies (NA, RG15, V755 F494483, Pt. 3, Harley to Smith, 14 February 1903]. In the North and South Colonies, 177 homesteads were reserved for 17-year old Doukhobor males (ibid., Smith to Scott, 17 November 1903).

challenging any of the names, so duplicates or underage entrants could easily be included.

Two other problems were raised regarding the acceptance of cultivation in community. In a letter to Greenway, F. FitzRoy Dixon pointed out that every time an application for cancellation came up, the entire amount of cultivation would have to be assessed in order to determine if the conditions had been met. (Once the minimum cultivation for a particular village had been met, there would be no further need to assess the amount of cultivation, if the land belonged to a resident of that village.) A second flaw was that patent could be granted to applicants for quarter sections "upon which there will be not a stroke of work done."[24] Such an occurrence posed a serious problem for the government, as it was already pressured by public demand to make available entered lands which were "idle." To think of countenancing the patent of such land was clearly unsupportable. To the Doukhobors, the critical point was that the right to work that piece of land, once cultivation had expanded to include it, be maintained. Their concern was with use, not ownership.

Speers was uncertain as to whether cultivation equivalent to the number of homestead entries was actually done, hence the detailed survey of 1905 which provides the data base for the "snapshots" of the colonies in Chapters 8-10. The findings of this survey indicated that considering all cultivation, slightly more than fifteen acres per homestead were cultivated, and that should have ended the matter, at least for those villages which met the standard (some villages had much more than the required fifteen acres per homestead, and some had much less), but Frank Oliver, who succeeded Clifford Sifton as Minister of the Interior in 1905, summarily dismissed Sifton's concession as having no binding authority. This decision was a clear violation of the rights and expectations of the Doukhobors. The remarkable progress made in the three years following Verigin's arrival was achieved under the assumption that the lands they were bringing under cultivation around the villages would fulfill the cultivation duties on the outlying homesteads, as Sifton had promised. When, in the course of a few months, they were given notice that this provision was invalid and that all homesteads having insufficient cultivation would be cancelled, the Doukhobors felt, justifiably, betrayed by the government.

It is quite possible that the conflict over cultivation was peripheral, and eventually inconsequential, to the core of the land ownership issue: swearing allegiance to the Crown. This matter was discussed at the general meeting of February 1903, and according to the government officials, the decision to become British subjects was wrapped up in, and more contentious than, the decision to register for the homestead lands.[25] The issue did not assume importance again until 1906.

---

24   NA, RG15, V755 F494483, Pt. 4, Dixon to Greenway, 6 July 1905.

25   "I wired you that all the Doukhobors had decided to become British subjects and to make entries for their homesteads .... We found it a good deal harder to have them to consent to become British subjects than to take up the land" (NA, RG15, V756 F494483, Pt. 8, Harley to Smith, 14 February 1903). Although Verigin later gave the impression of being uninvolved in the discussion — "at the moment, the Doukhobors are involved in discussions regarding becoming subjects of the English

Some of the villages now began to enter for their homesteads. The Good Spirit Lake Doukhobors had "broken the ice" in May 1902, when parties from three villages entered for their homesteads.[26] Crerar was optimistic that the rest of the Good Spirit Lake Colony would shortly follow suit. In the Saskatchewan Colony there was little resistance to registration on the part of many. Some 365 homesteads representing all but a few of the eligible homestead entrants in eight villages were entered by September 1902, according to an account in the *Manitoba Morning Free Press*.[27]

The initial indecision respecting the registration for individual homesteads was related to, and complicated by, the march of between 1,700 and 1,900 Doukhobor men, women and children in October 1902, the second major event of this pivotal year. This "pilgrimage" was the culmination of a series of disturbances (collectively called the "mania" by government officials) confined initially to a few of the most idealistic visionaries but which spread rapidly, in the context of confusion and disillusionment, to encompass a large component of the North and South Colony settlers. First a number of Doukhobors "liberated" ("set adrift" in Speers' colourful phrase) large numbers of their animals and then refused to use any animal products — milk, butter, wool or hide. Then they finally set out on a mass pilgrimage, determined to follow Christ's command to evangelize the world. The detailed events are described in Pedley's report based on Speers' observations.[28]

In early August, Speers reported "a strange religious craze" at work among the Doukhobors, apparently arising from the evangelistic work of a visiting New York agitator. They refused to work their animals, he said. They burned their sheepskin coats and women's boots, and talked about going to a warmer climate. They were also not preparing properly for the coming winter, saying that "the Lord will provide." He was unable to make out just what motivated this behaviour but relayed Crerar's hopeful opinion that the craze was confined to a few individuals and that they would "change their minds."[29] A large number of animals were "set adrift" as a consequence of the new regard for their animal brethren. After futile attempts to show that turning their animals loose in the bush to be ravaged by predators was hardly an act of Christian charity,[30] government officials gathered up the animals and auctioned them off, putting the money into a fund for the Doukhobors.[31] Some

---

king" [Verigin to Tolstoy, 20 February 1904 in Donskov, *Tolston-Verigin Correspondence*, 64] — Crerar stated that he was the spokesman for the group (NA, RG15, V756 F494483, Pt. 8, Crerar to Smith, 12 February 1903).

26 NA, RG76, V184 F65101, Pt. 6, Crerar to Turriff, 5 May 1902.

27 *Manitoba Morning Free Press*, 23 September 1902.

28 NA, RG76, V184 F65101, Pt. 6, Pedley, "Report," 25 October 1902.

29 Ibid., Speers to Pedley, 11 August 1902.

30 In a report describing his personal survey of the North Colony, Speers described the affected group as a "quiet, inoffensive, sullenly established people" who were "fully determined to stick to their new theory" (ibid., Speers, "Report," 10 September 1902).

31 The first auction of Doukhobor animals realized $14,500 owing to the "abnormally high prices."

285 cattle, 120 horses and ninety-five sheep were gathered up in the North Colony alone.[32] A sympathetic *Manitoba Morning Free Press* managed to infer that this episode was somehow a normal sale of surplus animals: "Public notice has been given of an auction sale of certain cattle which the Doukhobors did not desire to keep, and which the department, acting as their agent, is now selling."[33]

The final expression of this "new theory" was the pilgrimage to preach Christ. The notion of abandoning their villages and their work to "meet Jesus" and to preach the gospel, originated with a few influential people in the village of Terpennie Orlovsky and spread rapidly among the poorest villages of the Cyprus Doukhobors of the South Colony.[34] A group of 300 Cyprus villagers then toured the North Colony villages, inviting them to join their pilgrimage. About 800 responded and the combined group of 1,100 then marched south to Terpennie again. Harley noted that there was a good deal of the "religious mania" among them, but felt that the leaders were using this tactic as a scheme to bring pressure to bear on the government to have the Doukhobors transported to another place. Quite a number of women had left their families to join the pilgrimage, and husbands and sons attempted to persuade them to come home again without success.[35] By the time the group left Terpennie on its pilgrimage south, more than 1,900 men, women, and children were involved. An initial group of 1,160 led by 300 singers spread out over three miles. A second contingent of 768 followed about six miles behind.[36] Department officials intercepted the group at Yorkton and forced the women and children to abandon the march. This seems to have lessened the "ardour" of the group, and the numbers involved declined daily from that point on. As they approached the Manitoba border, a worried Premier Roblin wired Sifton for assurance that the Manitoba government would not be responsible for taking care of the Doukhobors.[37] Finally, in the face of -18°F temperatures and the possibility of many deaths, the remaining 450 men were intercepted at Minnedosa and returned to their villages.[38]

The general consensus seems to have been that the movement was the work of a few individuals who inflamed the emotions of a group of largely illiterate people who, Speers noted, "become the greatest enthusiasts" when they decided to join a

---

    Another sale of seventy-four cattle and ten horses was to have been held on 22 October (ibid., Pedley "Report," 25 October 1902.

32   Ibid., Smith to Pedley, 4 September 1902.

33   Ibid., 23 September 1902.

34   Ibid., Speers to Pedley, 11 August 1902. Woodcock and Avakumovic note that the movement split along lines of prosperity with the poorer Doukhobors accepting the new, more idealistic interpretation of Tolstoy's and Verigin's letters dealing with ownership of property while the wealthier Doukhobors ignored it (*The Doukhobors*, 168).

35   NA, RG76, V184 F65101, Pt. 6, Harley to Smith, 25 October 1902.

36   Ibid., Speers, "Report," 26 November 1902.

37   Ibid., Roblin to Sifton, 1 November 1902.

38   Ibid., Speers, "Report," 26 November 1902.

cause. Speers felt that the end result of the march would be beneficial. While "[t]hey exhibited a collective imbecility in their mad march that is rarely met with," he felt that they would now "resume their duty along right lines." He noted that many were embarrassed and ashamed they had participated in the march.[39] Philip Harvey agreed with this assessment in his report on fifteen of the northern villages of the Yorkton district:

> There is considerable preparation made by way of cultivation for the ensuing year and I observe that the returned pilgrims are in a state of practical contentment, expressing regret that they entered upon their foolish crusade. There are a few who are keeping up an agitation, but I think they will improve in time.[40]

Herbert Archer observed much the same response among the North Colony villages. "This stupid movement has left many of the villages quite poor again," he reported, but the pilgrimage movement was dead. The main body of Doukhobors were "regaining their sanity. One after another takes to horses again, some shave & cut their hair and lose the characteristic Pilgrim appearance." Most significant of all, in his opinion, the villages whose pilgrim members were being supplied by government flour hauled by government teams (paid for from the fund established by auctioning the freed animals) were one by one sending word to the officials to send no more.[41] The Doukhobors of Good Spirit Lake and the Saskatchewan Colony appear not to have been affected by this early manifestation of the mania.[42]

The mania proved to be a lingering phenomenon, however. The few remaining "agitators" who would not "change their minds" succeeded in continuing to disrupt the relative harmony of Doukhobor life and occasionally these protests broke out in public display. One of the ringleaders of the 1902 march moved to the Saskatchewan Colony and began to arouse some of the Doukhobors there. In the Redberry district, 100 Doukhobors turned their cattle loose and marched to the Elbow villages west of Saskatoon in May of the following year.[43] Nudity made its appearance in the villages of the Saskatchewan Colony at about the same time. Ivan Perapolkin of Troitzka (Troitzkaja) village was reported leading a small group who were afflicted by a "strange mania to divest themselves of clothing," and his influence caused others "to worship God in the manner before mentioned."[44] The dissident Doukhobors discovered more or less accidentally that this manner of worship was also a wonderfully effective, nonviolent protest against government (and societal) interference in their affairs, so what began as a religious urge quickly became a practical weapon of protest by hard-core radicals. A small group of twenty-six combined

---

39   Ibid.
40   Ibid.
41   Ibid., Archer to Turriff, 6 January 1903.
42   Ibid., Pedley, "Report," 25 October 1902.
43   Ibid., Smith to Scott, 2 May 1903.
44   Ibid., Speers to Scott, 4 May 1904 [sic] [1903].

nudity and fire by removing most of their clothes and making a bonfire of them just outside Yorkton in May 1903.[45] Arson as a corrective to the errors of wayward, materialistic Doukhobors began when a small group burned some binder canvases in protest of the owners using horses to reap their crop.[46] The wandering continued in 1904, although it involved many fewer people, perhaps fifty in all, and was not, according to Speers, a recurrence of the large pilgrimage of 1902:

> The first movement was very large and the people had some specific object, no matter how rediculous [sic]. This movement is small, a mere bagatelle, and is simply continuing the peculiar freaks characteristic of these people and this is a small element that never absolutely settled down.[47]

Such wanderings were not to attract significant attention until the long-distance pilgrimage of 1907-08, but they did provide the media with news items which stereotyped Doukhobors in the public eye as wild-eyed, discontented radicals who were unworthy of special concessions and who would never make good Canadian citizens.[48] At least one business was not above using the occasion to add what it considered a bit of humour to its advertising at the expense of the Doukhobors: McManus Jewellery used the headline "Doukhobors Go To Meet Christ," noting that some marchers went in their natural, unadorned state while "others, I am happy to say, are adorning themselves with watches and chains from McManus' Jewellery."[49] And one paper used the event to poke fun at a rival town: "The Doukhobors are not travelling in the direction of Regina. They know it would be useless there to seek a Messiah."[50]

It seems unlikely that the mania was related solely to the land question, although it is fairly clear that the leaders of the movement used the frustrations surrounding the land issue to motivate their followers. Verigin, professing personal ignorance as to the cause of the "pilgrimage," suggested three "mixed feelings" which prompted it: concern about the land — the government's land requirements were "too strict" and the pilgrims were in search of the truth, that is, a search for a more humane attitude on the part of government; concern about the cold climate which prompted people to go in search of a milder environment; and, concern about the problems of society which prompted them to leave home and work to preach Christ's teachings against the evils of tobacco, vodka, the military, and so on.[51]

The mania was also a general response to the confusion and frustration of attempting to make difficult ideological decisions (is registering for a homestead

---

45   Ibid., Smith to Scott, 21 May 1903.
46   NA, RG76, V184 F65101, Pt. 7, Smith to Scott, 27 July 1904.
47   Ibid., Speers to Scott, 27 July 1904.
48   See, for example, the *Star Phoenix* account of one of the marchers explaining the purpose of the march, "while the flickering light of lost reason gleamed from his eyes" (7 November 1902).
49   Ibid., 8 May 1903.
50   *Prince Albert Advocate*, 10 November 1902.
51   Verigin to Tolstoy, 12 January 1903 in Donskov, *Tolstoy-Verigin Correspondence*, 52-53.

abandoning the belief that land should be held communally with no divisions?) without any clear direction from their spiritual leader. They were a cooperative group, recently turned communal (in fact their experience in Canada was to be the first mass application of this way of life), and they had a long history of following leaders who were regarded as divine, or as having the authority of divinity. They were not habituated to making individual decisions — they followed the dictates of their leader. In the absence of a leader, they reverted to an Eastern face-saving or face-protecting stance in dealing with problems, conflicts and decisions. Things were not approached directly, answers were not given directly (not only because of this group's experience, but also for the very practical reason of protection against government manipulation), and conflicts were talked out — group consensus was extremely important. Individual decision making was foreign to their way of thinking. Without their leader and his personal instruction, they were "like sheep without a shepherd." They were forced to rely on written communications from their leader-in-exile which most of the group could not read, and which they were likely to interpret in ways opposite to their obvious meaning, reasoning that perhaps that was what Verigin intended so as to mislead the authorities who, they were convinced, were privy to these communications. Later, as a result of the confusions resulting from conflict with the government, conflict within their own ranks, and the oft-changing "suggestions" of their own leader, some were prone to interpret even direct communications in this way, again arguing that Verigin was trying to throw the authorities off track. The ultimate result was to produce confusion and unrest, even open conflict.

The majority of the Doukhobors would not commit themselves to practical decisions much less come to agreement on difficult matters of belief without direction from their leader. The growing frustration of the government and the growing confusion of the Doukhobors — leaderless and prodded by agitators and the idealistic letters from their leader — no doubt made them ripe for the kind of radical responses suggested by a few of their members.

The exhortations read into the vague and cryptic ideological ramblings of their leader,[52] distributed and distorted by a literate, non-Doukhobor anarchist, only increased their sense of confusion:

> Stimulated by government pressure to take out individual entry on land and obey statistical registration laws; plus misrepresentation of Verigin's anarchistic back-to-nature letters, Tchertkoff's Handbook for immigrants, Bodyansky's critique of governments, a few "seekers of freedom" release cattle and horses, pull wagons by human power, throw away their money and object to tillage of soil.[53]

The Doukhobors were increasingly persuaded that the "petty persecutions" they

---

52   A collection of the letters of Peter Verigin was published by Tchertkoff and circulated among the Doukhobors (NA, RG76, V184 F65101, Pt. 11, Maude, "Sketch of Doukhobor history," 1924).

53   Tarasoff, "In Search of Brotherhood," 259.

had to bear — the demands for reporting vital statistics, and the requirements of individual registration for homestead land — were all of a piece, that Canadians, collectively and individually, "wished to attack Doukhobor principles, to mock and destroy their pacifism, their vegetarianism, their preference for a communal way of life."[54] It is not surprising that what began as a more intense commitment to a literal interpretation of the communal way of life (and therefore a firm rejection of any attempt to persuade them away from a collective view of the land) quickly escalated into a full-blown religious fervour which encouraged them to abandon all aspects of the world, even their agricultural labour, to do the more important work of Christ. This "pure" motivation was leavened by rumours that their leader was waiting for them somewhere in a better land where their idealism could fully flower.

Whatever the motivations of the movement, its effect was to begin to change public opinion from pity to apathy to hostility. The mania showed a new facet of Doukhoborism: it was not just different, it was fanatical.[55] This strange behaviour implanted the seeds of negativism in minds which were initially favourable to Doukhobor settlement (or which at least were prepared to give the Doukhobors the benefit of the doubt), and it confirmed the judgements and increased the intolerance of those who were opposed to the Doukhobors (or any "non-white" group) from the beginning. It also was the beginning of a lasting schism in the community itself which crystalized when Peter Verigin arrived in Canada, a division among those who accepted his leadership and his idea of progress and the ideal community (the Orthodox or Community Doukhobors), the "free men" (the "Sons of God" and later, the "Sons of Freedom") who radically opposed material progress and what they saw as the abandonment of Doukhobor ideals, and the Independents who became disenchanted with both conservative and radical communalism.

The third significant event, in late 1902, was Peter Verigin's arrival in Canada to rejoin his followers. Government officials, frustrated in their attempts to explain and enforce homestead requirements, and puzzled and provoked by the fervour and flinty persistence characterizing the mass pilgrimage, looked forward to Verigin's arrival with great anticipation and considerable relief. Surely he would put an end to the bizarre behaviour of the few agitators, and would convince the bulk of the Doukhobors of the legitimacy of accepting homestead lands under the requirements which were uniformly applied to all land seekers. Released finally from exile in Russia, Verigin arrived in Canada in December 1902. His people welcomed him with joy and awe; government officials and the public were hardly less enthusiastic. Although noncommittal about whether Canada was the land of opportunity that it seemed to be, Verigin immediately set about to find every bit of information about the land question, seeking confirmation or denial even of rumours of requirements

---

54 Woodcock and Avakumovic, *The Doukhobors*, 166.

55 The government had equally passionate beliefs about the way society should be organized, but as an institution representing established authority, and using accepted methods of displaying its commitment, its passion was seen as nationalism.

or concessions, and then only from appointed officials.[56] Herbert Archer, the British Quaker who worked tirelessly among the North Colony Doukhobors and who prepared the lists of eligible homesteaders ready for the time when they would agree to sign individually for their land, was enthusiastic in his support of Verigin. "Since Peter Verigin came much has been done & the principle of individual entry is getting generally accepted," he was able to report just two weeks after Verigin's arrival. "[U]nless something quite unexpected intervenes, I think everything will be settled satisfactorily within the next month or two."[57] He commented on Verigin's "remarkable intelligence and power," and his extraordinary endurance.[58] On 7 January, Verigin met with government officials to discuss the details of the land question, and on 10 February, he brought together delegates from each village to a general meeting at Terpennie to decide on a course of action. Verigin convinced the delegates that signing for their land was a mere formality; the important thing was to resolve that the land be farmed communally.[59] The delegates unanimously agreed with their leader, and in April the registrations for the land, done by proxy by a "committee of three" for all the Doukhobors, went ahead. By November 1904, 422,800 acres representing approximately 2,640 homesteads had been entered,[60] leaving nearly 244,000 acres of the area originally reserved for the Doukhobors open for further homesteading.[61] These surplus lands were thrown open for public homesteading on 15 December 1904.[62]

Ignoring this problem was probably not simply a matter of buying time, although Verigin seems to have used the requirements and the patience of the government to good advantage in this regard.[63] The bulk of the people apparently went along with all of the registering in the misguided belief that they were indeed doing what

---

56 See Archer's complaint about the "muddling" of the land question by Ivin (NA, RG76, V184 F65101, Pt. 7, Archer to Moffat, 27 December 1902).

57 NA, RG15, V755 F494483, Pt. 3, Archer to Turriff, 6 January 1903.

58 NA, RG76, V184 F65101, Pt. 7, Archer to Moffat, 27 December 1902.

59 Woodcock and Avakumovic, *The Doukhobors*, 186-87.

60 This number, derived by dividing the total entered acreage by 160, is somewhat higher than the 2,330 entered homesteads reported by the 1905 survey, and the 2,383 homesteads recorded at the Yorkton Land Office. The discrepancy is largely explained by the fact that the total entered acreage on the reserves included entries by Independent Doukhobors while the 1905 figure included only Community Doukhobor homesteads.

61 NA, RG15, V755 F494483, Pt. 4, Goodeve to Smart, 29 November 1904.

62 Woodcock and Avakumovic, *The Doukhobors*, 204.

63 "As for taking the oath of allegiance to the Canadian government and the King of England, there is still three years to decide about that, and in the meantime we must live" (Peter Verigin quoted in Wright, *Slava Bohu*, 212). See also Verigin to Tolstoy, 20 February 1904: "This experiment [of determining what explanations the government would accept in the matter of land ownership and use] will take at least three or four years, over which time the Doukhobors, one would assume, will manage to save up at least some money, and if the government should decide to make life miserable for the Doukhobors over some question of citizenship, we shall be willing to agree to it" (in Donskov, *Tolstoy-Verigin Correspondence*, 64).

was necessary to obtain use of the land. The matter of oath taking either did not really enter into their thinking, or was brushed aside as one more requirement that could be modified as the cultivation requirements apparently had been. Owning the land was not a high priority in their thinking; using the land to support their Community and the coming generation was. And if there were problems in the future, they no doubt trusted their leader to take care of them. Their confidence in their future in Saskatchewan was ill-placed and the work of the Department in registering eligible and nearly-eligible entrants was for the most part wasted.

It is not entirely clear whether Verigin promoted this decision in order to have a "breathing space" of three years before a final decision on the oath of allegiance had to be made, whether he was assured that the oath of allegiance would not be obligatory, or whether an official merely noted that it was possible to affirm allegiance rather than swear it.[64] There is some support for suggesting that the officials, either by assurance or implication, conveyed to the Doukhobors the idea that swearing the oath of allegiance would not be required. In the same letter in which Herbert Archer expressed his optimism about the final settlement of the registration issue, he also noted that it had been agreed that the "Solemn Declaration" on the registration form would be omitted.[65] The Royal Commission of 1912 noted that the Doukhobors were assured by the government that they would be exempted from the requirement of naturalization but that public concern about any special treatment of the Doukhobors caused the government to change its position.[66] It seems likely that either the apparent understanding reached at the general meeting of February 1903 was all on one side (the government's),[67] or that the Doukhobors assumed the exemption from the "Solemn Declaration" (by oath) on the registration forms meant that the same exemption would apply to the final patent applications. At the very least, the Doukhobors could reasonably have assumed that the oath was not an unalterable part of the process of acquiring their land. The government had set aside what was clearly an official requirement on one form; it could certainly do so on another (the application for patent form).[68]

---

64 Woodcock and Avakumovic, *The Doukhobors*, 187.

65 NA, RG15, V755 F494483, Pt. 3, Archer to Turriff, 6 January 1903.

66 William Blakemore, *Report of the Royal Commission on Matters Relating to the Sect of Doukhobors in the Province of British Columbia* (Victoria: King's Printer, 1913), 25.

67 Peter Verigin wrote to Tolstoy in 1907, "I'm quite satisfied that the Doukhobors have accepted this proposal [that the government would cancel homesteads of those who would not become British subjects but would provide fifteen acres for each individual who wished to remain in the Community] with quiet equanimity, probably because the majority of them already decided the question of Citizenship about three or four years back — in the negative" (Verigin to Tolstoy, 9 March 1907 in Donskov, *Tolstoy-Verigin Correspondence*, 83).

68 Herbert Archer was perhaps aware of the possible complications of officially completing forms which included wording not applicable to the Doukhobors' special conditions. He requested direction on the three parts of the entry form that were problematic: the declaration that the homestead would be for the applicant's exclusive use and benefit, and the requirements for residence and cultivation. The modification related to the "Solemn Declaration" had been agreed

However, Harley's report emphasizes that the government representatives had been clear and firm about the necessity of the Doukhobors becoming British subjects, and "[w]hen they saw we meant business they decided at once to take up their homesteads and become British subjects."[69] Just exactly what the Doukhobors understood by becoming British subjects is not clear.

Having settled the land question, for the time being at least, Verigin turned to the task of reorganizing the Community on a grand communal basis. He brought back together in a cohesive group the factions that arose in the time of confusion. Agent Hugh Harley emphasized this new spirit of unity in his stream-of-consciousness report of the February meeting: "There is no two kinds of Doukhobors now they are all of one family again now and they look upon the money as belonging to them all now as they will all help one another from this time on. They told me they are all one family again."[70] Verigin's leadership also attracted some former Independents back to the fold.[71] Even many of the more Independent Doukhobors of the Saskatchewan Colony were drawn back into the Community, although as I have noted earlier, at least four villages seem not to have abandoned communalism even in the early stages. Under Verigin's reunification, perhaps as many as 500 felt strongly enough about the communal way of life that they were willing to abandon their lands and improvements in the Saskatchewan Colony to create three villages (possibly four) in the North Colony and a sizeable settlement in the South Colony near Veregin Station.[72]

Verigin used the inherent power of his position and his influential personality to consolidate his community. Some of his methods, however, were questionable. Hermann Fast, a preacher among the Russian Baptists and Mennonites near the Saskatchewan Colony, and a teacher in the Doukhobor school at Petrofka, was

---

upon already (NA, RG15, V755 F494483, Pt. 3, Archer to Turriff, 7 January 1903). Jeremy Adelman also alludes to possible inconsistencies in policy related to homestead entry and homestead patent, although he infers that Sifton ignored them, possibly because he thought that in three years, the Doukhobors would abandon the notion of communal ownership of land. See Jeremy Adelman, "Early Doukhobor Experience on the Canadian Prairies," *Journal of Canadian Studies* 25, no. 4 (Winter 1990-91): 114.

69   NA, RG15, V756 F494483, Pt. 8., Harley to Smith, 14 February 1903.
70   Ibid.
71   One of these was the avowed Independent, Ivan Ivin, who must have been a particularly vocal individual, judging by how frequently his name is mentioned in contemporary records. His return to the fold was short-lived, however. By late November 1904, he had again opted for the independent life, this time taking with him at least 100 acres of community cultivation (NA, RG15, V755 F494483, Pt. 4, Clark to Sifton, 26 November 1904).
72   The agitation for many of the Saskatchewan Colony Doukhobors to move to the Yorkton Colonies "to be with Petushka" began soon after Verigin's arrival, but the movement was delayed until 1905 (NA, RG15, V756 F494483, Pt. 8, Harley to J.Obed Smith, 14 February 1903). The village of Pavlovo (although not named) is noted as a fourth village set apart for the Saskatchewan Colony émigrés in the North Colony (NA, RG76, V184 F65101, Pt. 8, Smith to Scott, 23 April 1906). If indeed it was, it was the first settled of the four, having a population of 133 in the survey of 1905 (NA, RG15, V1167 F5412493, Pavlovo Village File).

critical of Verigin's authoritarian leadership. Verigin carried out his plans with "refined severity," said Fast, excommunicating from the benefits of community those who would not follow his slightest desire. Modestly playing down his absolute leadership publicly, he nonetheless encouraged the Doukhobors in their belief that he was indeed a stand-in for Christ. He appealed to the women by "promising them a shorter amount of labor hours, better raiment and food to gain their support for his ideas and through them to get over the husbands for the community system."[73] He also played upon the feelings of the young in his attempt to relocate the Saskatchewan Colony Doukhobors: "the young lads of 13 and 14 are promised to have homesteads reserved for them in the Yorkton district to incite their parents to follow them and move to Yorkton."[74] Fast ended his assessment of Verigin's leadership by noting that among the Saskatchewan Colony settlers, "there is a party who groans under the leadership of Peter Verigin" but they were "too oppressed and too shy" to take decisive action in breaking away.[75]

Whatever Verigin's methods, they produced results. He not only consolidated the majority of the group on a communal basis but applied this new enthusiasm and cooperation to produce the most vigorous progress of any immigrant group in the next few years:

> The result is the establishment of a very remarkable and very complete system of communism. It is doubtful whether at any time there has been in place quite so complete a system of community of goods on so large a scale as he has succeeded in establishing.[76]

Mavor goes on to describe the system in more detail:

> Otherwise [excepting purchases of machinery, stock and so on] they are absolutely self contained. They grind wheat grown by themselves in their own mills; they grind their flax also in their own mills, and press linseed oil. They grow flax for yarn and spin and weave it into linen. They spin and weave wool into woolen cloth, and, as a rule, they make their own garments, although, when they are working externally, the men buy

---

73 NA, RG15, V755 F494483, Pt. 3, Fast to Smart, 24 August 1903. Iwan Tchernoff, an Independent in the Saskatchewan Colony village of Petrofka who had recently left the Community, illustrates this problem: "Wife refuses to leave community, and threatens to leave him unless he returns to it. Wants to know whether if Peter Veregin [sic] advises his wife to leave him he can take another wife to look after his family" (NA, RG15, V1164 F5391335, Petrofka Village Files, 1905 schedule). This tactic is illustrated as late as 1911 in Smyrennie village: "Note: Discussion between Anna Chernoff and Nicholai Chernoff independent communist. The wife strongly objected to being counted with the independent communists and objected to being counted as having left the community. Husband requested that the two boys be counted with him. Wife and two girls counted with the community. Husband and two boys counted as ind communists. The woman was told this arrangement was only an understanding for this year" (NA, RG15, V1166 F5412431, Smyrennie Village File).

74 Many of the Saskatchewan villages reported young men entering for homesteads in the extreme northwest part of the South Colony.

75 NA, RG15, V755 F494483, Pt. 3, Fast to Smart, 24 August 1903.

76 Mavor, *Report to the Board of Trade*, 16.

ready-made clothes. Their threshing machinery, flour and flax mills, and their saw mills are all driven by steam power.[77]

The very success of Verigin's disciplined leadership caused Tolstoy to raise some cautious concerns. Responding to a letter from Verigin in which he detailed all the accomplishments of the previous year, Tolstoy cautioned him about getting "carried away" by the material success of the Community and reminded him that "this success is based on the unity stemming from the religious consciousness which brings everyone together."[78] The material progress of the Community was also raising concerns among other settlers:

> The local residents, especially, are beginning to regard the Doukhobors with some degree of envy, since the Doukhobors through their community organization are able to raise their standard of living more quickly and so get ahead of the English ... . The English[-speaking] farmers who all live on individual homesteads are upset because their own enterprises might fall behind, while the capitalists are upset because they don't get goods or money from [the Doukhobors] for interest.[79]

It was Mavor's assessment that group settlement had both advantages and limitations when compared with individual or "distributed" settlement. Group settlement "yields, at least on the margin of settlement, more immediately favorable results in material comfort and in amenity of personal life," but, on the other hand, is "less favorable to assimilation" than isolated settlement.[80] He might also have mentioned the psychological, social and religious benefits of community life in addition to the economic advantages. Community provided a great deal of security and social interaction. It also provided a context of sanctions and peer pressure which kept the group together as a functioning organization with common goals.

Organization

Despite the advantages of communal life, there was a good deal of organizational ambivalence in the villages in the period 1899-1905. Some villages started out communally, drifted toward cooperative individualism, were drawn back to communalism by the charisma of Verigin, and then reverted to complete independence. To characterize particular villages as organized in one particular way throughout this time of flux is misleading. It is especially dangerous to generalize on the basis of geographical areas. For example, it is conventional to characterize the Saskatchewan Colony villages as independent, and the North Colony villages as communal. While these statements are accurate as broad generalizations, they hide significant variations. Ashworth's report of 1901 (see Table 8) indicates that indeed nine of the

---

77 Ibid., 17.
78 L.N. Tolstoy to Peter V. Verigin, 2 January 1904, in Donskov, *Tolstoy-Verigin Correspondence*, 61.
79 Verigin to Tolstoy, 1 April 1905, in ibid., 71-72.
80 Mavor, *Report to the Board of Trade*, 21.

Table 8
Systems of Property Holding Among District of Assiniboia Villages

Colony	Number of Villages	Communistic*	Communal**	Partly Communal, Partly Independent	Independent
Thunder Hill	13	9	1	2	1
South Colony	24	12	3	8	1
Devil's Lake	10	—	—	5	5
Total: Assiniboia Reserve	47	21	4	15	7

* production and distribution.
** divided into more than one commune.

Source: Dawson, *Group Settlement*, 12 (from a report by John Ashworth, an English Quaker, 15 May 1901).

thirteen villages were fully communistic in the North Colony, but three were either partly or wholly individualistic, and one was divided among more than one commune.

At the other end of the spectrum, four of the ten villages in the so-called individualistic Saskatchewan Colony were fully communistic in 1900. And, after Verigin renewed the faith of many in the communal system, five of the thirteen villages were completely communal, only two villages had something approaching a balance between Independents and Community families (Oospennie and Petrofka), and fewer than 12 percent of the settlers in the whole Colony were classified as Independents.[81] The overwhelming majority of settlers in this supposedly "independent" Colony were living and operating in a communal context. Within villages, the variations were even greater. As perhaps an extreme example, Pakrofka village in the Saskatchewan Colony was comprised of no fewer than four identifiable groups in 1905: eight families (twenty-seven people) were Company (that is, Veriginites, holding to the large communal system), one group of two extended families (fourteen people) operated as an independent company (that is, a communal group separate from the Veriginites), another group of ten families (fifty-one people) formed yet another independent company, and fourteen families (sixty people) were classed as independent. It is not clear what relationship existed between the various communal groups, but they all lived together in the village (six company houses, nine independent company houses, and ten indepen- dent houses).[82] By 1905, then, some villages were totally communistic, some were totally independent (yet keeping the village format), and others included varying proportions of these and intermediate groupings.

---

81 NA, RG15, V1168 F5412499; NA, RG15, V1164 F5391335, Oospennie and Petrofka Village Files, 1905 Schedules.
82 NA, RG15, V1166 F5404690, Pakrofka Village File.

Movement

This period of flux was not confined to matters of attitude, organization or policy. The villages themselves were in flux:

> Another very damaging result of this intense communism, is that the individual having no special interest in the land or its product becomes extremely unstable and is constantly moving about. These people have moved their villages and moved themselves many times during their sojourn in Canada, and in this way have lost much labour and time.[83]

This assessment is one way of explaining the extreme mobility of the Doukhobors throughout this period of flux and later. Although this constant moving about caused consternation among the authorities as they attempted to apply conscientiously the modified provisions of the Hamlet Clause,[84] it does not seem to have had as much impact on the economic progress as the Commission thought. Certainly the Doukhobors expended a tremendous amount of labour on relocating their villages, but, in the main, it was time and energy expended in addition to the normal agricultural progress. In fact, most of the work in the villages during the period 1899 to 1905 was spent in rebuilding or replacing the original, crude houses and building new ones, as well as in adding granaries, workshops, barns, sheds and the like.

The magnitude of village relocation is surprising: twenty villages certainly relocated during this period, and there is good evidence that another seven did so as well. Some villages had erroneously settled on lands outside the Colony (five or six cases) and on lands not available for Doukhobor settlement (school lands, Hudson's Bay Company lands, railway lands), and these villages were, in nearly every case, forced to move to a location on reserved land. However, more than half the movements were voluntary and appear to confirm the lack of attachment to any specific location which the Commission noted.

In the North Colony, three of the thirteen original villages can be documented as having moved between 1899 and 1905: Bogdanofka, Teakomeernoe (Great Bodanofka) and Lubomeernoe.[85] Bogdanofka and Teakomeernoe relocated because they were outside the reserve in Range 32 and both moved far from their original location: straight-line distances of ten miles and 8.5 miles respectively. Whether Osvoborsdennie moved from its location astride NE1-34-32 and NW6-34-31 to a location fully within NW6-34-31 is uncertain. I can find no other documentation for the third village outside the reserve in Township 33, Range 32

---

83   NA, RG15, V755 F494483, Pt. 6, General Report of the Doukhobor Commissioner, n.d. [October-November 1906].

84   The Hamlet Clause allowed the homesteader to maintain residence in a village rather than on the homestead quarter, but it had to be residence in the village adjacent to the homestead land (technically within three miles). The Doukhobors, still under the impression that the land had been set aside for them to farm in any way they wished, felt under no obligation to remain in one particular village.

85   NA, RG76, V184 F65101, Pt. 5, "Doukhobor Statistics"; NA, RG15, V755 F494483, Pt. 4., Verigin to Greenway, 25 April 1905.

which Archer mentions, so I assume he is referring to Osvoborsdennie, since the original village was partially outside the reserve.[86] On the other hand, the location of one remaining house points to a village (the buildings at least) fully within NW6. No reason is given for moving Lubomeernoe diagonally from NW2 to SE2-34-31. Both Michaelovo and Vosnisennie are assumed to have moved early in this period, Michaelovo from McVey's timber camp about one mile to its permanent location, and Vosnisennie from its "blockhouse" location on a Hudson's Bay Company quarter section about one mile to its permanent location.[87] It is quite possible that the villages of Spasskoe (later renamed Hlebedarnoe) and Novotroitzkoe (Simeonovo) moved in 1900.[88]

Altogether, then, within the first few years of settlement, five of the original thirteen villages quite surely moved and two others quite possibly moved. That such a high proportion of the initial sites had to be relocated is likely due to the early arrival of the Doukhobors (beginning in February 1899) and the tardy subdivision survey of some of the lands of this reserve (see Chapter 2).

Eleven of the South Colony and Annex villages definitely relocated or were in the process of relocating in the years between 1900 and 1905. Some villages completed their relocations by 1905, leaving "ghost villages" in their wake (Troitska, Moisayovo, Kerelovka, Old Petrovo, and Old Slavenka); others were in the process of moving and occupied both the old and new sites (Old Kaminka, Old Riduonovo, Old Terpennie, and Old Voskriesennie), so thirty-nine South Colony and Annex villages are noted in the 1905 schedules. Lubovnoe and Old Efromovo were at work building structures on new sites in preparation for a move the following summer (1906), but they continued to occupy their initial sites in 1905.[89]

Some of the moves were a long distance — Old Kaminka moved thirty-nine miles from the southern section of the South Colony to the North Colony; Terpennie Orlovsky, Moisayovo, Kerelovka and Old Riduonovo each moved eighteen miles or more — and some were less than one mile. The villages left behind were substantial. Old Terpennie, a village of twenty-six houses and associated out-buildings, was described as "well built, streets graded and trees planted along each side … . The stables and other buildings used in common are well appointed and well built."[90] The village of Old Slavenka, abandoned in favour of a new site some twelve miles

---

86   NA, RG15, V754 F494483, Pt. 2, Archer to McCreary, 26 May 1900; pers. comm., Harry Vanin, 1991.

87   Bernard, *The Canadian Doukhobor Settlements*, 35; "Doukhobor Statistics."

88   A note written beside these two villages indicates they would be moving in the spring (of 1900) ("Doukhobor Statistics;" see also Tarasoff, *Plakun Trava*, 249).

89   Lubovnoe had built ten new houses ("these being of more modern type than the old"), "a splendid, large, new stable," and four other stables, a blacksmith shop, a carpenter's shop, three bathhouses and two granaries on its new location about one mile southeast (NA, RG15, V1165 F5404674, Lubovnoe Village File, 1905 Schedule). The new village of Efromovo, combining the former villages of Trusdennie and Old Efromovo, was to be occupied in the summer of 1906 (NA, RG15, V1165 F5404660, Efromovo Village File, 1905 Schedule).

90   NA, RG15, V1166 F5412443, Terpennie Village File, 1905 Schedule.

north and renamed Kapustina, left twenty-one empty houses and all the "necessary outbuildings for stock."[91] A remnant population of only six people occupied two of the thirty houses in the village of Old Petrovo.[92]

It is likely that at least four other villages moved as well, although the documentation is suggestive rather than conclusive. The villages of Nickolaievka and Petrofka (Cyprus) appear both on the "Doukhobor Statistics" schedule (which, unfortunately, does not give locations) and on Crerar's 1902 map, but I have not been able to discover the relationship, if any, to the villages on later maps and schedules. It is possible that these villages were abandoned in favour of already existing villages (although no villages show a sudden growth of people to support this conjecture), or it is possible that, like Trusdennie, they combined with an existing village to build on a new site. Crerar also identifies a village as Novo Slavanska, locating it outside the reserve of 1902 (later the reserve was enlarged to include this township). This may be the original site of Slavnoe, located just two miles south on later maps, or its fate was that of the other villages noted above. Finally, one unidentified village is surveyed by McCallum in 1902 and there is no indication of its fate thereafter; it may be the original site of Vosziennie since it is only one mile away, but no relocation is mentioned.[93] In summary, perhaps as many as twelve of the thirty-four South Colony and Annex villages relocated from their original sites in the period 1899-1905.

In the Saskatchewan Colony villages, Oospennie and probably Petrofka moved from crude, half dug-out villages on the banks of the North Saskatchewan to new sites on the plateau above the river early in 1900 (see the discussion in Chapter 5). Three villages were added in this period as well. Large Horelofka was composed of two groups in 1901,[94] and one group left to begin the new village of Small Horelofka two miles east sometime between then and 1904 (Speers lists Small Horelofka as a separate village).[95] Slavyanka was begun by settlers from the neighbouring village of Oospennie sometime after 1900[96] and Tonbofka was established sometime between 1901 and 1904 by a group of families from Pasariofka (not noted on Ens' list and present on Speers' list of 1904).[97] Apparently, although the villages remained

---

91   NA, RG15, V1165 F5404644, Kapustina Village File, 1905 Schedule.
92   NA, RG15, V1167 F5412491, Petrovo Village File, 1905 Schedule.
93   NA, RG15, V754 F494483, Pt. 2, N.G. McCallum, "Report."
94   NA, RG76, V184 F65101, Pt. 5, Ens, "Crop Report."
95   NA, RG76, V184 F65101, Pt. 7, Speers, "Report."
96   It appears that when Oospennie relocated from the original "dug-out" site, it divided into two villages: Oospennie and Slavyanka. The move took place about 1902 (*Bridging the Years*, 390-91, 597; pers. comm., Larry Orchansky, September 1992).
97   Ens notes that eight families from this village (Poserajeffka, Pasariofka) wanted to settle near Kirilovka and gives their names. The same names are listed in the 1905 schedule of Tonbofka village. Speers notes that several homesteaders who listed their residence as Tonbofka entered for their land in October 1902, so perhaps the village was established closer to 1901 than 1904. Ens' report also indicates that the move was contemplated for 1901.

fixed, people were mobile. Loyal Veriginites from some of the Saskatchewan villages moved to the Yorkton area beginning with Verigin's arrival, and they were joined by many others in a major relocation in 1905-06. As in all of the reserves, people moved from village to village within the reserve as well, although the volume of this movement cannot be ascertained with any degree of accuracy. There are only general complaints on the part of homestead inspectors and other officials that the movement was significant and continuous.

In the three reserves, then, a total of twenty villages relocated from their original sites to new sites, and it is likely that seven others did so as well, although these moves cannot be confirmed. Considering that all but two of these relocations were confined to the North and South Colonies, more than half the villages in those reserves abandoned their original sites and moved to new locations. Only eight of these moves were occasioned by locations on the "wrong land" — either outside the reserves or on nongovernment land. In addition, three new villages were established by people from existing villages within the Saskatchewan Colony. I have argued elsewhere[98] that, in fact, a good deal of this movement can be explained by Verigin's desire to consolidate his Community. The movement of villages in the South Colony consolidated locations around the nucleus of the South Colony, especially from the peripheral locations.

There is thus some basis for the Commission's judgement. The Doukhobors rejected any recognition of individual land ownership, and resisted also the division of lands into discrete segments. Their idea of a reservation might recognize external boundaries, but it could not tolerate or accommodate internal divisions. Removing survey posts (an activity of which they were accused more than once) was not so much to frustrate the government, perhaps, as to reaffirm their deeply held belief that such human divisions were not "God-honouring." In such a context, these were not acts of mischief as much as faith-affirming acts, a low-key civil disobedience in obedience to a higher authority. The Doukhobors were interested in using the land, not owning it, and consequently, while very much "sons of the soil" and committed to farming as their natural occupation, they did not attach themselves to a particular piece of land. Years of persecution and forced relocation strengthened their ties to the Community and weakened their ties to a particular location. They had a sense of usable space, but not of place. Thus, in the absence of real barriers to progress inherent in a particular place, one space was as good as another. And if some real or perceived problem with one chosen site arose, the villagers were quite ready to exchange it for a new one, even if it meant considerable extra work. Actually, the concept of "lost time and labour" probably meant less to the communal Doukhobors than it would have to the individual homesteader. Efficiency was not nearly as important as community, particularly in the light of the religious connotation of

---

98 Tracie, "Saskatchewan Community Doukhobors in 1913" (unpublished paper presented to a special joint session of the Canadian Sociological Association and Canadian Association of Slavists, Calgary, 1994). See Chapter 17 for a summary.

community. If a village move brought people into closer contact with the Community core, or if the move could be seen to benefit the concept of Community solidarity in one way or another, such a move made good sense. This attitude would have been enhanced after Verigin consolidated the Community since a relocation would be evaluated in the light of the larger community good, and any lost time and labour with respect to the commercial progress would be made up for by other members of the Community.

This attitude also meant that the Doukhobors disregarded artificial boundaries when they established their villages[99] and cultivated their land (although they generally adhered to the reserve boundaries where those were known). The combination of delayed surveys, misunderstandings regarding the reserved lands within the larger reserves, and their own lack of concern with surveyed subdivisions, meant that several villages had to be moved, and significant amounts of improved land were lost. Speers noted the loss of 400 acres of cultivated land by residents of the village of Tonbofka (Saskatchewan Colony) because the cultivation was done adjacent to the village on a section which was railway land. In his words, "it was sold over their heads by the C.P.Ry and they lost their work."[100]

Progress

Even before Verigin's arrival and in spite of the considerable ferment which disrupted many of the villages, the Doukhobor colonies made considerable progress. Thomas Dewan reported on the progress of the Doukhobors settled in the Redberry Lake area of the Saskatchewan Colony. "They are turning the whole country over," he commented, adding that in one village thirty-three ploughs were in use (all managed by women and boys since the men were away working), and that a water-powered gristmill ("runs smooth as a watch") ground up to forty bushels a day, powered by water brought by ditch over a mile long. A second mill was under construction in another village using water brought by a ditch two miles long.[101]

Hugh Harley reported on the thirteen villages of the North Colony in June 1900, although he could not include some of the statistics for Novotroitzkoe (Simeonovo) since he could not ford the river to visit the village. In addition to 165 houses, he reported twenty-two stables, eleven root houses, eight granaries and three blacksmith shops. They had added a few horses and thirteen oxen since the fall of 1899, and had nearly tripled the number of cows and calves. He also reported nineteen dogs in the thirteen villages. Harley estimated that the Colony had approximately

---

99 Many of the Doukhobor villages were sited across quarter-section lines, in some cases occupying parts of all four quarters of a particular section, and in others, occupying parts of two adjoining sections.
100 NA, RG76, V184 F65101, Pt. 7, Speers to Cory, 15 June 1904.
101 *Saskatchewan Herald*, 17 July 1901.

560 acres seeded to a variety of crops — barley, wheat, oats, rye and flax — including sixty-seven acres of potatoes, and twenty-six acres of other garden vegetables.[102]

Speers described the settlements of the North Colony in September 1902 as comprised of villages beautifully situated along the Swan River, with houses well built of

> good dimensions ... . Nice picket fences with shade trees with one long wide avenue, and a good deal of ability shown in the structure of their houses ... . Their gardens are excellent and they are building some three grist mills on the Swan River, they already have a trench dug for the mills and the flume for water and a small wheel of their own manufacture. They have purchased three sets of grinding stones, so that these mills would serve the purpose of the entire district. Some of these villages have as much as 500 acres of crop, and their crops are excellent and well matured.[103]

He notes that it was a pity that the harvest of the excellent crops was accomplished so slowly with small cradles and reaping hooks, because of the loosing of the animals. Tables 5, 6, and 7 provide a summary of the Doukhobors' progress in the North and South Colonies, and Annex, by the fall of 1902.

After Verigin's arrival and the formation of a committee to look after the affairs of the consolidated Doukhobor community, there was a new spirit of enthusiasm and progress. As a result of purchasing "the best horses in the country" on a Winnipeg buying trip to replace animals turned loose in the fervour of the previous summer, the Doukhobors were equipped "with a better class of horses than can be found in any other community."[104] Speers went on to say that the Doukhobors were dressing like Canadians, observing Canadian holidays and were expressing a desire to conform to the customs of the country. His optimistic conclusion was that the "Doukhobors will yet be considered among our most progressive settlers ... . They are making excellent progress."[105]

An account of receipts and expenditures by the Doukhobor community for 1903 shows purchases of a variety of implements, harnesses and provisions, including four portable engines with thresher machines, two traction engines with thresher machines, two sawmills, fifty binders, thirty-two mowers, 10,000 pounds of twine, forty-five disc harrows, twenty seeders, sixteen wagons, 190 ploughs, 234 sections of harrows, twelve fanning mills and 152 sleighs, as well as lands to the value of $13,445 purchased by Peter Verigin. The purchases totalled $215,544.92.[106]

Speaking of the 8,000 members of the Doukhobor Community in 1904, Speers noted amazing progress:

---

102 NA, RG76, V184 F65101, Pt. 5, Harley, "Report."
103 NA, RG76, V184 F65101, Pt. 6, Speers, "Report."
104 NA, RG76, V184 F65101, Pt. 7, Speers to Scott, 13 April 1903.
105 Ibid.
106 Ibid., Verigin to Smith, 19 February 1904.

This community have [sic] graded 10 miles of good turnpike road in their district. They have about 20,000 acres of crop looking excellent. They have about 1,000 men at work on railroads and other places, besides teams. The women have picked 2,000 lbs. of sennaca [sic] root which is worth $10,000. They are starting a brick-yard and some other industries. They have established saw mills and gristmills among themselves. They have a steam plough working and they intend to cultivate a large area next to the railroad and go extensively into wheat-raising. They have every material want supplied and excellent equipment for their work in their district. There is an air of prosperity among these people and a great promise for the present year.[107]

The crop of 1904 for the Assiniboia, Swan River and Good Spirit Lake districts also gave substance to Speers's optimism: 67,663 bushels of wheat, 78,648 bushels of oats, 39,715 bushels of barley and 5,454 bushels of flax. In addition, they had gathered a large amount of Seneca root which yielded an income of $2,600.[108]

This was a period of flux. Leaderless and powerless, the Doukhobors established their villages and began cultivation of the land in the midst of confusion, misunderstanding, and growing internal and external conflicts. Released from exile in late 1902, Peter Verigin brought with him a vision of Doukhobor Community and strong leadership which focussed the energies of individual villages in support of the larger Christian Community of Universal Brotherhood. The results, in the midst of simmering conflicts within the Doukhobor ranks, were impressive. Despite the progress, and the resolution of the land registration problem, however, Verigin's leadership also hardened the divisions among the Independents, the Freedomites, and the Community. And, as events in the next few years would show, the land problem was far from being resolved. It is not unreasonable, however, to identify 1905, the year at the end of this period of flux, as a year of temporary equilibrium.

Summary: Land Entry

The initial agricultural settlement of the Canadian West depended on two essentials: a rapid, efficient, and unambiguous method of identifying parcels of land, and a policy to transfer these parcels from public to private ownership. The township and range survey system, based on townships of thirty-six sections of one square mile, each section further subdivided into four "quarters" of 160 acres, accomplished the first. The Dominion Lands Act, centred on the "free" homestead, addressed the second. Both were adopted, with some modifications, from the United States.

After the land was surveyed, it was available for disposal. There were various ways by which a settler could acquire land, but the main attraction for hundreds of thousands of intending settlers was the quarter-section homestead. Homestead land was "free" land in that it was given to settlers rather than sold, but in lieu of cash, the homesteader had to satisfy several requirements. First, the entrant had to register the homestead in his name and pay a nominal entry fee. This ensured that he had legal possession of the land until he abandoned it or it was cancelled for some lack in fulfilling the homestead requirements.

---

107 NA, RG76, V184 F65101, Pt. 7, Speers to Scott, 27 July 1904.

108 Verigin gives a figure of 17,000 pounds but this does not match his calculation of sixty cents a pound yielding a total of $2,600 (ibid., Verigin to Moffatt, 17 January 1905).

Beyond that, the homesteader had to satisfy certain residence and cultivation duties. Although there were variations in these requirements over the years, in general the entrant had to live on the homestead quarter at least six months each year for three years, and to break and crop a certain acreage of land. Upon completion of these duties, the homestead entrant would apply for a patent (title) for the land. A homestead inspector would determine that the requirements had indeed been satisfied, and a patent for the homestead quarter would be issued. Both the entry form and the patent form required the swearing of an oath, certifying that the information was accurate, and the patent form required an oath of allegiance to the Crown.

The Doukhobors had problems with every step of the process. At base was their belief that land belonged to God and any human division of the land that recognized individual ownership was a violation of God's sovereignty. Exacerbating this basic belief conflict was the Doukhobors' misunderstanding about the way in which land would be granted and the government's misconception of the full implications of the Doukhobor commitment to the communal way of life.

When the Doukhobors began to settle their land, they did so as occupying reserves of common property, ignoring interior divisions (building villages and cultivating land across quarter-section boundaries), and, in a few cases, ignoring even the reserve boundaries (although this seems to have been at least partially due to the slow pace of survey in a few areas). When they were informed that they would have to make homestead entry for individual quarter sections of land, most refused to do so. Some even removed survey markers in protest of the human artifice of dividing the indivisible.

Peter Verigin's arrival brought a temporary solution. He assured his followers that registering for their homesteads was just a formality and to aid in the process, the government allowed Verigin and two others to make entry on behalf of all the Doukhobors, and the land was entered en masse. There was still the matter of residence and cultivation duties, however. The first was not a problem since the Hamlet Clause which had been introduced to attract the Mennonites was reapplied to the Doukhobors. This allowed the residence requirement to be fulfilled while living in a village within three miles of the homestead quarter section. The second seemed to have been satisfied in February 1903, when Clifford Sifton promised a similar concession in the matter of cultivation. In this critical policy statement, he noted that the cultivation could be done in common around the village as long as the total amount equalled the amount required for the number of homesteads in the village. The government inspectors were still frustrated by finding a complete lack of concern about attachment to a particular piece of land (people moved from one village to another without regard for the land which was registered to them). However, it appeared that over the next three years, the Doukhobors were working toward fulfilling the requirements as understood by both parties.

An abrupt end to this period of apparent agreement came in 1906 when the new Minister of the Interior, Frank Oliver, overruled the cultivation concession granted by Sifton, and threatened the cancellation of all homestead entries where cultivation on the individual homestead was not performed. To make matters worse, those who might be willing to comply with this requirement had to make a new entry for the land, which included the intention to become a citizen and involved swearing allegiance to the Crown. In 1907, these regulations were enforced and the homestead entries of the Doukhobors not willing to conform to these requirements were cancelled and the lands thrown open to general homesteading (with first opportunity given to other Doukhobors). To avoid the spectre of bringing the Doukhobors to economic ruin by completely eliminating their agricultural base, the government set up reserves around each village for the Community Doukhobors based on fifteen acres of land for each villager. The Doukhobors had no legal claim to this land and occupied it only "at the pleasure of the government." As some Doukhobors left the Community to take up land individually and many others moved to British Columbia, these village reserves dwindled from year to year and in 1918, the land remaining was sold (or in some cases rented) to individual members of the Community — often with the help of mortgages which were underwritten by the Christian Community of Universal Brotherhood (CCUB).

The last lands to be disposed of in each village reserve were the village sites themselves. Eventually, the site (normally about twenty acres) was added to the homestead entry for that quarter section or sold to the homestead entrant at $3 per acre. A meeting house in the village tended to delay the process: the building had to be purchased from the Community before the land could be deeded. In villages where both Community members and Independent Doukhobors occupied lots, licenses of occupation were issued as an intermediary step between Community use and either homestead entry or sale. They confirmed the right of an individual or family to occupy the lot until it was deeded. Licenses of occupation were also issued for acreages in the village reserve smaller than a quarter section. As the reserves and villages were phased out, these licenses were cancelled. Throughout the various stages of this process, the government officials were plagued by problems stemming from the Doukhobors' basic disregard for individual landholding. In the homesteading phase until 1907, entrants moved from village to village and from reserve to reserve, ignoring the residence requirement of the Hamlet Clause that residence must be in a village within three miles of the homestead quarter. In the village reserve phase, interprovincial movements were added to the other relocations, making it difficult for officials to maintain accurate village lists upon which the allocation of reserve land was based. By 1918, however, almost all of the original homestead land in the reserves had been disposed of, and the Community's agricultural and commercial base consisted of purchased land.

Chapter 7
Stasis ~ 1905

Choosing a time to represent stability in a fifteen-year period which is most characterized by change is a difficult and uncertain task. If 1905 does not quite reflect stability, it does represent a turning point for the Community Doukhobors.[1] By almost any measure, the Community as a visible body in Saskatchewan was at its zenith in 1905; adherents to the communal way of life peaked at 8,400 in 1905, declined to 7,700 in 1906, and continued to decline thereafter.[2] Later, as Cormie observed, whole villages abandoned the community way of life "and every village has its house with the stained wall," a reference to the abandoned houses left in the village by Independent Doukhobors moving out onto their own homesteads.[3] And, of course, even those who remained in the villages were not necessarily of one mind. Independents who farmed their individual homesteads from farmsteads in the village, and not-quite-Independents working within a communal structure but disillusioned with Verigin's Community, lived side by side with those committed to Verigin's leadership in every aspect of life. In the years following 1905, departures to British Columbia of the totally committed and conflicts among the others sapped the economic and spiritual vitality of the Community body and reduced its size.

The amount of cultivated land controlled by the Community also peaked in 1905: cultivated acreage declined from 42,400 acres in 1905 to 40,650 acres a year later.[4] There was some continued growth after 1905, however. Oxen increased fourfold, sheep by 35 percent, and cattle marginally, although the number of horses decreased

---

[1] 1905 is also the first year in which the government collected detailed statistics for each of the Doukhobor villages. Thereafter, almost annual visits (two in 1913) until 1913 by the Doukhobor Commission created in 1906 continued to provide information on population, cultivation and movement for each village.

[2] All statistics for 1905, unless explicitly noted, are derived from the 1905 survey of the Doukhobor villages (fifty-nine were villages surveyed, with some information provided for seven others).

[3] Cormie, "Will the Doukhobor Survive?," 596.

[4] These figures do not include cultivation on land purchased by the Community.

by 20 percent between 1905 and 1906. The Community in the North Colony continued to grow at a modest rate for the next two years, while the Saskatchewan Colony registered the greatest decline in Community adherents. While 1905 was the zenith of development for the Community Doukhobors as a whole, there was a decline "lag" in some parts of the Community as forward momentum and Community consolidation sustained economic growth for the next year or two — then decline began in earnest.

If 1905 can be seen as a turning point in the development of the Doukhobor Community, it was also a turning point in governmental and societal attitudes. The successes of earlier settlers and a series of wetter-than-average years combined to sustain the flow of settlers into the West. The government's focus shifted from attracting new settlers to providing policy and structure which would integrate the existing settlers into the Canadian way of life and into the developing Canadian economy. National goals were to be achieved through a Canadianized western population of farmers and businessmen committed to an individualistic, free-enterprise economy. Sustained economic growth would depend on increasingly prosperous farm families buying greater quantities of consumer goods from local businesses. The model was based on a symbiotic dependence between local businesses and institutions in the incipient urban centres, and the progressive farm family on its quarter-section or half-section farm. On a larger scale, the same model applied to the nation. Central Canada relied on the growing prosperity and consumption in the newly-developing western hinterland as markets for the manufactured goods and machinery produced in the industrial heartland.

The Community Doukhobors did not fit this mould either regionally or nationally. Their communal way of life produced economies of scale which bypassed local businesses and contributed little to the local economy. Like the Hutterites who would bear the same social and economic stigma fifty years later, the Saskatchewan Community Doukhobors were charged with being a closed community with very limited involvement in local affairs.

---

5   The decline here was caused not only by disillusioned Doukhobors leaving the Community but by a significant number of the faithful (as many as 500) relocating to newly established villages in the North and South Colonies. This movement also contributed to the increase of communal members in the North Colony noted above.

6   I must emphasize that "decline" is used in reference to Community Doukhobors on government land, that is, a decline of their original settlements. The Doukhobor Community remained a viable part of the Saskatchewan landscape on purchased land until the late 1930s.

7   See Donald T. Gale and Paul M. Koroscil, "Doukhobor Settlements: Experiments in Idealism," *Canadian Ethnic Studies* 9 (1977): 53-71. Also see Verigin's assessment of this state of affairs noted previously (Verigin to Tolstoy, 1 April 1905, in Donskov, *Tolstoy-Verigin Correspondence*, 71-72).

8   In the words of W.S. Fielding in his budget speech of 1903, "The best way you can help the manufacturers of Canada ... is to fill up the prairie regions of Manitoba and the Northwest with a prosperous and contented people, who will be consumers of the manufactured goods of the east" [quoted in Robert C. Brown and B. Ramsey Cook, *Canada 1896-1921: A Nation Transformed* (Toronto: McClelland and Stewart, 1974), 50].

The factor most critical to Doukhobor fortunes in 1905 was, however, a change in the Ministry of the Interior; Clifford Sifton resigned and was replaced by Frank Oliver. As Woodcock and Avakumovic point out, Oliver "had no prestige at stake in the question of Doukhobor immigration," in contrast to Sifton's "proprietary interest," and had earlier proven to be antagonistic to the Doukhobors.[9] Oliver's disallowance of the cultivation concession, granted by Sifton in 1902, led most directly to the decline in the Doukhobor Community after 1905.[10]

Although Peter Verigin's charismatic leadership was welding his followers into a powerful economic machine, he was less successful in persuading the government to keep its word with respect to the fulfillment of the modified homestead requirements. The shift in government personnel and attitude, the pressure on the land created by the continuing influx of settlers, and the spirit of the times, all combined to militate against any compromise respecting land policies. The government could hardly eliminate these "undigested and undigestable"[11] lumps in the ethnic stew of the Canadian West, but it could make certain that no special advantages were given to them. This policy, it was hoped, would force them into the individualistic, free-enterprise mould which both government and Canadian society supported. That it failed to do so for the bulk of the Doukhobor Community reflected both the injustice of government policy decisions and its failure to recognize the strength of religious conviction.

Despite the looming problems concerning both land and society, the Christian Community of Universal Brotherhood (CCUB) in 1905 was a vibrant, if not totally cohesive, community which had created from the prairies and parklands a truly distinctive cultural landscape in the new province of Saskatchewan. Chapters 8-10 present a colony-by-colony portrayal of life and landscape in the CCUB-dominated lands in that year of (temporary) stasis.

---

9   Woodcock and Avakumovic, *The Doukhobors*, 204. It was Frank Oliver who, as owner of the *Edmonton Bulletin*, spearheaded the local opposition to Doukhobor settlement in the Beaver Lake area northwest of Edmonton in 1898, which forced them to look for lands in other parts of the Prairies.

10 This is discussed in detail in Chapter 11.

11 This was Stephen Leacock's inelegant assessment of several groups of immigrants, including the Doukhobors, in *My Discovery of the West* (New York: Hale, Cushman and Flint, 1937), 161.

Chapter 8
The North Colony - 1905

Fifteen villages dotted the landscape of the North Colony in 1905 (see Map 8). The two new villages added to the original thirteen were Kaminka, just being established by Cyprus Doukhobors relocating from the South Colony, and Pavlovo.[1] Bogdanofka and Tichomeerofka (Teakomeernoe) were forced to abandon their original sites just outside the west boundary of the reserve to relocate inside the reserve, despite Herbert Archer's strong appeal to the Department that they be left in their original location; in 1905 only two families remained in Old Bogdanofka, and Tichomeerofka was deserted, leaving about 120 cultivated acres.[2] For a time, the villagers of Stradaevka were contemplating a separation which would create two villages: the original village for Independent Doukhobors, and a new village, to be called Libedevo, for the Community members. I have noted that Michaelovo and Vosnisennie had moved from their original sites in 1899 or early 1900, and that "Doukhobor Statistics" suggests that both Novotroitzkoe and Spasskoe (later called Hlebedarnoe) would be relocated in spring 1900 (see Chapter 6). These villages did not move again in the intervening years to 1905.

---

1   As I have noted in Chapter 6 (note 72) there is some evidence that Pavlovo was the first of *four* villages established in the North Colony by relocated Saskatchewan Colony Community members. The others — Archangelskoe, Perehodnoe, and Gromovoe — were not established until 1906.

2   Statistics and other village information are compiled from the 1905 schedules of the village files unless otherwise noted. These schedules provide a very detailed assessment of all aspects of the villages. In conveying the instructions of the Department of the Interior to those who would gather this information, Speers wrote: "you shall visit each Village, accurately measure the cultivated land appurtenant thereto, ascertain the exact population of each Village, including women and children, giving the number of houses, distinguishing between those occupied and unoccupied, and any other informa- tion of importance that will be of service to the Department. In giving the population it would be well to give the ages of all inhabitants, both male and female." He noted also that the report be "absolutely accurate and reliable" particularly with respect to the assessment of the cultivated land since "these people are permitted to live in Villages and cultivate en bloc" (NA, RG15, V755 F494493, Pt. 4, Speers, "Instructions," 16 October 1905).

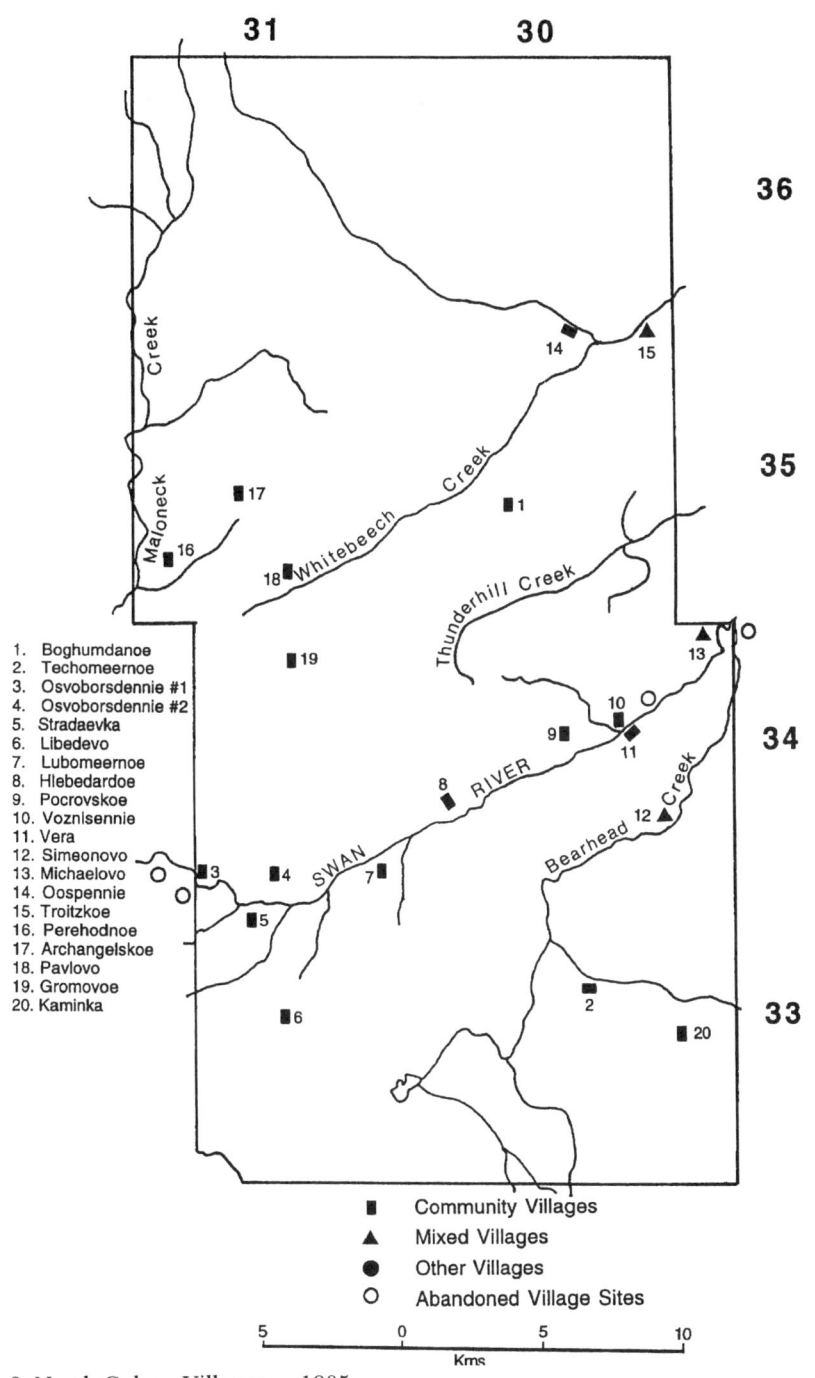

1. Boghumdanoe
2. Techomeernoe
3. Osvoborsdennie #1
4. Osvoborsdennie #2
5. Stradaevka
6. Libedevo
7. Lubomeernoe
8. Hlebedardoe
9. Pocrovskoe
10. Voznisennie
11. Vera
12. Simeonovo
13. Michaelovo
14. Oospennie
15. Troitzkoe
16. Perehodnoe
17. Archangelskoe
18. Pavlovo
19. Gromovoe
20. Kaminka

■ Community Villages
▲ Mixed Villages
● Other Villages
○ Abandoned Village Sites

Map 8. North Colony Villages — 1905.

Figure 35. Doukhobor village east of Canora, 1908 (BCA HP96801).

By 1905, the villages had assumed a more permanent look and bore the unmistakable stamp of the motherland. The older buildings were either upgraded or replaced, new houses and supplemental structures were added, and prayer homes were begun in three of the villages.[3] The average North Colony village had twenty-five houses — twenty occupied and five unoccupied or unfinished on average — although the larger villages had more than thirty and the smallest fewer than fifteen. The exotic architectural styles which attracted comment from early observers were clearly evident. Nearly every village had a bathhouse (sauna), a carpenter's shop, a blacksmith's shop, an implement shed, several stables (barns) and granaries, and often a chicken house. Lubomeernoe had an oil house for its flax press, and Vosnisennie had a grist mill with associated blacksmith's shop, storehouse, stable and boarding house. These were substantial log buildings with sod or thatched roofs, and carefully plastered with a clay-straw paste inside and out (see Figure 35). Trees were planted along the street and between houses, and fences (woven willow, pole or sapling "pickets") outlined the front yards, adding to the atmosphere of permanence.

The community or prayer homes which were to be the core of many of the North and South Colony villages were just being built in 1905. A good deal of care was given to their construction, and their placement within the village was of some significance. Of the three structures begun in 1905, two were being delayed by such

---

3 An indication of the pace of construction at this time is that forty-six of the 383 houses reported on the 1905 survey were under construction.

concerns. In Spasskoe (Hlebedarnoe) the foundation had been laid but it was to be moved about 100 yards because it was not in the exact centre of the village. The foundation of the prayer home at Michaelovo was also being moved, apparently owing to the close proximity of an Independent's house across the street. At Oospennie, the unfinished "Club House" was apparently completed without any serious problems (see Figure 13, Chapter 2).

Speers classified forty-four villages in the Yorkton and Swan River (North Colony) settlements in terms of Verigin's ideal of a "uniform" village size — forty families: fifteen villages were classed as "large," twenty-two as "small," and only seven as uniform. Unfortunately, it is difficult to match up the names of the villages with known villages because of the spelling,[4] so the designation of some North Colony villages is uncertain. Twelve of the fifteen villages can be reasonably identified and two more with some certainty — "Plovo," a large village, is likely Pavlovo, and "Besticdofka" is likely Bogdanofka (Boghumdanoe).[5] Kaminka is not mentioned.[6] The population of the average North Colony village was 158 in 1905. By this standard, eight villages were very near the average, two were somewhat smaller, and four somewhat larger. Kaminka, with a population of eighty-eight, was anomalously small, no doubt because the inhabitants were in the process of moving from their original location in the South Colony.

Few contemporary photographs of the North Colony villages are available, but those of Simeonovo (see Figure 8, Chapter 2) and Vosnisennie (see Figure 9, Chapter 2) show the degree to which the Doukhobors had succeeded in fashioning a familiar cultural landscape in this new environment.

The settlers had also been busy in extending their plots of cultivated land. While the total cultivated acreage of the Colony fell short of the amount needed to fulfill the modified requirements laid out by Sifton in February 1902,[7] by 1905 the North Colony Doukhobors had cultivated just over 7,400 acres, an average of nearly 500 acres per village. Two of the villages, Osvoborsdennie and Simeonovo, would have fulfilled the fifteen-acre requirement at this date (see Table 9). Of course, the real

---

4   Speers notes: "The above names seem to be in the Russian language, there [sic] are as nearly accurate as I could get them after revising them, but I feel impressed that they would stand a little more revision" (NA, RG15, V755 F494483, Pt. 4, Speers to Department of the Interior, 16 October 1905).

5   Speers no doubt used the 1905 Commission's information in classifying these villages. If these two villages are indeed Pavlovo and Bogdanofka, the two villages had identical populations (133) but Pavlovo had forty-four families whereas Bogdanofka had only thirty-three.

6   NA, RG15, V755 F494483, Pt. 4, Speers to Department, 16 October 1905. One of the uniform villages is termed merely "Sawmill," perhaps a reference to the settlement in the North Colony in 34-36-31 where Verigin had established a modern sawmill in the substantial timber of the North Colony, although Speers's classification would indicate a larger settlement than would be expected at a sawmill (NA, RG15, V755 F494483, Pt. 6, Archer to Smith, 10 December 1906).

7   According to the 1905 schedule, the fifteen villages entered a total of 674 homesteads. To fulfill the homestead cultivation requirements, fifteen acres for each homestead were to be broken. The total cultivation for all villages was 7,416 acres or just over eleven acres per homestead.

Table 9 North Colony, 1905*										
Village	Horses	Oxen	Cows	Sheep	Ploughs	Cult. acres	Hsds.	Ac/hsd	Pop.
Boghumdanoe	15	10	43	30	7	317.5	46	6.9	129
Hlebedarnoe	14	12	41	37	9	561	50	11.2	153
Kaminka	9	6	44	28	6	318.5	24	13.3	88
Libedevo	14	—	59	40	8	491	50	9.8	163
Lubomeernoe	16	—	66	41	10	596.5	50	11.9	178
Michaelovo	16	10	40	40	8	547	41	13.3	153
Oospennie	19	3	76	46	10	500.5	57	8.8	194
Osvoborsdennie	16	8	62	35	7	728.5	46	15.8	159
Pavlovo	16	8	50	34	8	219	45	4.9	133
Procovskoe	15	9	45	42	8	617	49	12.6	181
Simeonovo	14	11	41	30	7	644	42	15.3	122
Teakomeernoe	16	12	47	35	7	325.5	49	6.6	156
Troitzkoe	13	8	46	30	5	467	35	13.3	128
Vera	15	4	53	24	5	395	42	9.4	144
Vosnisennie	18	10	50	33	9	653	48	13.6	158
Totals	226	111	763	525	114	7,416	674	11.0	2,239

* all data refer to the Community component of these villages — 95 percent of the total population of 2,364.

Source: Village Files, 1905 schedules.

problem was that this cultivation was concentrated in certain areas of their homesteaded land. Even though the Doukhobors' practice of cultivating their land in scattered blocks was not confined to land immediately surrounding the village, they did focus on these more proximate lands to the neglect of almost all of the lands further away. Osvoborsdennie, for example, entered for forty-six homesteads, but its 728.5 acres of cultivation was done on only seventeen quarters, and nearly 75 percent was done on only six quarters. Simeonovo entered for forty-two homesteads, but its 644 acres of cultivation was done on thirteen quarters and 55 percent of that was done on only four quarters. Table 10 provides an indication of the pace of progress in the years since 1899.

Table 10 Animal and Implement Ratios — North Colony, 1905*	
1 draught animal per 7.0 persons (1/18)	1 cow per 3.1 persons (1/47)
1 sheep per 4.5 persons (n/a)	1 binder per 57.7 persons (n/a)
1 mower per 62.2 persons (n/a)	1 wagon per 28.1 persons (1/61)
1 plough per 20.7 persons (1/83)	1 harrow per 30.7 persons (n/a)

* bracketed figures indicate 1899 ratios.

Source: 1899 - "Doukhobor Statistics"; 1905 - Village Files.

Organization

Although I have stressed the point that generalizations about the organization of villages in a particular geographic area mask a host of variations within villages, the North Colony settlers in 1905 appear as a near-monolithic communal group. Only five of the fifteen villages surveyed (the three "Prince Albert" villages of Archangelskoe, Gromovoe and Perehodnoe had not been formally organized yet) contained any Independents and they were a decided minority. Simeonovo and Troitzkoe, both of which were originally settled by those wishing to break away from the communal way of life, had returned to the Community: Independents comprised just under 30 percent of Simeonovo's population and just over 20 percent of Troitzkoe's. Three other villages — Libedevo, Michaelovo, and Vera — had only two or three families of Independents each. Overall, Independents comprised only 5 percent of the North Colony population in 1905. This was a Veriginite reserve.

Michaelovo in 1905

Michaelovo probably enjoyed an advantage over the other North Colony villages in that it was the core from which the whole Colony dispersed in the early summer of 1899. A large complement of houses and other buildings was built to house the hundreds that used this village as temporary quarters before building their own villages (see description in Chapter 3). By 1905, Michaelovo was a mature village with a more complex plan of three central streets radiating outward from the hub of the village which eventually focussed on the meeting house (see Figure 3, Chapter 2). Twenty-six "comfortable" houses were occupied by 162 people, many of the older structures having been replaced by new ones "of more modern style." Two granaries, two large stables, an implement shed, a carpenter's shop and a blacksmith's shop, as well as a bathhouse completed the built landscape of the village. The Community had sixteen horses, ten oxen, forty cattle, forty sheep, and 250 chickens, a more-or-less average complement of animals for a North Colony village with somewhat fewer cattle and more chickens. Michaelovo was one of the five North Colony villages with an Independent component. Although only two Independent families lived here, the family of Ivan Ivin being one of them, the conflicts between the Community members and the Independents were intense enough that the foundation of the meeting house was in the process of being torn up and moved because it was on a lot immediately across from an Independent's house.

Michaelovo's residents had cultivated a total of 547 acres, again about average for the Colony as a whole (see Table 9 for the lands homesteaded). And as with most

---

8   NA, RG15, V1167 F5412457, Michaelovo Village File. I have noted the vagaries of Ivan Ivin earlier. Given the low regard the Community had for him, it is quite likely that it was his house that occasioned the relocation of the meeting house. An additional item in the report confirms how high feelings ran in this conflict; it notes that the village wanted to move its location: "the only discoverable reason being that they might be removed from the Independents." The fact that there were only two Independent families in the village underlines the animosity between the two groups.

other villages, the cultivation was concentrated on a small portion of the forty-one homesteads — 95 percent of the cultivation was done on only ten quarter sections, and fully 60 percent was done on only four quarters. The lands were farmed with a full range of equipment — binders, mowers, discers, harrows, ploughs, a seeder, a roller, and a fanning mill, as well as wagons and sleighs — but the Doukhobors were restricted, nonetheless, in their agricultural progress by the amount of equipment available. The single Independent family of Ivan Ivin, for example, owned approximately one-third the amount of equipment, excluding sleighs and wagons, "owned" by the entire village of Michaelovo. He also had his own bathhouse, stable and implement shed, along with his house on his village lot.[9]

Although the 1905 schedules do not report the amount of acreage seeded, they do indicate crop expectations. Michaelovo, as almost all Doukhobor villages, seeded most of its improved land to some combination of wheat, barley and oats, with a lesser acreage devoted to flax. Michaelovo did not seed any land to rye, a crop which, in small acreages, was common to many villages. In addition, Michaelovo's large garden plots were seeded to a variety of vegetables, with potatoes, carrots, and cabbages figuring especially prominently. The villagers expected to harvest some 3,500 bushels of potatoes, 800 of carrots, 200 each of turnips and beets, 160 of onions, three of cucumbers, as well as 2,000 heads of cabbage. Again, a comparison with Ivin is instructive. His family of five (wife, son, and two grandchildren) expected to harvest eight times as much wheat per capita as the village, four times as much oats and barley, but only about a quarter of the potatoes.

---

[9] The schedules make a careful distinction between the buildings, equipment, and improvements of the Community and the Independents, although in some cases it is not easy to distinguish between the improved acreage on Independents' homesteads as a result of Community efforts before they left the Community, and the breaking done on their own after leaving the Community. The comparison between Ivin and the Community may provide more contrast than was normally the case. Ivin had started out as an Independent and his conversion to the Community was apparently short-lived and superficial. Consequently, his material assets were no doubt much greater than those Independents who had left the Community only a year or two before.

Chapter 9
The South Colony and Annex ~ 1905

The structure and organization of the villages in the South Colony bore the impress of Verigin's influence. This was the nucleus of his empire; Otradnoe, and later, Veregin, his headquarters. Despite earlier compromises with the delights of independent ownership of livestock and goods, these villages now returned *en masse* to the community way of life. All twenty-seven South Colony villages were communal in organization and only four villages — Novoe, Pakrofka (Prokuratovo), Trusdennie and Slavnoe — had any Independents at all in 1905, and in these they represented the obdurate resistance of only a handful of families. It was a time for a return to their leader both in spirit and body, most forcefully characterized by the flow of settlers from the Saskatchewan Colony "to be with Petushka" (see Chapter 10). But the villages of the South Colony drew closer physically too, as the southernmost villages relocated from the periphery of the reserve to more central locations near the "heartland" around Veregin Station (see Map 9). One perceptive homestead inspector, commenting on the move-in-progress of Old Terpennie, the southernmost of the South Colony villages, noted that the reason for desertion was that the village was built on a school section but added, "and I think perhaps, a desire to draw within closer bounds the different villages of the community."[1] He did not speculate as to whether this desire was that of the villagers or of their leader. This particular move was to a site more than eighteen miles away, and it left substantial, well-constructed buildings and about eighty acres of cultivated land at the former location.

Old Petrovo (Petrovka Orlovsky) joined Old Terpennie in relocating from the southern periphery to the core. The remaining peripheral villages also moved. Old Kaminka was in the process of moving to its new site in the North Colony; both sites were included in the schedules as were the two sites of Terpennie. Nickolaievka had

---

[1] NA, RG15, V1166 F5412443, Terpennie Village File, 1905 Schedule. All village information is taken from the 1905 schedule, from each of the village files, unless indicated otherwise.

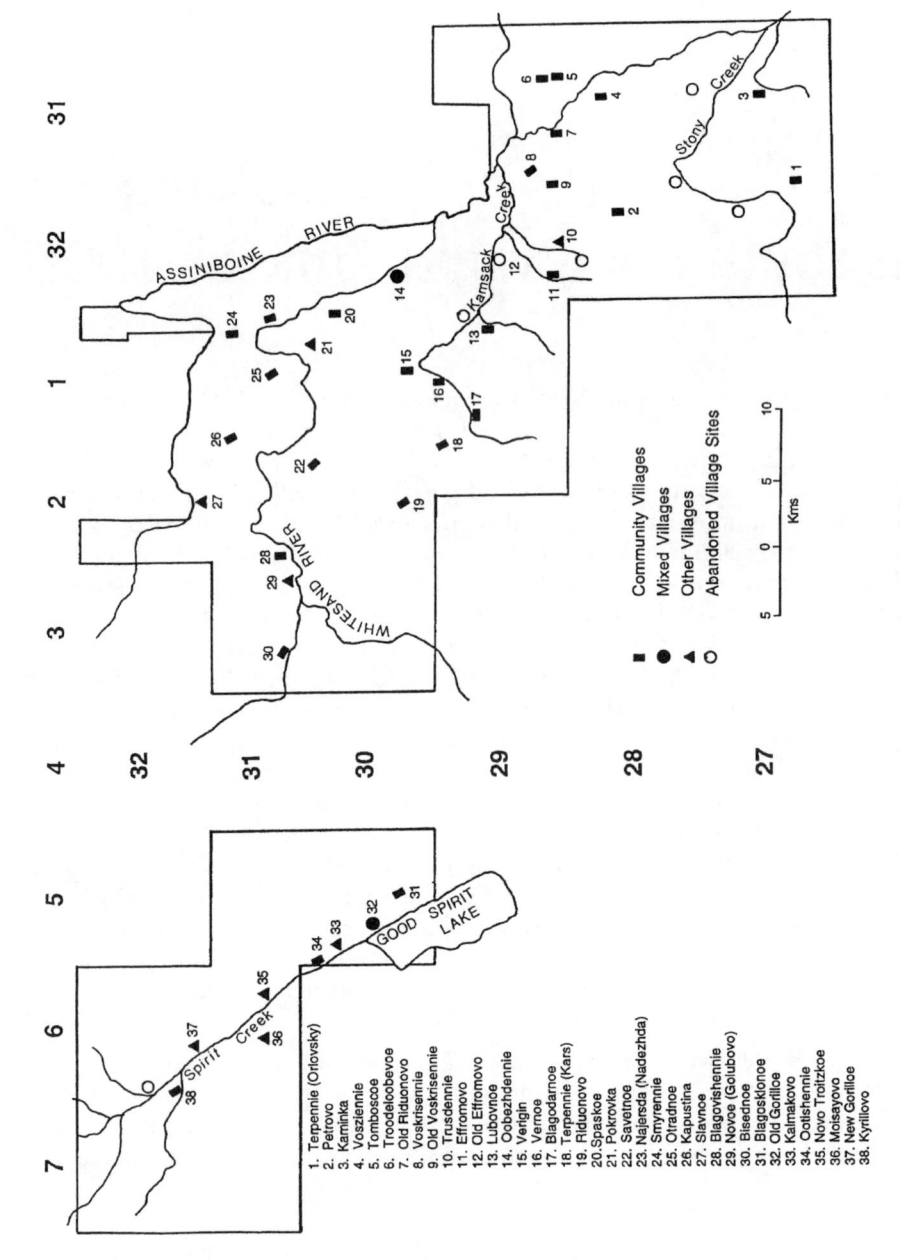

Map 9. South Colony and Annex Villages — 1905.

1. Terpennie (Orlovsky)
2. Petrovo
3. Kaminka
4. Vosziennie
5. Tomboscoe
6. Troodeloobevoe
7. Old Riduonovo
8. Voskrisennie
9. Old Voskrisennie
10. Trusdennie
11. Effromovo
12. Old Effromovo
13. Lubovnoe
14. Oobezhdennlie
15. Verigin
16. Vernoe
17. Blagodarnoe
18. Terpennie (Kars)
19. Riduonovo
20. Spaskoe
21. Pokrovka
22. Savelnoe
23. Najensda (Nadezhda)
24. Smyrennie
25. Otradnoe
26. Kapustina
27. Slavnoe
28. Blagovishennie
29. Novoe (Golubovo)
30. Bisednoe
31. Blagosklonoe
32. Old Gorilloe
33. Kalmakovo
34. Ootishennie
35. Novo Troitzkoe
36. Moisayovo
37. New Gorilloe
38. Kyrillovo

Community Villages ■
Mixed Villages ●
Other Villages ▲
Abandoned Village Sites ○

also relocated by 1905, but the relocated site is not indicated in the records. Most likely the villagers joined an existing village. Novo Petrofka (Petrofka Cyprus as distinct from Petrofka Orlovsky) relocated from a site near Nickolaievka on Stone Creek, but it is not clear to what site. Verigin's 1904 village list locates a Petrovo on SW32-28-32-W1, but his 1905 list locates Petrovo on NW22-28-32-W1, the same location noted for the second site of Petrovo (Orlovsky) in the village files.[2] Old Riduonovo was also in the process of moving in 1905, occupying both the old site near the eastern periphery and a new site closer to the heartland west of Veregin Station.

The villages of the South Colony were by now mature settlements with a full complement of houses, shops, utility sheds, granaries and stables. The average village had twenty-six houses, of which eighteen were occupied and eight unoccupied or unfinished. The somewhat larger proportion of unoccupied and unfinished houses here reflects the moves-in-progress noted above. Old Terpennie, Old Riduonovo and Old Kaminka were in the throes of long-distance moves, leaving large numbers of unoccupied houses in the abandoned villages (forty-one unoccupied houses in the three villages) and building new houses in their destination villages (twelve unfinished houses in the three villages). The move of Old Petrovo (see notes 2 and 6) was nearly complete at this time — all but two of the thirty houses were unoccupied. The fields around these villages also reflected the changes taking place. Some of these "transitional" villages were cropping land on both old and new sites. Kaminka, slowed in the move from the South Colony to the North Colony by a lack of horses, was still cropping 150 acres around the old village site and had another 230 acres broken around the new site. Others were surrounded by "go back" land — fields which were abandoned and allowed to revert to natural vegetation. Old Petrovo's 200 acres, for example, were "mostly deserted" in 1905, but some of this land was being used to pasture cattle owned by the village.

In other villages, replacing the original houses with better and more substantial ones left the old houses unoccupied, and families abandoning the Community also left houses "with the stained wall." Every village had a bathhouse — Lubovnoe and Otradnoe had three, six other villages had two — and nearly every village had a blacksmith's shop and carpenter's shop. Six villages had grist mills, and three had flax presses and oil houses. Veregin Station (Veregin Siding),[3] a market-oriented village recently constructed at a railway siding on the newly extended Canadian Northern Railway, had a large brick store, a storehouse, and a brickyard (which turned out 1.5 million bricks in 1905), among other buildings.[4] Perhaps the most

---

2   Two Petrovos are listed in "Doukhobor Statistics," one an Orlovsky village and one a Cyprus village. Crerar's 1902 Map locates both villages — Petrofka Cyprus, and Novo Petrofka (presumably Petrovo Orlovsky) — the latter on the site indicated by the village files.

3   The siding and village are officially named "Veregin," a departure from the original spelling of the station and from the accepted spelling of the leader's surname. I have held to the official spelling when referring to the railway siding and the village associated with it.

4   It is not clear from the files if this is the brickyard located near the village of Vernoe just a mile

significant additions to the villages were the prayer homes or community homes which were in the process of construction in eight South Colony villages. With the exception of the prayer home at Otradnoe which served as Peter Verigin's residence, the prayer homes were built to much the same exterior plan as the high-lofted houses with small "porches" in the boxed gable ends (see Figure 12, Chapter 2). The community homes built in Voskrisennie and Vosziennie are quite typical: brick-clad structures 22' x 56' and 20' x 50' respectively. Spaskoe's community home, begun after 1905, was somewhat larger at 24' x 58'. Verigin's residence at Otradnoe not only differed in plan — it was a highly decorated, two-storey, nearly square structure patterned after the Orphan's Home in the Caucasus — but in placement. It occupied a position of imposing dominance on a rise at the head of the central street of Otradnoe. All other prayer homes were placed in a central position on one side of the central street.

The South Colony had a much larger proportion of "large" villages according to Speers' classification.[5] Of the twenty-three villages he listed for the South Colony, ten were classified as large, nine were small, and only four were uniform. Again, there is not a good correlation between number of families and number of people. The average village size was 157 people, about the same as the average North Colony village, and most villages were close to the average. Some were considerably smaller, ranging from sixty-seven to ninety-one people in the four smallest villages, and three were considerably larger, with populations of 199 to 223.

The largest villages were Blagodarnoe, a well-established Kars village, and Petrovo Orlovksy. Blagodarnoe was the first village Peter Verigin visited on his arrival in Canada, and may well have been one of the first South Colony villages to be established.[6] Blagodarnoe's 223 people occupied thirty log houses beautifully situated on a level flat beside Kamsack Creek. In addition to the normal complement of bathhouse, carpenter's shop, blacksmith's shop and chicken house, it had nine stables, a sheep pen, and was in the process of erecting a large "club house." Petrovo had nearly completed its move from its original site (Old Petrovo) by Stone (Stony) Creek to a site about twelve miles north.[7] The thirty houses of Old Petrovo were long, low structures (14' x 30') constructed with poles and clay, and were largely

---

    south of Veregin Station which was to be moved to Veregin proper, or a separate brickyard (NA, RG15, V1165 F5404668, Vernoe Village File, 1905 Schedule).

5   NA, RG15, V755 F494483, Pt. 4, Speers to Department, 16 October 1905.

6   Verigin to Tolstoy, 12 January 1903 in Donskov, *Tolstoy-Verigin Correspondence*, 52. The villages of Blagodarnoe and Vernoe were both close to the site of the blockhouses built for South Colony settlers in the Whitesand portion of the reserve. As in the North Colony, these blockhouses became the raw materials for houses in adjacent villages, although unlike the North Colony, no village was established on the blockhouse sites.

7   McCallum's survey of 1902 shows well-established villages at both sites with twenty houses (slightly smaller than those of the first village) and three stables at the "new" village, with twenty acres cleared and fenced. Both houses and stables were built of poles and clay (NA, RG15, V754 F494483, Pt. 2, McCallum to Secretary, 25 October 1902).

Table 11
Animal and Implement Ratios, South Colony, 1905*

1 draught animal per 8.7 persons** (1/20)	1 cow per 2.5 persons (1/55)
1 sheep per 4.8 persons (n/a)	1 plough per 22.8 persons (1/75)
1 wagon per 22.2 persons (1/57)	1 binder per 52 persons (n/a)
1 mower per 63.7 persons (n/a)	1 harrow per 29.9 persons (n/a)

* bracketed figures indicate 1899 ratios.
** this figure includes a herd of 70-75 mares and colts at Old Riduonovo; without these the ratio is one draft animal per 10.6 persons.

Source: "Doukhobor Statistics"; Village Files, 1905 Schedules.

abandoned at the time of the survey. One of the six people who occupied two houses of the village was 100-year-old Ivan Mahortoff, one of the group of delegates who spied out the land in 1898 and who figured prominently in subsequent discussions of the land question and village organization. Six pole-and-clay stables were still used by the remaining residents who pastured a portion of the village cattle nearby. Two hundred acres of cultivated land on four quarter sections around the village were described as "old and deserted." None was cropped in 1905 and only a small part had been sown in 1904. The 213 people who had moved to the new site (Petrovo) occupied twenty-six houses, were constructing ten new houses, and had a bathhouse, a blacksmith's shop, a carpenter's shop and one stable. They were apparently unsatisfied with this site too, and while still finishing the second village, were in the process of building a third village on a site a mile distant. They intended to feed 200 head of "outside" cattle over the 1905-06 winter. Table 11 provides some measure of the increasing "prosperity" of the South Colony villages since they were begun in 1899.

The Community had almost 16,000 acres under cultivation in the South Colony, which amounted to fifteen acres per entered homestead (omitting 420 acres cultivated at Veregin Station which could not be linked to any homestead entries, and 282 acres cultivated on purchased land). On a village-by-village basis, however, fourteen villages had at least fifteen acres of cultivated land per homestead but twelve fell below this requirement (see Table 12). This should have assured the South Colony of a significant land base but, again, the village residents limited their cultivation to a few homesteads near the village, leaving the bulk of the homesteaded land "untouched," in the words of a homestead inspector. Under the provisions of Sifton's concession, this should not have made any difference, but according to the legal regulations, this meant that most villages satisfied the homestead requirements on a very few quarter sections. Only four villages had cultivation on 50 percent or more of their homesteads; the rest had cultivation on between 25 and 35 percent of their homesteads. And since the Doukhobors cultivated only small patches of land on many of these quarter sections, the concentration of cultivated land on a very few homesteads was even more pronounced. For example, the villagers of Tomboscoe registered for fifty-five homesteads but nearly 60 percent of their cultivation was on only three quarter sections. The villagers of Troodoloobevoe registered for fifty-four homesteads yet 75 percent of their cultivation was on only four quarter

Table 12
South Colony — 1905[a]

Village	Horses	Oxen	Cattle	Sheep	Ploughs	Cult.	Hsds.	Ac/Hsd.	Pop.
Bisednoe	17	6	60	37	6	1,036.5	39	26.6	135
Blagodarnoe	18	0	91	37	7	683	56	12.2	223
Blagovishennie	15	10	51	36	8	841	55	15.3	170
Efromovo	10	0	40	22	6	339	29	11.7	75
Kapustina	17	10	80	30	7	650	47	13.8	171
Lubovnoe	13	0	61	38	6	630	42	15.0	150
Najersda	14	0	60	36	8	864	44	19.6	152
Novoe	8	4	15	37	4	305.5	20	15.3	60
Old Kaminka	8	0	51	0	3	250	21	11.9	84
Old Petrovo	2	0	20	0	0	200	1	200[b]	6
Old Riduonovo	75	0	9	0	ni	111	8	13.9[c]	32
Old Terpennie	1	0	35	0	1	80	6	13.3	35
Old Voskrisennie	16	0	53	36	6	472	50	9.4	174
Oobezhdennie[d]	ni	ni	ni	ni	ni	ni	ni	ni	ni
Otradnoe	34	0	75	37	7	912	58	15.7	199
Petrovo	17	0	61	37	6	583	50	11.7	213
Prokuratovo	16	0	85	37	7	680	31	21.9	138
Riduonovo	14	0	46	0	8	568	35	16.2	125
Savetnoe	22	8	72	37	8	809	54	15.0	169
Slavnoe	14	9	65	36	7	581.5	26	22.4	145
Smyrennie	16	0	67	37	7	997	46	21.7	156
Spaskoe	18	0	71	37	8	715.5	50	14.3	163
Terpennie	15	0	33	0	7	378	47	8.0	136
Tomboscoe	19	0	66	37	8	670	55	12.2	186
Troodoloobevoe	15	0	63	36	7	714	54	13.2	175
Trusdennie	8	0	31	15	4	268.5	24	11.2	75
Veregin Siding	ni	ni	ni	ni	ni	420	ni	ni	56
Vernoe	14	0	53	37	8	778.5	53	14.7	187
Voskrisennie[e]	ni	ni	ni	ni	ni	ni	ni	ni	ni
Vosziennie	18	0	56	37	8	673	51	13.2	157
Totals	454	47	1,470	699	158	16,210[f]	1,052	15.4	3,693

a) all data refer to the Community component of these villages — 98 percent of the total village population of 3,752; b) Old Petrovo and Petrovo combined would have had 15.4 acres/homestead; c) Old Riduonovo and Riduonovo combined would have had 15.8 acres/homestead; d) an Independent village; e) see Old Voskrisennie — village in the process of relocation; f) this figure includes 702 cultivated acres on purchased land.
ni = no information.
Source: Village Files, 1905 Schedules.

sections; in Otradnoe village the inhabitants registered for fifty-eight homesteads but 60 percent of the cultivation was on five quarter sections.

The South Colony villages relied much more on horses in their agricultural operations than did the North Colony villages, where oxen were more prevalent (see Table 9, Chapter 8). Most of the North Colony villages had at least four yoke of oxen, while only six of the South Colony villages had any oxen at all. This seems to be further evidence that Verigin, in his commercialization of the agricultural enterprise, was concentrating his efforts on the core lands of the CCUB, which were also, by and large, the best lands. In terms of rapid transformation of the prairie and parklands into agricultural lands, horses were much more efficient. And, of course, even they were being supplanted on the larger fields by huge steam traction engines and gang ploughs.[8]

Good Spirit Lake Annex

Need and group pressure initially held the Kars and Elizavetpol Annex villages to the communal way of life, but many leaned toward individualism and were among the first of the South Colony people to come forward to register for their homesteads, even before Peter Verigin arrived in late 1902.[9] His persuasive ways and grand plans drew the bulk of the Good Spirit Lake villagers back to a communal way of life, but in all but three villages, varying proportions of Independents remained in 1905, and Old Gorilloe was fully individualistic. New Gorilloe and Novo Troiztkoe each had a significant Independent component, and Kalmakovo and Moisayovo each had a few Independents. Despite the individualism of these villages, 90 percent of the total Annex population belonged to Verigin's Community in 1905, and was communal in practice if perhaps not wholly convinced in spirit.

The survey of the Annex village of Novo Troitzkoe (see Figure 20, Chapter 4) provides the most detailed portrayal of a 1905 Doukhobor village, although it is impossible to determine just how representative it is. Since it was newly established (sometime between 1902 and 1905), and since about a third of its population was Independent, it may have differed in some respects from the longer-established villages or those which were wholly communal. In general plan, however, Novo Troitzkoe replicated the pattern of the street-village followed by all the villages. While not as rigidly uniform in the spacing and orientation of buildings as some of the villages — see, for example, the photos of Voskrisennie in the South Colony (Figure 24, Chapter 4) and the Annex village of Moisayovo (Khristianovka, Figure 10, Chapter 2) — there is clear evidence of order. All the major structures (stables and houses) on one side of the street, and most on the opposite side, are aligned, and all but two of the houses are oriented with their gable ends toward the street. It is true that two of the granaries and the engine house are set right along the fence line, and that a house and granary are set much further back than the other structures, but overall, in plan and general appearance, it probably differed little from Terpennie (see Figure 25, Chapter 4). The back of the village lots were given over to fenced garden plots and beyond that, to larger cultivated fields.

---

8 As early as February 1904 Verigin was considering the purchase of steam tractors for ploughing, and he reported to Tolstoy that ten such engines pulling either eight-bottomed gang ploughs or four bottoms with a discing "cutter" behind, were working in the summer of 1905 (Verigin to Tolstoy, 20 February 1904; ibid., 3 July 1905 in Donskov, *Tolstoy-Verigin Correspondence*, 64, 76).

9 NA, RG15, V754 F494483, Pt. 2, Crerar to Turriff, 5 May 1902.

A few interesting points warrant consideration. In 1905, Novo Troitzkoe was a "mixed" village with 106 Community Doukhobors and forty-two Independents. Aylsworth identifies some of the granaries and the grist mill as belonging to the Doukhobor Company, while the other structures are noted only by function. The only exception is the identification of the house and granary of Ivan Schoukin (Shukin), an Independent who had never belonged to the Community, according to the 1905 schedule. Schoukin's granary, a large stable (20' x 60') and a well were located across the central street from his house rather than beside it, as was the more common practice in the Independent villages of the Saskatchewan Colony. Perhaps he was laying claim to unoccupied land across the street.

Aylsworth makes the distinction among "occupied," "abandoned" and "vacant" houses. The distinction between the last two terms is not explained, but it might mean that the "vacant" houses were only temporarily unoccupied (possibly because Independent homesteaders left these houses for makeshift dwellings on their homestead land to fulfill the residency requirement, but returned to reoccupy them for the winter), whereas the "abandoned" house may have been left by an Independent taking up full-time residency on his homestead.

Almost all of the houses in the village were long and narrow, ranging from an unusually long and narrow one (10' x 100') — no doubt belonging to an Independent with house and barn built together in the manner of the Saskatchewan Colony settlers — to the more common 15', 18' or 20' x 60' house. Two of the vacant houses were much more compact at 12' x 30' and one occupied house was nearly square (15' x 20'). The plan identifies the same number of granaries as are listed in the 1905 schedule but locates only five of the eighteen stables, nineteen of the twenty-two houses (seventeen occupied and five unoccupied), and neither of the two bathhouses listed on the 1905 schedule. Nor are the two implement sheds, the blacksmith's shop and the chicken house identified on the plan, although two large structures — an "engine house" and an unidentified structure of the same dimension — might be the implement sheds.[10] It is possible that many of the stables were located outside of the thirty-acre village site which Aylsworth surveyed, or that the schedule identified separately the stables which were built as extensions to the houses. Since this village housed several families of Independents, and since most of the houses were considerably longer than the Community houses in other villages, it is quite possible that these families built the traditional house-barn combination in this village. The village buildings were constructed of log, as were all the buildings of the Annex villages.[11] Table 13 indicates relative growth in the Annex villages in the period since 1899.

---

10 NA, RG15, V1168 F5412501, Novo Troitzkoe Village Files, 1905 Schedule.
11 NA, RG15, V754 F494483, Pt. 2, N.G. McCallum, "Report." The buildings of Novo Troitzkoe were built of sod according to the 1899 "Doukhobor Statistics." Whether this was an error, a particular use of the term "sod" (see Chapter 2, note 29), or whether the initial buildings of sod were replaced by those of log by 1905, is unclear. The same uncertainty exists for the Annex village of Novo Gorilovka (New Gorilloe).

Table 13
Animal and Implement Ratios, South Colony, 1905*

1 draught animal per 4.7 persons (1/12)	1 cow per 2.1 persons (1/159)
1 sheep per 4.6 persons (n/a)	1 plough per 20.7 persons (1/47)
1 wagon per 21.1 persons (1/42)	1 binder per 50.0 persons (n/a)
1 mower per 55.9 persons (n/a)	1 harrow per 31.7 persons (n/a)

* bracketed figures indicate 1899 ratios.

Source: "Doukhobor Statistics"; Village Files, 1905 Schedules.

In general, the Annex villages were slightly smaller on average than the villages in the other reserves. The average village contained 138 Community Doukhobors, with an additional eighty-six Independents scattered among the four "mixed" villages. The average Annex village had nineteen occupied and two unoccupied or unfinished houses, and ten stables of varying sizes, all constructed of log. The number of stables gives an indication of a somewhat greater dependence on livestock: Ootishennie and Kalmakovo had twenty-six and sixteen stables respectively, and the seven Community villages had seventy-two stables in all. In common with the other Doukhobor villages, each had a bathhouse (Blagosklonoe had two), a blacksmith's shop, and one or more granaries, and most had a carpenter's shop, an implement shed, and a chicken house. Four of the six also had an oil house with a flax press (in contrast to only three among the twenty-six villages of the South Colony).

Despite a somewhat greater emphasis on livestock, the Annex villages expanded their cultivated land base more rapidly than did the North Colony villages. The seven Community villages had cultivated a total of 4,801 acres by 1905, an average of 800 acres per village or an average of twenty acres per homestead (see Table 14). Every village of the Annex met the minimum requirements of fifteen cultivated acres

Table 14
Good Spirit Lake Annex — 1905*

Village	Horses	Oxen	Cattle	Sheep	Ploughs	Cult.	Hsds.	Ac/Hsd.	Pop.
Blagosklonoe	24	12	68	36	7	966	46	20.9	185
Gorilloe	20	10	37	25	7	639	26	24.6	72
Kalmakovo	24	10	78	37	10	775.5	43	18.0	140
Kyrillovo	27	8	77	37	7	592.5	37	16.0	140
Moisayovo	24	8	85	37	7	868.5	46	18.9	141
Novotroitzkoe	20	12	46	36	8	852.5	31	27.5	105
Old Gorilloe				— Independent Village —					
Ootishennie	13	22	98	37	8	960	47	20.4	181
Totals	152	82	489	245	54	5,654	276	20.5	964

* all data refer to the Community component of these villages — 88 percent of the total population of 1,100.

Source: Village Files, 1905 Schedule.

per homestead, but again, the Doukhobors concentrated their cultivation on a small fraction of the homesteads they had entered for. New Gorilloe had cultivated 639 acres on ten quarter sections, but nearly half of their cultivation was on only two quarter sections. They had no cultivation at all on sixteen of their homesteads. Ootishennie had cultivated 902 acres on sixteen quarter sections, and half of the cultivation was on only four. Twenty-one homesteads had no cultivation. Blagosklonoe had cultivated 951 acres — the most of any Annex village — but half of the cultivated land was on only six quarter sections, and twenty-three of its forty-six quarter sections were "untouched."

It is nearly impossible to make any regional comparisons despite the extent of the reserve and its varied natural environment. Many of the "peripheral" villages were slowed in their progress by relocating, abandoning well-built villages and quite extensive cultivated lands to start anew in a more satisfactory location. These relocations, in fact, make a regional separation of the peripheral Wet Mountains villages and the "core" region meaningless, since their new locations were on the fringes of the core area. There appears to be little in the way of major differences between the clearly defined region occupied by the Annex villages and the South Colony proper.

Chapter 10
The Saskatchewan Colony - 1905

The thirteen villages of the Kars Doukhobors in the Saskatchewan Colony in 1905 (see Map 10) shared some general similarities with the North and South Colony villages, but differed from them in other respects. All were built on the *strassendorf* plan and all but one were fully or predominantly communal. On the other hand, these villages were much better equipped in livestock and implements and the farm buildings were built along more traditional lines, although a good deal of variation in building styles is evident in contemporary photographs (see Figures 31 and 33, Chapter 5).

As he did with the villages of the North and South Colonies, Speers classified the thirteen villages of the Saskatchewan Colony in three categories according to the ideal of forty families: three "large" villages, four "small" villages, and six "uniform" villages.[1] Although these spellings are in as much need of "a little more revision" as the others — "Kriille" for Kirilovka, "Horilo" for Horelofka, "Pesirifoka" for Pasariofka — the villages can be matched with known villages without difficulty. While almost half of the villages were uniform in terms of numbers of families, village populations were as variable here as in the other colonies. The average village was somewhat smaller — 146 people — but this average included villages as small as sixty-six people and as large as 224. Only three villages were close to the average; five were much larger and five were much smaller.

The average village had twenty occupied houses, although here again there was wide variation around the average. Four villages had near the average number of houses (eighteen to twenty-three), five had far fewer (nine to seventeen), and four had somewhat more (twenty-five to twenty-seven). Either because the homestead inspectors who provided this information were not as thorough as in other areas, or because the identification of stables and sheds would have been meaningless in an area where house, stable and shed were all one connected unit, only houses were

---

1   NA, RG15, V755 F494483, Pt. 4, Speers to Department, 16 October 1905.

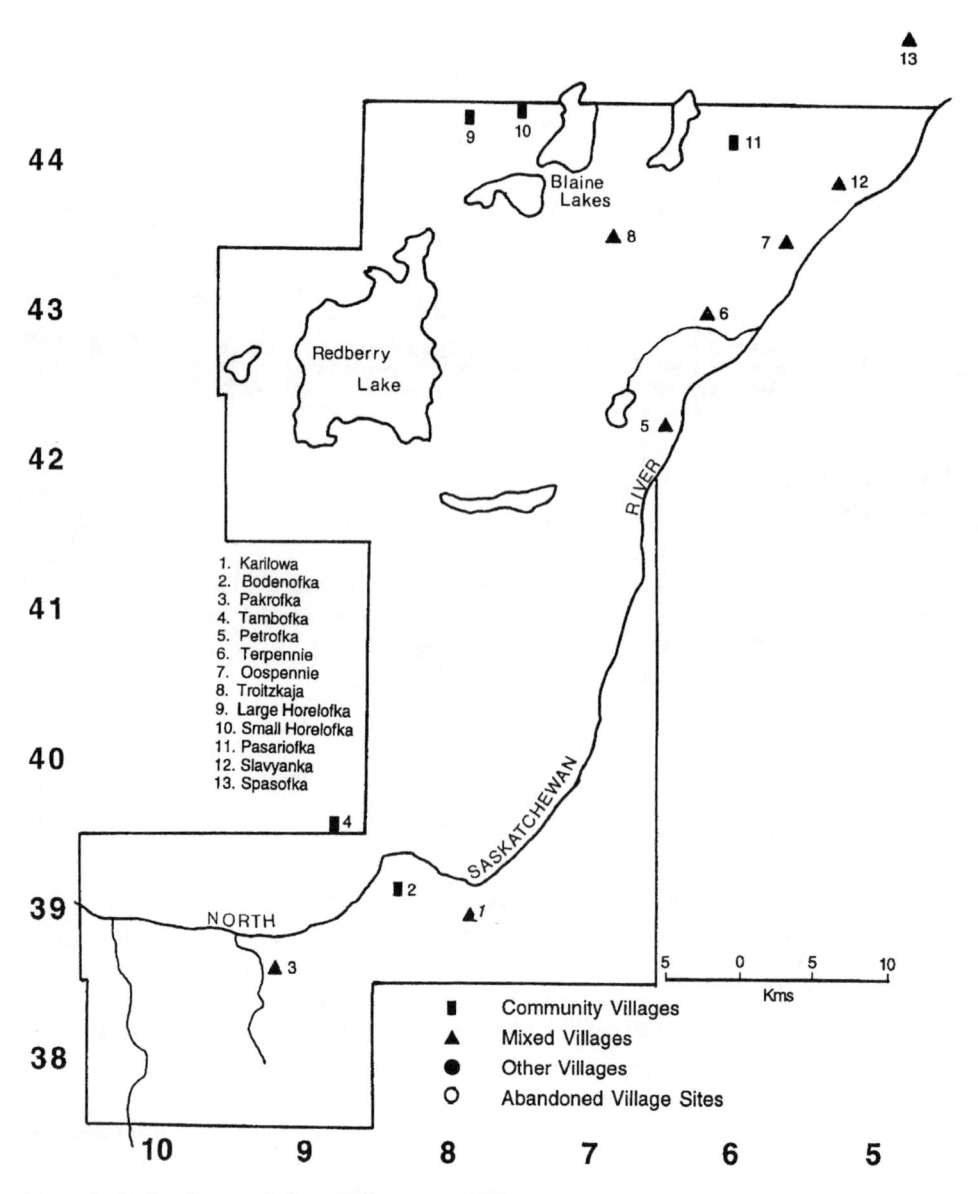

Map 10. Saskatchewan Colony Villages — 1905.

identified in the 1905 schedules. Petrofka was the only exception: the Company's large stable and several small granaries were identified separately. These structures were likely built after Verigin called the bulk of the people back to a communal way of life, and after most of the traditional house-barns had been completed.

Contemporary photographs show a variety of architectural styles and materials in use at this time, including the long, low house-barn combinations; high-profile,

Table 15 Animal and Implement Ratios, Saskatchewan Colony, 1905	
1 draught animal per 3.5 persons (1/7.7)	1 cow per 1.4 persons (1/20.2)
1 sheep per 3.5 persons (n/a)	1 plough per 10.0 persons (1/33.5)
1 wagon per 8.7 persons (1/22.6)	1 mower per 27.6 persons (n/a)
1 harrow per 17.0 persons (n/a)	1 binder per 41.4 persons (n/a)
* bracketed figures indicate 1899 ratios.	
Source: Village Files, 1905 Schedules.	

full-lofted houses with perimeter porches (quite rare); medium-profile, double-purlined houses with eave extensions along one side (the most common style); and a few one-and-one-half-storey "western" houses. Mud-plastered log houses with thatched or sod roofs are predominant in these photographs, but there is an occasional building of sawn lumber with a shingle roof as well.

Table 15 shows the pace of progress in terms of livestock and equipment between 1899 and 1905. It is clear that the initial relative "prosperity" of the Kars settlers overcame the penalties of their late start. In 1905, as in 1899, they were much better off than other Colony villages, better even than the relatively prosperous and progressive Annex villages (compare with Table 10, Chapter 8, and Tables 11 and 13, Chapter 9).

The Saskatchewan Colony was the only reserve to fulfill the requirements of Sifton's cultivation concession (see Table 16); every village exceeded these requirements. Oospennie had progressed most rapidly, with sixty-five cultivated acres for each of its seventeen homesteads, while even Karilowa, with the least cultivated acreage per homestead, still had more than double the required acreage (nearly thirty-two cultivated acres for each of its forty-four homesteads). Overall, the Colony cultivated an average of forty-one acres for each homestead registered. Here too, however, the cultivated acreage was concentrated on a small proportion of the total homesteads entered. The proportion of entered homesteads on which some cultivation was done was higher here than in the other colonies, but in several villages the proportion was below 50 percent (Bodenofka - 33 percent; Large Horelofka - 30 percent), and most were below 65 percent. At least one village, Karilowa, was obviously preparing to comply with the initial cultivation requirements of the homestead law, as the villagers cultivated thirteen acres on each of twenty-eight homesteads. This, however, represented less than 30 percent of the 1,399 acres cultivated; almost all the rest was done on eleven homesteads.

The Saskatchewan Colony villages in 1905 reflect both the early individualism which dominated in the original village organization, and the great impact of Verigin's call back to communal life. Although the communal way of life dominated

---

[2] As noted in Chapter 9, the Annex villages also met the requirements as individual villages and as a group, but the South Colony as a whole, of which the Annex was a part, did not.

Table 16 Saskatchewan Colony — 1905[a]								
Village	Horses	Oxen	Cattle	Sheep	Ploughs	Cult.	Hsds.	Ac/hsd.	Pop.
Bodenofka	31	0	100	45	12	1,340	30	44.7	131
Karilowa	50	0	129	50	18	1,399	44	31.8	161
Large Horelofka	80	0	200	64	20	1,025	30	34.2	168
Oospennie	29	0	87	31	9	1,108[b]	17	65.2	60
Pakrofka	18	0	47	15	9	445	13	34.2	110
Pasariofka	36	0	112	37	13	1,067	25	42.7	105
Petrofka	41	0	93	38	15	1,257	28	44.9	85
Slavyanka	20	0	67	30	7	791[c]	16	49.4	82
Small Horelofka	44	0	71	26	8	650	14	46.4	74
Spasofka	70	0	150	67	30	1,620[d]	47	34.5	217
Terpennie	56	0	125	60	23	1,954[e]	44	44.4	191
Tonbofka	23	16	54	24	11	800	19	42.1	66
Troitskaya	42	0	145	55	15	1,210[f]	17	71.2	179
Totals	540	16	1,380	542	190	14,666	347	41.1	1,629

a) all data refer to the Community component of these villages — 1,629 persons, or 86 percent of a total of 1,904 persons; b) includes 430 acres of "go back land"; c) includes 150 acres of "go back land"; d) includes 275 acres of "old breaking"; e) includes 380 acres of "old breaking"; f) includes ninety acres of "old breaking."

Source: Village Files, 1905 Schedules.

this area as it did every other colony, the proportion of Independents was higher here (14 percent of the Colony's population), and five villages had a substantial population of Independents (Petrofka had an Independent majority). Nonetheless, twelve of the thirteen villages in 1905 were either fully or predominantly communal. Considering that in 1900 only four of ten villages were communal, this shift is indicative of Verigin's appeal, even to the more individualistic of the Doukhobors. Not all of the communal Doukhobors belonged to the Veriginite Community, however. I have noted the case of Pakrofka (Chapter 6), which had three different communal groups in addition to a group of Independents.

I have alluded already to Verigin's strategy of consolidating his Community around the core of the South Colony by relocating whole villages from peripheral areas to locations nearer the centre of activity around Veregin Station. This strategy also included relocating people from peripheral villages (particularly those of the North Colony) to more central villages within the South Colony. An even more ambitious part of this strategy involved relocating more than 600 Saskatchewan

---

3   These figures, as all statistics relating to Colony populations in 1905, reflect only those Doukhobors residing in the villages and do not include Independent Doukhobors who were living on their own homesteads.

4   NA, RG76, V184 F65101, Pt. 5, Ens, "Crop Report," 1900.

Colony settlers to the core areas. As early as March 1903, Verigin was petitioning the government to allow those who wanted to become more fully integrated into the Community to take up lands in the eastern reserves. The Saskatchewan faithful were to move to two major areas: as yet unsettled lands in the North Colony and, according to the homestead registrations made, an area on the western periphery of the South Colony/Annex lands. Three new villages — Archangelskoe, Gromovoe and Perehodnoe (and possibly a fourth, Pavlovo) — in fact were being constructed in 1905 on lands which had, until then, been avoided. Yet there is no record in the 1905 schedules of any homestead entries for lands in the North Colony. The movement of Saskatchewan Colony Doukhobors to the North Colony appears to have taken place no earlier than 1906, for the village schedules of 1905 do not include these villages.

In the South Colony, no settlements were ever established on the lands for which homestead entries had actually been made (Townships 31 and 32, Range 7). According to later schedules, the Saskatchewan settlers ended up at Veregin Siding. There was a settlement at Veregin Station in 1905, but it is not at all clear how many, if any, of the people there in 1905 were from the Saskatchewan Colony. The 1905 and 1906 lists apparently include only those persons who were temporarily absent from their villages while working at Veregin; these lists would be needed to confirm their status as residents in their own villages for homestead purposes. The list of fifty-six names for both years gives the village origin and homestead location but no Saskatchewan Colony villages are listed. However, the reserve set aside for this village in April 1907 includes land for immigrants from Langham (apparently thirty-one from Tonbofka village), which would suggest that the movement of Doukhobors from the Saskatchewan Colony to this area began after 1906. By 1909, all 315 village residents are designated as Saskatchewan Colony emigrants.

The lack of association between homestead entries and actual locations of the relocated Saskatchewan settlers may underline again the Doukhobors' understanding of the way the land was to be allocated. They apparently made these homestead entries with the understanding that location with respect to actual

---

5   NA, RG76, V184 F65101, Pt. 7, Harley to Smith, 31 March 1903.

6   Although there is no evidence of any movement taking place at this date, more than 100 homesteads were entered in this area by Saskatchewan Colony Doukhobors. Verigin seems to have targeted especially the young men between the ages of 17 and 23, and there are many instances of homesteads being entered for by young men of 15 and 16. These last were cancelled, but homesteads registered for 17-year-old men were maintained until June 1907 (see the 1905 schedules of the Saskatchewan Colony villages where the ages of those making entry for homesteads in the Yorkton area are given).

7   If indeed Pavlovo was one of the villages (see note 72, Chapter 6), the movement began in 1905 with the major movement occurring in 1906.

8   This figure matches the number of residents in Tonbofka village in the survey of 1907. They indicated they did not want to take up the land they entered for in the Saskatchewan Colony, but wanted land "somewhere in the Yorkton district" (NA, RG15, V1166 F5412433, Tonbofka Village Files).

settlements was not important. The entry was merely to comply with the regulations and to ensure that land would be reserved for the next generation of Doukhobors. And the Doukhobors surely believed that no matter where the new settlers located, as long as the cultivated acreage of the Community as a whole amounted to fifteen acres per entered homestead, they had fulfilled the government requirements.[9] Of course, this scenario disregards the whole matter of citizenship, without which the land could not be patented, but it is not clear just how this issue was viewed by the Community Doukhobors at this time. Perhaps if the cultivation requirement had been honoured, the Doukhobors might have felt more comfortable about affirming their allegiance to the Crown. This lack of concern for the relationship between residence and homestead land represented the kinds of irregularities which Oliver referred to in his later interviews with Doukhobor delegates and which made unlikely any concessions on his part respecting the homestead requirements.

In 1905, then, there was great anticipation on the part of many Veriginite Doukhobors of a move either to the North or South Colony, and in fact, construction of the new villages to receive them in the North Colony was underway. The departure of those most loyal to Verigin and to his vision of a shared community left the Saskatchewan villages without the leavening of the communal bent, so the subsequent slide into individualism was precipitous. By 1909, only Bodenofka and Karilowa were communal villages (the communal village of Tonbofka had been relocated in stages, some to Gromovoe in the North Colony, and some to the South Colony); the rest were either Independent villages or comprised of a mix of Independents and Independent-Communists.[10]

Summary for 1905

1905 marked the peak of Doukhobor dominance in the three reserves set aside for them, at least potentially. They claimed nearly 423,000 acres of homestead land and another 13,000 acres of purchased land. Their impress on the land was to expand in the next period, in acres cultivated and investments in land, machinery and stock, even in the midst of uncertainty, but the numbers of the Community Doukhobors and their land holdings in the original areas of settlement never exceeded those of this period.

Their progress since their arrival in 1899 is little less than astounding, given their poverty and the "wasted" years of 1899-1902 when they were leaderless and without direction. In 1905, 8,417 Community Doukhobors and 554 Independent Doukhobors occupied 2,000 houses (with an additional 125 in the course of construction) in at least sixty-six villages. Except for a handful of newly occupied

---

9   Canada, *Papers*, 16-18.

10   In the schedules of 1905 through 1907, the distinction is made between Communists and Independents; thereafter, a further distinction is made between Independents and Independent-Communists. I have been unable to find a formal definition of the latter, although it seems to refer to people who wished to maintain a communal way of life, but who did not want to be associated with the larger Verigin Community. Thus they practiced their communalism on a smaller scale, again on lands set aside under the fifteen-acre-per-person allotment, but distinguished from the larger Community reserves.

or newly abandoned villages, these were fully functioning and fully equipped. The Community increased their cultivated acreage nearly fortyfold to over 42,000 acres from the garden-size plots totalling 1,100 acres in 1899, and with fine draught horses and steam traction engines, the prospect for even more rapid growth was very promising.

A regional comparison of Doukhobor settlement in 1905 reveals some variation in cultural landscape, and a good deal of variation in agricultural development. While all villages adhered to the traditional strassendorf *plan and built structures within traditional architectural styles, the variations that would distinguish the eastern colonies from the Saskatchewan Colony on the plans drawn up by Fairchild in 1909 were already evident. The prayer homes that were to be the core of the eastern villages, and which would appear on the 1909 plans as large buildings on large lots near the centre of the villages, were being constructed in several locations. The Saskatchewan Colony village plans, on the other hand, show the unmodified regularity of the traditional* strassendorf *plan. And while the traditional house-stable combination was not entirely absent from the eastern villages, especially in those of the Good Spirit Lake Annex (see the discussion in Chapter 2), the dominant style of house built here was a truncated version of a traditional style. The reverse was true of the Saskatchewan Colony villages where the traditional low-profile house-stable combination was the norm, and the individual, high-lofted house the exception.*

Regional variation in agricultural progress and prosperity is quite evident in 1905. The Kars settlers of the Saskatchewan Colony were by far the most prosperous of the groups, having two or three times the stock and farm equipment per capita as the next most prosperous Annex settlers. The North Colony by most measures was the poorest of the colonies, but even here the progress was considerable. The Saskatchewan Colony also had the highest per capita and per homestead cultivated acreage, and, except for the South Colony (which by this time was using steam traction engines for cultivation), had the most cultivated land per draught animal. The North Colony, relying primarily on oxen for cultivation, had the lowest ratios in all these categories.

Despite regional variations, Verigin had unified his followers around a single vision of toil and peaceful life that harnessed their energies and bent their wills to a common purpose. Every prospect pleased; only the government was to prove vile. The government was as convinced that the Doukhobors would comply with the homestead requirements when faced with the loss of their lands (or it did not care) as the Doukhobors were convinced that the government had betrayed them (or shown its true colours: governments, no matter what they promised, could not be trusted) by going back on its promise to grant them land under the modified cultivation concession. The "stasis" of 1905-06 was short-lived. Decline was imminent.

Chapter 11
Decline ~ 1906~1913

The continuing influx of land-hungry settlers in the years following 1905 not only rapidly filled up the better lands and created a sustained demand for homesteads, but put pressure on the government to ensure that all settlers were being treated equitably. Concessions, especially to "non-white" settlers or groups, were an affront to resident or intending settlers who either were, or were willing to become, British subjects. The pressure to have the uncultivated lands of the Doukhobors opened for homesteading came not only from intending homesteaders, but "from people concerned in the business interests whose success depends on the settlement and cultivation of the adjacent land."[1] Also, the continuing negative publicity surrounding the occasional displays of arson, nudism, and periodic "treks" by a tiny but increasingly radical element of the Doukhobors tended to draw attention away from the very real advances made by the larger group; in fact, as today, these sporadic displays came to characterize, and stigmatize, the Doukhobors as a whole.

In view of the continuing shift in attitudes toward the Doukhobors and the changing societal context, their appeal for the government to keep faith with its commitments produced no softening in the rigid interpretation of the homestead regulations, and roused little public sympathy. In light of the "developments during the season of 1905," it was apparent that the government felt it needed to embark on a course which would "satisfy public opinion on the one hand, and protect the legitimate interests of the Doukhobors, on the other."[2] The course it chose was to satisfy the former and frustrate the latter. It was to culminate in a decision which gave the committed Community Doukhobors little choice: compromise what they felt to be an essential element of true Doukhoborism by recognizing individual land ownership and swearing allegiance to the Crown, preserve the Community on token plots of government land to be held "at the pleasure of the government," or leave.

---

1   Canada, *Papers* (1907), 6.
2   Ibid.

Most of the committed left, either for what would become the "Second Community" in British Columbia, or for new villages on purchased land in Saskatchewan. Many of those who chose to go along with the government requirements also eventually left the villages to take up residence on their individual homesteads.

It is useful to treat the decline of this period in two stages, each of which involved the two major elements of people and land. The early decline of 1906-10 was initiated when, in 1906, Frank Oliver, the Minister of the Interior, rejected his predecessor's cultivation concession and demanded proof of allegiance to the Crown as a prerequisite to continued homestead entry. This decision resulted in the loss of homestead lands in 1907, and the decline it precipitated in the Doukhobor settlements might be characterized as slow in terms of the Community, rapid in terms of Community land. The later decline was initiated by Verigin's purchase of land in British Columbia in 1908, although the impact of that decision was not significant until 1911-13. This stage of decline might be characterized as rapid in terms of Community and relatively slow in terms of Community land.

First Stage of Decline

At the beginning of this period, the Doukhobor Community appeared to be coasting on the apparent successes of earlier agreements reached between Verigin and the government. Upon arriving at the various reserves, the Doukhobors set up their villages and began cultivating the most favourable areas adjacent to, or within a reasonable distance of, the village. While the Doukhobors adhered in the main to the boundaries of the stipulated reserves, there was little attention given to any restrictions or reservations within the reserves (school lands, Hudson's Bay Company lands, railway lands), for, either from real (the interior subdivision of many of the reserves was not finished until after the villages were established) or willful ignorance, they assumed that all the lands were for their use. When faced with the choice of making formal entry for individual quarter sections of land, almost all refused to do so, as they perceived this act to be a violation of their principle of communal land use, and of their commitment to God's ultimate ownership of the land. Peter Verigin joined his followers in 1902 and assured them that making entry for individual pieces of land was a mere formality, no more than satisfying a harmless government regulation. What was essential was to live and work as a community on the lands the government had set aside for them.

To facilitate the process of homestead registration, the Department allowed a Committee of Three — Peter Verigin, Simeon Reiben and Pavel Planidin — to make proxy entries for each eligible entrant and the land was entered *en masse*. This procedure no doubt helped Verigin allay some of the fears of his followers since they were not directly involved in the registration process. The individual Doukhobors, most of whom could neither read nor write, did not even know, or care, what quarter sections they were laying claim to. Communal life went on as before, in the villages and in the fields.

The authorities subsequently found some irregularities in the procedure: some names appeared more than once — a problem that was difficult to detect given the similarity of names and the difficulties of communication — and there were many underaged entrants included in the entries. Verigin explained that some parents intentionally gave younger than actual ages to the inspectors because they suspected the government was going to call up their sons for military duty. This was an entirely understandable concern in light of the intense persecution the Doukhobors experienced in Russia as a result of military conscription. Giving their sons' ages as 15 or 16 instead of 18 or 19 meant that they would have an additional two or three years to see whether this government could be trusted when it said that this procedure had nothing to do with military conscription. There certainly was inadequate communication as to the age requirements when the Doukhobors were first asked to make entry. Leo Sulerzhitsky wrote out of some frustration in early August 1899:

> We have done nothing yet about the age of those who can take a homestead; 18, 17 or 16. I do not know who is responsible that the people on Thunder Hill have not yet been told about the conditions on which they can occupy land, but the fact of the matter is that they do not know yet anything about it .... Now I would like to know for sure what is the age at which a homestead can be taken.[3]

This uncertainty had been dealt with by 1903.

There seems to have been no particular rationale for the choice of lands by the members of the villages, although the entered lands, in general, were in the vicinity of the village of residence. Blagodarnoe village, for example, entered lands that were in three different townships, with some of the quarter sections more than five miles from the village site. This seemingly "careless" attitude reflected the Doukhobors' disregard for the niceties of official policy. They did not pay much attention to the location of individual quarter sections, believing that the whole of these lands were reserved for their use. If having their names beside some piece of land satisfied the authorities, so much the better. At least it would allow them to get on with their work, now that Verigin was with them and they could hear his directives first-hand. The desultory manner in which they had cultivated their land up to now gave way, under his leadership, to a concentrated push for progress.

The authorities, however, viewed the Doukhobors' attitude towards land, and the disregard for the homestead regulations, with annoyance and frustration. Charged with supervising the agricultural settlement of a vast area and with regularizing the way in which land could be taken up, they could not, or would not, sympathize with, much less countenance, the beliefs and motivation of the group. When the authorities tried to match entrants with quarter sections, they found confusion. Some had entered on land attached to one village, had moved to another village, but had not changed the entry to match the new village. In other cases, the land entered upon by the villagers was not contiguous to the village; sometimes, as in the case of Blagodarnoe just noted, it was several miles distant. The Doukhobors either did not know or did not care about the three-mile limit for fulfilling the residence

---

3   NA, RG15, V754 F494483, Pt. 1, Soulerjitzky to McCreary, 3 August 1899.

requirement in a village under the Hamlet Clause. By virtue of their belief in the community of land, they rejected anything smacking of individual ownership. By virtue of the government's promises, they continued to cultivate land on a village basis, ignoring the human artifice of the subdivision survey. Besides, the great majority of the Doukhobors could not read, and even had they been literate, they would soon have occasion to distrust the written word as well.

In any case, Verigin had at least put the land entry question to rest, and the homesteads beyond the three-mile limit were a small part of the whole. The next issue to raise concern was the cultivation requirement. In response to the Doukhobors' communal cultivation practice, Clifford Sifton had decided to allow cultivation *en bloc* in fulfilling the homestead requirements.[4] This concession did nothing to allay the continuing concerns with respect to land ownership, but it did set in place a policy that the Doukhobors could justifiably view as one which supported their communal lifestyle. That the general pattern of cultivating the lands in close proximity to their villages at the expense of leaving peripheral lands untouched did not change between 1902 and 1906, is evidence that the Community believed it could fulfill this requirement on any part of the land a particular village held.

While all seemed settled from the Doukhobors' perspective, the government was having a change of heart, or rather, a change of Minister. Frank Oliver, well-known opponent of Sifton's strategy of filling up the West with Eastern Europeans, took over the Interior portfolio. Of immediate concern was the "Doukhobor Problem." Land which had been occupied for six years was no closer to being patented, apparently, than at the beginning. There was no attempt to apply for patent even on homesteads for which, under the most rigorous interpretation of the homestead law, all requirements had been fulfilled.

In October 1905, Oliver sent out homestead inspectors to determine the amount of land the Doukhobors had cultivated. Besides this information, they also made a general census of the population and reported on buildings, stock, machinery, and the location of cultivated land. They found the people in the villages "a hospitable, industrious, resourceful people, well pleased with the country and the treatment which had been accorded to them, and full of hope for the future."[5] It is clear from the correspondence relating to the land question that while the task of the 1905 survey was to determine whether the amount of cultivation might fulfill the *en bloc* requirements which Sifton had promised, there was a more serious obstacle standing in the way of the Community Doukhobors: their refusal to become naturalized citizens. The homestead inspector N.G. McCallum, who accompanied the 1905 Commission on its survey, stated that the Communists they saw were "very pronounced" in their refusal to ever become British subjects.[6]

---

4 NA, RG15, V755 F494483, Pt. 6, Sifton to Ivan and Feodor Suchorukoff, 15 February 1902.
5 NA, RG15, V755 F494483, Pt. 4, J.B. White, Thos. Young, and D.C. McNab to Secretary, Department of the Interior, 12 January 1906.
6 NA, RG15, V755 F494483, Pt. 6, McCallum to Cash, 27 November 1906.

Oliver presented his general course of action respecting the cultivation concession in a memorandum issued in March 1906, outlining the conditions under which Doukhobor entries within the reserved lands would be maintained "for the time being."[7] All entries would be maintained except for entrants whose residence could not be established, and where the entrant was under 17 years of age. Homestead entries would be maintained for those between the ages of 17 and 18, and for those who had entered while under 18 but who had since attained that age, but legal entry was to be made after turning 18. Oliver also ruled that lands which were not entered, but had "substantial improvements" done by the Community, could be entered by a Community member, "and the privileges which have been exercised by the Doukhobor community may be continued." He further made the distinction between "the standing of privileged entries made previous to this date[8] and entries made by Doukhobors subsequent to this date to which no special privileges are attached."[9] For all entries, he emphasized the fact that the Dominion Lands Act was the standard:

> No promise of patent can be made nor can patent be issued unless the requirements of the Dominion Lands Act have been fulfilled. This is not a ruling but a statement of the law as it existed when the Doukhobor reserves were set apart and as it still exists.[10]

This last sentence sets out what would be Oliver's standard argument when charged with reneging on the cultivation concession promised by Sifton.

The mandate of the Doukhobor Commission under the leadership of John MacDougall, however, was directed precisely to the second and more basic issue. The Commission, in its tour in August and September 1906, not only took detailed information on where and how much cultivation was done, but also whether the homesteader was willing to swear allegiance to the Crown. Cultivation was not the sticking point; acknowledging allegiance to the Crown was:

> Q. Do you know that unless you naturalize and become citizens of this country, you cannot secure patents to these homesteads you have applied for?
>
> A. Yes, we know that, but we can't become subject to the government, "God is our King."[11]

After the survey of the sixty-one Doukhobor villages, the Commission presented Oliver with a list of recommendations among which was the cancellation of all

---

7   NA, RG15, V755 F494483, Pt. 4, Oliver to Greenway, 7 March 1906.
8   A handwritten note at the bottom by Greenway underlines the fact that the date referred to is the date of this memorandum — 7 March 1906.
9   NA, RG15, V755 F494483, Pt. 4, Oliver to Greenway, 7 March 1906.
10 Ibid.
11 John MacDougall's example of a "typical" conversation between the Commission and the Community Doukhobors (NA, RG15, V755 F494483, Pt. 6, "General Report," Doukhobor Commission [1906]).

Community Doukhobor homestead entries with the provision of re-entry for those willing to become naturalized and to fulfill all cultivation and residence requirements; this last could still be done in a village as long as the homestead land was within the "vicinity" of the village. It also recommended that reserves of seventeen to twenty acres per capita be set up around the villages for those who wished to remain "in community."[12]

Oliver decided to act upon these recommendations, and the Commission, in two whirlwind tours of the villages in early 1907, first ensured that the Doukhobors understood what was proposed, and then cancelled homestead entries, accepted re-entry applications, and set aside land for the intransigent Community members as village reserves on the basis of fifteen acres per capita.[13]

The Doukhobors addressed the two aspects of the Dominion Lands Act which formed the heart of the ultimatum John MacDougall left in every village in his January 1907 visit, in their "Petition to the Minster of the Interior and All People in Canada." In an eloquent and moving document, they argued that they had complied with the requirements as had been documented:

> We have been allowed to be exempted from the military service, we have been permitted to live in villages and to cultivate the soil in common for all of this we possess documents issued by the Government.[14]

They pointed out that they respectfully declined to take the oath of allegiance on the basis of their belief in Christ's teachings. Oliver was unmoved.

It is probably fruitless to attempt to separate the issues of cultivation duties and allegiance in assessing their impact on the cancellation of Doukhobor lands. The noncultivation or subcultivation of the majority of Doukhobor lands was what caught the intending homesteader's eye, and the government, knowing that there was a deeper problem involved, used this obvious and more immediate delinquency (if in fact it was such) to force the land issue, rather than to have it drag on for three more years, when it would have to deal with the issue of allegiance.

The decline of the Community land base on government land as a result of these policy decisions can only be described as precipitous. Some 2,500 homesteads representing approximately 400,000 acres were cancelled in June 1907;[15] 766 quarter sections (or approximately 122,500 acres) were returned to the Community in the form of reserves, on the basis of fifteen acres per Community member. In addition, 384 entries were either made or maintained for Doukhobors "who were desirous of acquiring title thereto by compliance with the law," that is to say, those

---

12 Ibid.
13 NA, RG15, V756 F494483, Pt. 7, MacDougall to Oliver, 14 May 1907.
14 Ibid., "Petition."
15 Canada, "Reports and Maps," 1907. MacDougall's original figures show some 2,386 homesteads cancelled with 768 of these quarter sections set aside as village reserves (NA, RG15, V756 F494483, Pt. 7, MacDougall to Oliver, 14 May 1907).

who would fulfill the cultivation requirements on their homestead quarter section and who would become British subjects.[16] In total, the land held by the Community (apart from land purchased from other vendors) was reduced from about 406,000 acres to about 123,000 acres in June 1907 — a loss of approximately 283,000 acres. In 1910, government land used by the Community further declined to just under 99,000 acres.[17]

It is much more difficult to trace changes in the amount of cultivated land actually used by the Doukhobor Community. There is a persistent notion that the acreage lost in 1907 consisted largely of improved lands, however, these were primarily lands on which little or no cultivation had been done. The village reserves of fifteen acres per person were chosen to retain as much of the cultivated land as possible,[18] nonetheless, the loss was not insignificant: the Community lost nearly 40 percent of their improved lands in the South Colony.[19] The village Community members were involved in the choice of which lands would be retained as part of the fifteen-acre allotment,[20] and which reserve lands would be given up to Community members deciding to go out on their own. For example, in Lubomeernoe,

> The communists were asked what three quarters they would select to be disposed of in case the commission desired to grant entries to applicants for the surplus area. They selected the N.E. 35-in 33-31 W 1st (no cultivation), and the North Half 1-34-31 W1st (twenty acres ready for crop, five of which are on the N.W. 1/4.).[21]

---

16 "Extract from a Report of the Committee of the Privy Council, 7 December 1907," *Canada Gazette*, 10 October 1908.

17 This total is based on a fifteen-acre allotment for the 6,585 people listed as Communists in the 1910 Commission survey. The lands reserved for the villages were reduced as people left the village, either to go to British Columbia, or to become Independents. The amount of land in the village reserves may have been slightly more than this, since there was a surplus in a few village reserves, that is, the reserve was larger than the fifteen-acre per capita allotment (village files for the three colonies).

18 "The quarter section upon which each Community village is situated, and such adjoining or adjacent quarter sections not exceeding in total area 15 acres to each resident of the village, exclusive of Independents, or approximately three times as much land as they have brought under cultivation during eight years [Oliver apparently could not refrain from emphasizing his generosity to the Doukhobors] so adjusted as to include as much of the Community cultivation as possible, but in no case exceeding a distance of three miles from the village, shall be held from re-entry for the purpose of protecting the Community of Doukhobors in their residence and cultivation during the pleasure of the Government" (NA, RG15, V755 F494483, Pt. 5, Oliver to MacDougall, 28 December 1906).

19 I estimated the cultivated lands lost by comparing the quarters on which cultivation occurred in 1905 (the nearest comprehensive survey to the June 1907 loss of lands) to the quarters maintained in the village reserves in 1907. The actual amount of cultivated land lost would be somewhat larger than this estimate since some new breaking on lands that were to be forfeited no doubt occurred in 1906.

20 The fifteen-acre reserve could not include lands more than three miles from the appropriate village, so the cultivation done on distant quarter sections could not be retained as part of the reserve.

21 NA, RG15, V1167 F5412461, Lubomeernoe Village File, May 1910 Report.

In some cases, to maintain the cohesiveness of the village land, the Community sacrificed quarter sections which were well-cultivated for others on which little cultivation had been done.[22] That this situation prevailed in some villages — more distant land cultivated while land closer to the village was left uncultivated — bolsters the claim that the Community chose the easiest and best lands upon which to focus their energies, rather than merely proximate lands.

There were problems in some cases, however. In the village of Otradnoe, a disposition of land was made which was not agreeable. The villagers apparently thought that a fair division had been made, but that the agreement was later changed by the Commissioner to give two Independents entry to quarter sections which were almost totally cultivated by the Community. The problem was resolved by a further exchange which allowed the Community to retain the cultivated land.[23]

In any case, the loss of cultivated land owing to the decision of 1907 did not result in an overall decline in cultivated land. While the total amount of land controlled by the Community declined precipitously, the amount of improved land actually continued to increase until approximately 1910. This seemingly anomalous situation reflects the rate of expansion of cultivated land on the remaining village reserves, a situation which could suggest either that Verigin still hoped that the village reserves would remain part of his prairie land base, or that he wished to get maximum returns from these lands in order to finance the move to British Columbia.[24] Community cultivation in the North Colony increased from approximately 5,370 acres to at least 8,250 acres by 1910 (this latter figure is cropped land and seems not to include any summerfallowed land). Unfortunately, the village files do not record the cultivation totals consistently for the villages in the other colonies after 1906; when the government decided to reserve a per capita allowance of land to keep the Doukhobors from being totally dispossessed, the only important statistic was the number of people on the census list (that is, those who were legitimately eligible for the allotment). If cultivation increased on the poorer lands of the North Colony, it is reasonable to assume that the amount of cultivated land would also have increased on the better lands of the South Colony where Verigin was focussing the energies of his Community. The only qualification to this conclusion is that more cultivated land was lost in the South Colony in 1907 than in the North Colony.

C.C. Fairchild, Dominion Lands Surveyor, was sent to survey lot lines and roads in the fifty-eight villages which were occupied in 1909. Initially, the plan was to allow the Doukhobors to purchase these lots, but in 1910, licenses of occupation were allocated instead. It seems the Department realized that in most villages, the Community members in residence were there only temporarily, and it needed some less permanent method of allocating land. These instruments confirmed the use of

---

22 In the case of Blagodarnoe, whose reserve was somewhat dispersed, more than 200 acres of cultivation were lost.
23 NA, RG15, V1167 F5412467, Otradnoe Village File.
24 Tarasoff, *Plakun Trava*, 94.

Table 17
Population Changes, 1905-1910

Colony	1905	1906	1909	1910
North Colony	2,239 C (95%) 125 NC[a]	2,549 C (95%) 129 NC	2,854 C (95%) 146 NC	2,541 (90%) 272 NC
Saskatchewan Colony	1,564 C (82%) 340 NC	1,162 C (80%) 282 NC	319 C (37%) 532 NC	297 C (30%) 709 NC
South Colony	3,693 C (98%) 59 NC	3,317 C (92%) 302 NC	3,467 C (91%) 353 NC	3,175 C (85%) 544 NC
Annex	859 C (90%) 93 NC	703 C (77%) 211 NC	729 C (77%) 219 NC	572 C (66%) 301 NC
Totals	8,355 C (93%) 617 NC	7,731 C (89%) 924 NC	7,050 C (85%) 1,223 NC[b]	6,585 C (78%) 1,826 NC[c]

a) Non-Community (includes both Independent and those classed as Independent-Communists); b) this total does not include the village of Oobezhdennie (South Colony), a village of Independents with no population data given, nor the Saskatchewan Colony villages of Petrovka and Terpennie, of which the former had a large population of Independents (117 in 1906); c) this total does not include the village of Oobezhdennie.
Source: Village Files.

particular pieces of land (both village lots and surrounding quarter sections) by particular individuals or groups of individuals (as in the case of the Independent-Communists). As Community members left, or as the Independent-Communists registered for individual pieces of land in the manner of the Independents, these licenses were cancelled.

While the decline in the land base was drastic, the decline in village population was much more moderate, from a peak of just under 9,000 in 1905 to about 8,400 in 1910. More significantly, the Community component of the village population declined from about 93 percent (8,355 people) in 1905 to about 78 percent (6,585 people) in 1910.[25] The speed of decline varied from village to village, and from Colony to Colony (see Table 17). The North Colony was the lone exception to this trend: the numbers of Community members in its villages actually increased; nonetheless, the proportion of communal Doukhobors in the villages decreased slightly. The increase of 300 Community members largely reflected the influx of Community Doukhobors from the Saskatchewan Colony villages, which more than offset the numbers of Community members who left for British Columbia or for the heartland of the South Colony, or who abandoned the Community to take up land independently. The Saskatchewan Colony decreased most dramatically, both numerically and proportionately for the same reason. In addition to those Community members who relocated to the North Colony, some 365 moved to the South Colony (see below for detail), and just over 200 moved directly to British Columbia. Between 300 and 400 left the Community to become Independents, but retained farmsteads in the village.

---

25   The statistical data, unless otherwise indicated, are derived from the schedules compiled by the various commissions which visited the villages from 1906 to 1913, and are consistently part of each village file.

Second Stage of Decline

The second stage of decline in the last two or three years of this period was a mirror image of the first — a rapid decline in Community members and a more modest decline in land. It reflected the delayed impact of Verigin's purchase of lands in British Columbia in 1908. Whatever Verigin's assessment of the continued success of his Community on government lands in the years of conflict immediately before and after his arrival in Canada, by now it was clear that he could not fully realize his vision of community on government land. After considering relocations to Russia and California, Verigin purchased land near the present-day communities of Castlegar and Grand Forks which would become the "Second Community."[26] Representatives from each of the Community villages (five to eight men) began the work of building the necessary structures and clearing the land for permanent settlement soon after Verigin acquired the land. Somewhat later, other men supplemented, or in some cases replaced, these first recruits; later still, their wives and children joined them. By 1912 or 1913, the British Columbia lands were ready for full occupation and the largest exodus occurred (see Table 18).[27] The massive relocation ultimately involved nearly 5,000 people and was to empty most Saskatchewan villages of their Community members.

A consideration of Table 18 reveals that the major movement to British Columbia was from the villages of the North and South Colonies. By 1908, most villages in the Saskatchewan and Annex Colonies were populated by Independents, so there was little potential for a large-scale evacuation of these Colonies.[28] Table 18 also suggests a more detailed strategy of relocation to British Columbia within the dominantly communal villages. The relocation of North Colony migrants was earlier, and proportionately larger, than occurred in the South Colony. This suggests a plan to abandon the poorer and more peripheral lands first, and to maintain the economic base in the better lands and more consolidated Community presence of the South Colony villages. This was Hugh Harley's view:

> Peter Verigin is a long headed man. There will be about 400 of the Douks.
> go to B.C. this Spring, and I want to inform you of Peter's plan. He is

---

26 Woodcock and Avakumovic, *The Doukhobors*, 225-26.

27 It is difficult to assess accurately both the time of emigration and the numbers involved. The village files of a particular year may note the number of Doukhobors who had left for British Columbia, but in some cases, the figures of the next year may state a revised number, so it is sometimes difficult to determine whether the first figure indicated an actual, or a proposed, migration (usually, however, this is indicated) or whether the second figure is merely a correction of a previous movement. For example, the 1912 entry for Archangelskoe indicates that eighty-one left for British Columbia, but the May 1913 Commission notes that seventy-five left for British Columbia, twelve for elsewhere. In this particular case, the village population figures confirm the 1913 report as a correction of the 1912 report.

28 In the Saskatchewan Colony, only Bodenofka and Karilowa were communal; the movement of the Community faithful to the North and South Colonies between 1905 and 1907 had emptied all the other villages of Community members. Only three Annex villages — Blagosklonoe, Kalmakovo and Moisayovo — were communal.

Table 18 Emigration to British Columbia, 1909-1913						
Colony	1909	1910	1911	1912	1913	Total
North Colony	126	230	405	1,085	163	2,009
Saskatchewan Colony	7	33	26	128	18	212
South Colony	126	186	306	331	778	1,727
Annex	27	46	47	364	—	484
Total	286	495	784	1,908	959	4,432
Source: Village Files.						

taking all of these 400 from the villages that have the poorest lands, but the villages that have first class lands he is not taking any families from there, so that these villages will always be full of men and will always be able to hold and keep the best for them to cultivate and grow their grain on. But the poor lands around the other villages where he is taking the folks from he is quite willing for the Department to take this land and give it to the other Doukhobors that are not going to B.C. and to English speaking settlers, so you will see by Peter's plan he will still keep all the good lands for some time to come.[29]

Even in 1918, when most of the villages had been abandoned, and those that still existed did so with a population of Independent Doukhobors and non-Doukhobors, this presence persisted. Five villages in the heart of the CCUB farmlands in the South Colony maintained their communal organization — Blagovishennie, Kapustina, Najersda, Otradnoe and Riduonovo — and, along with the beginnings of new villages on purchased land, formed the prairie core of the CCUB.

While it is possible to identify fairly accurately the number of people who moved to British Columbia, it is much more difficult to determine how many relocated there permanently. There are sporadic references in the village files to people returning from British Columbia to take up residence in the village they had left, or, in some cases, returning to an original Saskatchewan Colony village after Community sojourns in both the North Colony and British Columbia. In Moisayovo, "a great many of the communists have returned from BC and more are expected back shortly." (Some 158 persons had left Moisayovo for British Columbia between 1911 and 1912).[30] Twenty-six entrants representing 116 persons filed for homesteads according to the Commission's November 1913 Report, so it appears that many of those returning abandoned the Community to begin independent farming. In Najersda, "Feodor Zarelookoff with 6 of a family was taken by the Community to B.C. a year ago and has returned and wants his acres again."[31] In this case, the

---

29 NA, RG76, V184 F65101, Pt. 9, Harley to J. Bruce Walker, Commissioner of Immigration, 27 February 1909). Hugh Harley was sub-agent of the Dominion Lands Branch, Swan River, Manitoba.
30 NA, RG15, V1165 F5404642, Moisayovo Village File, 29 May 1913 Commission Report.
31 NA, RG15, V1167 F5412459, Najersda Village File, 1912 Commission Report.

family either wanted to continue as Community members, or they desired to live as Independent-Communists in a small-scale village commune. No doubt there were many similar cases.

Individuals and families continued to return from British Columbia in the following years. The Commission reported that seven people were to return from British Columbia to their home in Novoe.[32] At Voskrisennie, the Commission noted:

> Population of village, seventy-two people, nineteen of whom are temporarily absent according to the community here. May be moved back from reserves in B.C. anytime now.[33]

As late as 1918, many of those who had left in the previous eight to ten years were still being recorded by the Community as "temporarily absent in British Columbia and Alberta."[34] These people, having done their part to establish the Second Community, seem to be returning to their place within the prairie component of the Veriginite Community.

The village files do not indicate the number of these transplants who returned to their villages in the Saskatchewan Colony, but it is clear that many became disenchanted with the Community, either in eastern Saskatchewan, or later in British Columbia, and returned to take up homesteads around their original villages.[35]

Throughout this period of general Community decline there was a continued consolidation of the faithful in the areas of Veriginite dominance in the North and South Colonies. Most significant was the relocation of approximately 300 Saskatchewan Colony settlers to three new villages in the North Colony, apparently at Verigin's insistence,[36] in the early part of this period. A year or two later approximately 365 more went to villages in the South Colony, 315 of whom settled at Veregin Station and on the nearby "Post" reserve. This last figure included the thirty-one remaining residents of Tonbofka (Saskatchewan Colony) who abandoned their village and joined the move east by other Saskatchewan Colony settlers in 1910. A few other destinations were involved. An unspecified number of Saskatchewan Colony settlers, along with Community members from the old village of Blagodarnoe, were resident in the new village of Novo Blagodarnoe in 1911.[37] Other

---

32 NA, RG15, V1168 F5412497, Novoe Village File, 1917 Commission Report.

33 NA, RG15, V1167 F5412469, Voskrisennie Village File, 1917 Commission Report.

34 NA, RG15, V757 F494483(14), Cazakoff, 1918 Schedules, South Colony Village Files.

35 The histories of at least fourteen families recounted in Bondoreff, *Bridging the Years* include such moves. In two cases, the various relocations included some time in the Alberta Colony, begun in 1915. Peter Bludoff also related how his parents, and many others, were so persecuted by the "true" Community members when they moved to the North Colony, that they returned, and would not even take up residence in the village since it reminded them of the communal way of life (personal communication).

36 "From the Independents we learned the real cause of this recent migration [to the North Colony] was that 'Verigin so ordered these people to move' " (NA, RG15, V755 F494483, Pt. 6, General Report of the Doukhobor Commission).

37 The village of Novo Blagodarnoe is not listed in the village files, nor is it mentioned beyond the

Saskatchewan Colony settlers came to Otradnoe (a total of twenty-one between May 1909 and June 1911) and to Vernoe (thirteen in 1911).

These were not always one-way relocations; the ebb and flow of people to and from the eastern reserves was almost continuous in this period of decline. The village files do not provide a consistent base from which to determine the total number of returnees, but they provide some suggestion of the movement: in 1909, twenty-nine people returned to Slavyanka, ten to Pakrofka, eight to Pasariofka, six to Large Horelofka, and eight to Small Horelofka.[38] In addition, five came to Petrofka from Yorkton in 1910 (although it would appear that these were "new" settlers who joined the returnees), and some of the Saskatchewan Colony settlers in the village of Novo Blagodarnoe were intending to return in 1911 (although about forty from the Saskatchewan Colony were still there in 1912, and were intending to move to British Columbia in the fall).[39] The largest (and perhaps most surprising) movement was that of approximately fifty Terpennie (South Colony) residents to the village of Bodenofka (Saskatchewan Colony) in 1908. There is no indication that these people were originally from the Saskatchewan Colony, so this appears to be a reversal of the normal flow of Community Doukhobors.[40]

The consolidation of the faithful occurred within the colonies as well. Among the Annex villages, Moisayovo was the focus for the consolidation of the Community members. Community members from Novotroitzkoe, New Gorilloe and Kyrillovo all moved to Moisayovo in 1908, more than doubling its population from 139 in 1906 to 321 in 1909. Kalmakovo and Blagosklonoe absorbed the other Community Doukhobors, with the Community members of Oospennie merging with nearby Kalmakovo in 1911-12. The remaining Annex villages were Independent. In the North Colony, the Veriginites of Vera moved to Simeonovo in 1911[41] and 104 Communists from Troitzkoe moved to Oospennie in 1908 or early 1909.[42] There

---

two references in the Blagodarnoe village file. However, in the 1906 schedule of lands and cultivation, a note beside the entry of Gregorie Krazokoff for SE28-29-32 says "broken by proposed new village from Prince Albert 2 miles from Kamsack. Probably NW33." This may refer to Novo Blagodarnoe; the location is within eight miles of Blagodarnoe which also contributed settlers to this new village. The note on the 1906 schedule for Efromovo, indicating that some new cultivation on land near the village was "broken by proposed new village from Prince Albert 2 miles from Kamsack NW33 [29-32-W1]," is a reference to this same village (NA, RG15, V1165 F5404660, Efromovo Village File).

38   These people are no doubt included in the fifty "Prince Albert" people noted as having returned to their villages from Veregin Station in 1909 (NA, RG15, V1166 F5412427, Verigin Village File).

39   NA, RG15, V1165 F5404656, Blagadarnoe Village File.

40   NA, RG15, V1166 F5412443, Terpennie Village File, January 1908 Report. While the village population of Terpennie does not show a significant decline in the next year, the village of Bodenofka shows a significant increase in 1909.

41   See a note made in NA, RG15, V1166 F5412449, Simeonovo Village File, 3 April 1907.

42   This is an interesting move since originally Troitzkoe was established as an Independent village by those more independently minded from the village of Oospennie. Apparently Verigin was able to persuade many of these people to rejoin his Community.

was less consolidation of this kind in the South Colony since most villages were dominated by Community members. The Veriginites of Prokuratovo moved to Spaskoe in 1907, and about sixty from Blagodarnoe moved to the new village of Novo Blagodarnoe, but this was more an expansion than a consolidation since the older village continued to be dominated by Community members. The only indication of any consolidation within the Saskatchewan Colony was a movement of forty-five people from one of the villages "across the river near Langham" to Spasofka, the most northerly of the Saskatchewan villages, and these were identified as Independent-Communists, rather than Community members.[43]

As we have seen, the movements were not confined to individuals within and between the various villages and colonies; whole villages were involved. Relocations which were begun in the earlier period of flux — Old Kaminka, Terpennie Orlofsky, Old Petrovo, Old Riduonovo, Trusdennie, Old Efromovo, Old Slavenka, Lubovnoe and Old Voskrisennie — were for the most part completed in the early part of this period of decline. Prokuratovo was abandoned in 1907 with the Independents building a new village (Pakrofka on NE28-30-1) and the Communists moving to nearby Spaskoe. This latter consolidation coincided with the removal of the Spaskoe Independents to another new village (Oobezhdennie).[44] Petrovo's second site on NW21-28-32 (Petrovo #2) was erroneously located on nongovernment land, so the village had to be relocated to yet a third site.

Beyond these movements, there seemed to be an almost constant interchange among the villages throughout this period. Almost every Commission report makes mention of some movement in or out of the villages. A sampling will suffice to hint at the magnitude of this movement: in 1909, twelve persons from Voskrisennie to Terpennie (South Colony), twenty from Veregin Station to Smyrennie, twenty-six from Veregin Station to Najersda, and nine from Veregin Station to Novoe. Ten persons moved from Veregin Siding to Vernoe in 1910. Twelve Russian families came to Canada in 1911 (ninety-five persons according to a 1916 letter)[45] and purchased homes left vacant by Doukhobors in the village of Petrovo.[46]

This constant movement of Doukhobor individuals and families among villages, colonies and provinces nearly drove the homestead officials to distraction. With the constant movement, many common family names, and the difficulties of language,

---

43 NA, RG15, V1166 F5412429, Spasofka Village File, May 1909 Schedule. The source village could have been Karilowa (Kyrillovo). There seems to have been a good deal of movement between these two villages. A note in the Karilowa file indicates that seven people moved to Spasofka (3 May 1910), and an earlier note indicates that twenty-three people from Spasofka moved here in 1908 (NA, RG15, V1165 F5404666, Kyrillovo Village File, 1908 Report). The Spaskoe Village File notes that eighty-one people moved to Kyrillovo (1908 Report). The village populations at this date, however, are not in accordance with these figures. The other possibility is that Pakrofka was the source village. It was the only village to lose a significant number of Community members from 1907 to 1909.

44 NA, RG15, V1166 F5412447, Spaskoe Village File, 30 March 1907 Report.

45 NA, RG15, V1167 F5412491, Secretary to J. Bowes, 18 April 1916, Petrovo Village File.

46 Ibid., Storosjeff to Department of Interior, 24 January 1915, Petrovo Village File.

the officials found it almost impossible to match homestead entries to village residence, and to keep track of the people once the match had been made.

While hundreds of thousands of acres of land were lost in the first stage of decline, the loss in the second stage of decline was in the order of tens of thousands of acres. Although slower, the loss was still significant and resulted from people leaving the Saskatchewan village reserves (either moving to the Second Community in British Columbia, or leaving the Veriginite Community for some form of small-scale communalism or to become Independent farmers) and, in a very real sense, "taking their acres with them." For each member leaving the Community, the village reserve was reduced by fifteen acres, so the decline in Community membership translated directly into a loss of land. The village reserves declined from the 99,000 acres of 1910 to slightly more than 14,000 acres in 1913.[47]

As some members of the Community moved to British Columbia and others became Independent, the village reserves became smaller and smaller. Land taken out of the reserves was usually entered by Doukhobors who were becoming Independent, and some land was also retained by the government for the so-called Independent-Communists on the same basis of fifteen acres per person. The problem of keeping the census lists accurate affected both the Community members and the would-be Independents. The Community wished to retain as much land as possible to support their main settlements in British Columbia, so the more people retained on the lists, the better. The would-be Independents, however, were waiting for land. The good land had already been either patented or entered, so they relied on land released from the village reserves for their chance at homesteading.

The reserve land was calculated on the basis of census lists kept by the Doukhobor Commission, which were updated annually so as to fairly apportion the reserved land. As had been the case with the original homestead entrants, the Doukhobors' penchant for moving from village to village (or in the case of the Saskatchewan people, from reserve to reserve) and the proxy nature of the information given on behalf of people "temporarily away," created problems in accurately apportioning the amount of land which each village required. The lists of villagers were prepared by the village foremen, and could not be checked easily because of language difficulties and the natural reticence of the villagers. The village files are sprinkled with complaints raised by Doukhobors who had moved from one village to another, had lost their allotment in the original village, and then had tried to be put back on the list when they returned to their original village. The Saskatchewan Colony Doukhobors who had left their lands and improvements to join Verigin in the North or South Colonies were especially disadvantaged. For many, their experience with the Community convinced them to become Independents, yet when they returned to their home villages, the lands had been taken up. Those returning from British

---

47 This calculation is based on a Community population of 949; again the actual reserved land was probably slightly larger than this figure since several village reserves had surplus land and only a few had less land than required by the allotment.

Columbia found the same situation, although the Community attempted to hold their lands by keeping them on the village lists while they were absent.

The communal aspect of their economic enterprise also created difficulties in maintaining accurate lists. Some men from each village put in time in the various enterprises at Veregin — in the brickyards and in the farming operations especially. Others were at work on Community lands in British Columbia and Alberta. The authorities found it difficult to track these "temporarily absent" workers. Just what did "temporarily absent" really mean, when did the absence become permanent, and when could the name be eliminated from the list to free up land for those Doukhobors (and others) who were waiting for homestead land? The Community was loath to let any name slip from the list (each name represented fifteen acres), so it interpreted these absences in the most liberal terms.

The government has been wrongfully taken to task for attempting to force the closure of the reserves, and in so doing, deprive some Doukhobors of their rightful allotment. In fact, it was extremely difficult to determine which people belonged to which reserve. When people moved out, their allotment was lost, and if they decided to move back, or if others came in from another village, there was no land for them. Unless the Department was willing to keep some sort of land "slush fund," these movements could not be accommodated. If the Department had undertaken this course, those Independents who were waiting for land would have been disadvantaged. In the light of the times, and of the government's policy of individual homesteads, it is not surprising that it refrained from exercising this option.

One other complication arose during this transitional period. Whereas in 1905 there were three rather distinct groups of Doukhobors — Communists (Veriginite Doukhobors), Independents, and "Wanderers" or "Pilgrims" (the term used by the Commission to refer to the "Sons of God") — a fourth group, the Independent-Communists, appeared in the Commission schedules as early as 1910. This group appears to represent an intermediary position between the communalism of the Community — the CCUB, and a fully independent status. The Independent-Communists were allocated land on the basis of fifteen acres per member — like the Community members — but most opted for individual entry for land, including, apparently, taking the oath of allegiance to gain title to their land. Unlike the Independents, however, they shared among themselves the work and returns from those lands. The appellation "Independent-Communist," then, was an appropriate designation for this intermediate group, who abandoned Verigin's vision of community, but retained some form of communal sharing of the returns from the land.[48] The November 1913 Commission Report for Simeonovo provides some clarification as to the distinction between the three groups by noting the case of three families

---

48   The process is hinted at in the Commission report of September 1912 for the village of Troodolobevoe (NA, RG15, V1165 F5404680) when it notes that the previous population of eighteen Independent- Communists had grown to thirty-four by the addition of those who had "turned Ind Communist."

who were calling themselves Independent-Communists but who were really Independents, "as they are living as any other family does, the head providing for his wife and children."[49] This would suggest the communal basis of the Independent-Communists, but unfortunately does little to clarify the "independent" aspect of their hyphenated status.

Summary

It is clear that Verigin bent the energies of his Community to focus on commercial agriculture and subsidiary activities (brickmaking, flour milling, and so on). The rapid and substantial progress made in these areas might give credence to the idea that Verigin knew he could not maintain the viability of his Community in Saskatchewan very much longer. The requirement of citizenship, if not cultivation, was very clear by 1905, and this element was non-negotiable.[50] Money would be needed to finance a move to some more favourable area. Yet Verigin himself discounted this suggestion. If the Community was going to abandon the lands it had settled, he argued, why would it have spent a good deal of money on purchasing more land, getting the best stock, and acquiring the most modern machinery? Why was it engaged in brickmaking, milling and gristing, and other enterprises? Perhaps Verigin entertained the hope that this commitment to growth and prosperity would prove that the CCUB was a legitimate part of the emerging western vision and would convince Canadians — and the Canadian government — that allowing the Doukhobors to stay on the land, even if it meant further concessions, would be advantageous to the region and to the country.

Although this was a period of general decline in Community members and in land base, there was, at least in the early part of this period, other evidence of a commitment to continued development than the increase in cultivated land. Perhaps the most obvious in the cultural landscape was the continued upgrading of many of the villages. Village residents completed houses unfinished in 1905, and replaced thatch and sod roofs with shingles. They added stables, implement sheds and granaries. Of special significance, they completed Community homes in at least twenty-one villages. These structures were the heart of the village and completing them signified a stability and permanence that made their rapid abandonment paradoxical.

The decline of the Community from the peak of progress in 1905-06 to the complete abandonment of the agricultural villages occupied little more than a decade. Some villages did remain beyond 1915, but many were in the last stages of dissolution, and only a few of the core villages maintained the vitality of the communal system. Almost all were occupied by Doukhobors who had left the Community and/or non-Doukhobors (Russians, "Galicians," Germans) who moved into the houses left vacant by people moving to British Columbia or to their homestead land. Those few villages that remained a vital part of the Community clustered in the Doukhobor heartland of the South Colony near Veregin Station.

---

49 NA, RG15, V1165 F5404680, Simeonovo Village File.
50 NA, RG15, V756 F494483, Pt. 7, "Petition to the Minister of the Interior and all People in Canada from the Christian Community of Universal Brotherhood The Doukhobors in Canada."

Chapter 12
Transition ~ 1913

The positions taken and decisions made between 1905 and 1912 by both the Doukhobors and the government essentially determined the destiny of the Doukhobor villages built on government land. While some villages continued to survive as settlements for non-Community Doukhobors and some non-Doukhobors, with plan and architecture generally unchanged from the time of peak occupation, the village as a functioning community, integrated and vitalized by common cause and communal practice, had largely disappeared. The agricultural base of government-reserved lands had shrunk as well, since most of the Community Doukhobors had relocated permanently to their new lands in British Columbia, and many who remained in Saskatchewan had abandoned the Community for their own homestead land. Only in the Community "heartland" — a tripartite "core" of Community-dominated villages in the South Colony — did the villages retain their communal vitality, and did so until at least 1918. The rest of the Community members occupied newly formed "villages" on land purchased by the CCUB.

A number of villages had been abandoned even by this time, however, an irony inasmuch as Fairchild had been sent to survey the villages into lots in 1909 so licenses of occupation could confirm continuing use of the farmsteads of those Doukhobors still on the village lists. Seven of the fifty-eight villages Fairchild surveyed had only one or two families in the fall of 1913, and most of the other fifty-one villages were non-communal, occupied by Independents or by outsiders — mainly Russians, "Galicians," and German-Russians. Thus, while the external structure of many villages remained essentially intact, village life and village composition had changed radically.

The last year for which consistent information is available for the remaining villages of the three colonies is 1913. The Commission which gathered information on population changes and cultivation visited almost every village twice that year, once in May or early June, and once in November or December. The detailed statistics given in the reports suggest thorough and accurate population counts, but the figures must be used with some caution since, in some villages, the Commission did not distinguish clearly between people actually resident in the village and people on the village census list (that is, those who were entitled to "acres" in the village reserve under the provision of the government for communal Doukhobors), but temporarily absent.[1] In the latter case, people remained on the census list until it could be determined that they were permanently absent from the village, or until they had entered for their own quarter section of land. People who were temporarily absent in the British Columbia settlements, at work on farms in Alberta, or at Community work at Veregin, were kept on the village lists. In most cases the Commission indicated those "here" and those "away," and also made the distinction between the census population and the village population, so it is possible to arrive at a reasonably accurate estimate of the village population.[2]

As noted in the previous chapter, after the sharp decrease in 1907, the land base declined steadily over this period. The number of people actually resident in the villages also declined in each reserve and in almost every village during this period. The cross section of 1913, then, generally portrays villages in various stages of abandonment with some significant exceptions. The landscapes of abandonment were most evident in the "peripheral" colonies — the North Colony, the Good Spirit Lake Annex, and the Saskatchewan Colony. Four of the eighteen North Colony villages had only two or three families resident, and many of the larger villages had populations inflated by "Galician" and Russian residents. Only two Annex villages had more than two or three families: Kalmakovo, a village of Independent farmers, and Moisayovo, a village of Independent-Communists. In the Saskatchewan Colony, Terpennie, Tonbofka, and Small Horleofka were vacant by 1913, and Pasariofka had only three families. Pakrofka and Petrofka, the largest and most viable villages, were being maintained by an influx of non-Doukhobor Russians and Germans who had moved into abandoned houses.

In contrast, many of the villages of the South Colony, especially in the core area around Veregin Station, maintained their populations of Community members and some were actually growing as a result of a consolidation of Community members within the Colony. Most South Colony Veriginites who relocated to British Columbia did not leave until 1912 or later (see Table 18, Chapter 11), so several villages were nearly as large in 1913 as they had been at their peak. Fifteen of twenty-three[3] South Colony villages had Community majorities (Kapustina and Vosziennie were made up entirely of Community members) and one more had a significant component of

---

1   These discrepancies could lead to errors in both directions. In villages where many people were absent from the village but were still regarded as belonging to the village reserve, the population of the census list could be larger than the actual population resident in the village at the time of the survey. Where a number of families entered for their own land (either as Independents or Independent-Communists) but continued to live in the village, or where a number of outsiders had taken occupation of some of the abandoned houses, the actual village population could be larger than the population given on the census list.

2   Births were not always added to the population on the census list. This omission would have offset somewhat the error made in resident village populations by counting absent people.

3   Of the twenty-three, Oobezhdennie was an Independent village for which no information was given.

Community Doukhobors. Despite this, an increasing amount of the agricultural activity and settlement was on purchased land.

What were these villages like in 1913? In general form, they were little different from the villages of 1905. Although most villages had lost residents to British Columbia, to CCUB villages on purchased land at the centre of the South Colony, or to farmsteads on homestead land, their place and their houses were often taken by "outsiders," non-Doukhobors — Germans, "Galicians," Bulgarians, Russians and occasionally English — or Doukhobors from other villages who, despite frequent warnings and notices by the new Doukhobor Commissioner, John Bowes, either bought, rented or appropriated the vacated houses and worked on farms as labourers. Since this was a decidedly tenuous arrangement, the inhabitants spent little effort in maintaining these properties.

In some cases, even the plan of the village was modified gradually. Abandoned houses and outbuildings which were not reoccupied by outsiders gradually fell into disrepair and were finally unusable. These either collapsed or were torn down. Occasionally, villagers would take the more substantial and well-maintained buildings with them when they left their village lot for a farmstead on their own land, sometimes moving them several miles. The abandoned or neglected lots were soon overrun by weeds, creating a problem for nearby crops. In several cases, this was serious enough that steps had to be taken to break up and sow these plots to keep adjacent crops from being contaminated. And, of course, the changing residential composition of the villages invited internal squabbles among the villagers. There were charges and countercharges of gardens and crops being savaged by animals left to roam freely over the village, and of unauthorized use of some of the vacant lots for crops:

> There is some trouble between the straight Communists and Independent-Communists owing to living together in the village ... . In those villages where there is a number of Independents doing business for themselves and keeping poultry in the village which destroys the gardens of the Communists who keep none has caused some quarrelling. I have tried to show them that it is better to live peaceably together and think it may have some effect but I think it was poor policy to have those villages surveyed at all.[4]

Thus, while many of the villages retained a skeletal form of the original plan, the appearance of most changed from the tidy houses and yards of 1905 to the unkempt appearance of villages in slow decay in 1913. The externalities of architecture and plan remained, but the vigour of community village life had drained away with the Community members.

---

[4] NA, RG15, V1167 F5412469, John Bowes, 1912 Commission Report, Voskrisennie Village File.

Chapter 13
The North Colony ~ 1913

The North Colony was peopled by some of the most conservative of the Doukhobor migrants. As part of the eastern "core" of Saskatchewan communal Doukhoborism, one might expect that the communal village settlement would persist here, especially since a substantial number of Saskatchewan Colony Doukhobors moved to the North Colony following the establishment of three new villages in 1906. It was, nonetheless, peripheral to the heartland of the Community in the South Colony, and occupied somewhat poorer agricultural land. These factors were responsible for rather more change here than would otherwise be expected. North Colony people were among the first to move to British Columbia following the purchase of land there in 1908, and in the years up to 1913, more than 1,000 left their villages (see Table 18, Chapter 11 and Table 19). Even in 1913, between visits in the spring and fall, the Commission recorded some significant movements both to British Columbia and to CCUB-purchased land at Veregin.[1]

In 1912, the village population of the North Colony was 926, made up of 449 "Communists" or Community members, 401 Independent-Communists, forty Independents, and thirty-six others.[2] The Community members were concentrated in

---

1 The 5 November 1913 Commission Report for Perehodnoe, reported sixty-five to British Columbia, thirteen to Veregin (the 9 May 1913 report had indicated that some were going to go to British Columbia, some "to purchased land at Veregin") (NA, RG15, V1168 F5412973). The Pavlovo Commission report of 8 May 1913 (NA, RG15, V1167 F5412493) reported 112 to British Columbia and five to Veregin; the Osvoborsdennie Commission report of 8 May 1913 (NA, RG15, V1167 F5412455) reported sixty-six to British Columbia and four to Veregin. It is not clear in some cases whether the May figures refer to an emigration in 1912 or in 1913. John Bowes, the Doukhobor Commissioner, apparently took some general information about the changes in village population in 1912, and on his visits in the spring and fall of 1913 gave a more detailed and accurate breakdown of these changes. For some villages it is possible to determine how much of the movement took place in 1912 and how much in 1913 by comparing the adjustments to the census list in the two years. For several villages, however, it is difficult to make this distinction (see note 27, Chapter 11).

2 All individual and cumulative village data are taken from the village files unless noted otherwise.

Table 19
North Colony Village Population

Village	1912 Population	1912 Reserve	1913 May Pop.	1913 May Cult.	1913 Nov/Dec. Pop.	1917
Archangelskoe	37 C	2,400 on 15 quarters	23 IC (4 families)	n/a	23 IC	16 (2 Galicians)
Boghumdanoe	24 IC	1,600 on 10 quarters	19 IC	370 acres on 10 quarters	21 IC	11 (homesteader & father in law: 9 & 2)
Gromovoe	132 C; 1 IC	2,560 on 16 quarters	90 C	n/a	7 (2 families)	2 (Galician homesteader)
Hlebedarnoe	52 IC; 5 ref. W.; 25 Wand.	2,080 on 13 quarters	51 IC; 6 ref. W.; 5 Ind.	858 on 11 quarters	104 (39 D; 15 Wand.; 4 Russians; 1 Gal. family)	77 (includes 7 Russian families
New Kaminka	56 IC	1,600 on 10 quarters	59 IC	255 acres on 7 quarters	41 IC	16
Libedevo	10 IC (3 families)	2,080 on 13 quarters	22 IC and 5 outsider families	530 acres on 11 quarters	47	18
Lubomeernoe	29 IC	2,480 on 15.5 quarters	126 (28 IC; 21 Russians +?)	835 acres on 14.5 quarters	54	5 (2 families) (no reserve)
Michaelovo	76 C; 29 IC	1,680 on 10.5 quarters	56C; 21 IC; 7 Russians	1,300 acres on 10.5 quarters	11 IC; 37 others	21
Oospennie	26 IC	3,520 on 22 quarters	19 IC; 13 others	864 acres on 15 quarters	28 (no reserve)	12 (3 families) (1915 - 59 IC)
Osvoborsdennie	26 IC	1,880 on 11.75 quarters	2C; 27 IC; 7 doubt.; 3 Gal. families	695 acres on 11 quarters	71 (14 from B.C. and 2 Gal. families)	25
Pavlovo	11 IC (2 families)	2,240 on 14 quarters	13 IC	n/a	10 IC; 3 Ind.	13 (2 families Gal. homesteaders)
Perehodnoe	115 C	2,720 on 17 quarters	89 C	n/a	10 IC or Ind.	8 Ind.
Procovskoe	37 IC	2,160 on 13.5 quarters	27 IC	342 acres on 11 quarters	63 (no designation)	17 (no reserve)
Simeonovo	64 IC	3,040 on 19 quarters	59 IC; 2 Ind.; 3 Russian families	1,230 acres on 13 quarters	37 Ind.; 70 others	50 (including 3 Russians)
Teakomeernoe	24 IC	1,760 on 11 quarters	26 IC	n/a	4 IC; 22 Ind.	5 Ind. (homesteader family)
Troitzkoe	40 Ind. (7 families)	n/a	51 Ind. (9 families)	n/a	Est. 51	25 Ind. (5 families)
Vera	6 (1 family)	n/a	n/a	n/a	n/a	1 (H. Archer)
Vosnisennie	89 C; 12 IC	1,920 on 12 quarters	73C; 6 IC	895 acres on 10 quarters	4 IC; 6 Ind.	4 (homesteader family)
Totals	928 (449 C; 406 IC; 73 others)		966 (310 C; 400 IC; 53 I; 203 others)	8,174	720*	326*

* No breakdown of total population can be calculated.

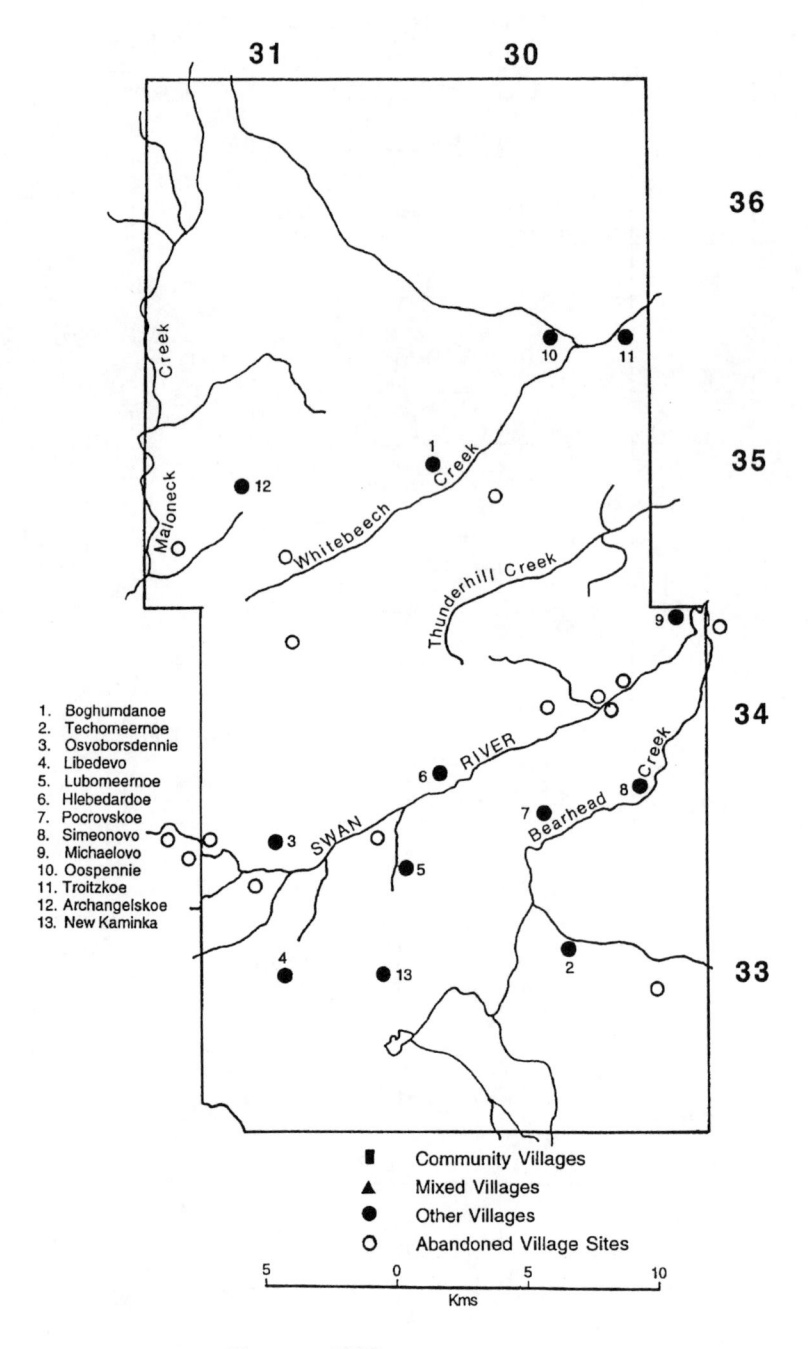

1. Boghurndanoe
2. Techorneernoe
3. Osvoborsdennie
4. Libedevo
5. Lubomeernoe
6. Hlebedardoe
7. Pocrovskoe
8. Simeonovo
9. Michaelovo
10. Oospennie
11. Troitzkoe
12. Archangelskoe
13. New Kaminka

■ Community Villages
▲ Mixed Villages
● Other Villages
○ Abandoned Village Sites

Map 11. North Colony Villages — 1913.

five villages: Archangelskoe, Gromovoe and Perehodnoe (the three villages built for the relocated faithful from the Saskatchewan Colony), and Michaelovo and Vosnisennie, the two original North Colony villages (see Map 11). Three of the remaining thirteen villages were almost completely abandoned by this time; the others were occupied by Independent-Communists, Independents, or non-Doukhobor families.

Seventy-five Veriginites had moved to British Columbia from Archangelskoe in 1911-12, leaving a population of four families (twenty-three persons) of Independent-Communists in May 1913. They did not want homestead entry here as the land was very poor, bushy, and full of sloughs. Gromovoe and Perehodnoe had sent several families to British Columbia by May 1913, and the remaining 179 villagers were still fully communistic. They were merely marking time, however, as they moved away from the villages in the summer: 128 to British Columbia and thirty-three to other locations — some to Veregin, a few to homesteads, and some to unidentified destinations.[3] By November 1913, only two families, either Independents or Independent-Communists, were left in each of the two villages.

These three "Prince Albert" villages and the village of Pavlovo were established several years later than the other villages in the North Colony, and consequently were forced to choose sites in an area which had been avoided up to that time. As these lands were generally quite poor agriculturally, it is not surprising that they did not have the problem of other settlers moving into the vacant houses of the village as did those villages sited more favourably along the Swan River. In fact, only Perehodnoe maintained a Doukhobor presence in the years following (and that by a returning family from British Columbia); the other three village sites eventually were homesteaded by "Galician" settlers.

The other two CCUB villages in 1912 — Michaelovo and Vosnisennie — had been focal points for the Community from their beginnings as the initial "block-house" sites for the North Colony settlers before the individual villages were established. Vosnisennie, home of staunch Community supporter Nikolai Ziebaroff, who operated the communal store which served all the North Colony villages for a short while, remained the centre of communal activity. By November 1913, however, the CCUB members in both villages had either left the villages, or had left the CCUB and remained in the villages as Independent-Communists. Michaelovo was still a viable settlement in 1913, primarily because several Doukhobor families had returned there, probably from the Community in British Columbia. They returned, however, as Independents.

Although the Community presence was limited both geographically and numerically in 1912, and would disappear by the end of 1913, by May 1913, the total village population had actually increased to 966[4] by virtue of a substantial

---

3   It is quite possible that this number may have included some who, disillusioned by the treatment they received at the hands of the more zealous members of the North Colony Community, returned to their homes in the Saskatchewan Colony (Peter Bludoff, personal communication).

4   It is impossible to arrive at a precise figure since only the Doukhobor population is given as

increase in the number of non-Doukhobor residents who had temporarily (and illegally) occupied some of the vacant houses in the village. There was a decline in the number of Community members (to 310 from 449 in 1912), and a slight increase in the Independent component, from forty to fifty-three. The number of Independent-Communists remained about the same.

The influx of non-Doukhobors and returned ex-Community members could not make up for the exodus of the remaining Community members in the summer of 1913. By November, the village population of the North Colony declined to about 720 people, of whom at least 40 percent were non-Doukhobor, and the rest either Independents or Independent-Communists. The Community presence had disappeared from this bastion of communal settlement. Five North Colony villages were nearly empty and many of the surviving villages were being maintained temporarily by the influx of non-Doukhobor families and individuals. Even the former strongholds of Michaelovo and Vosnisennie were in rapid decline. Michaelovo's population of forty-eight in November 1913 was made up of returning Doukhobor "outsiders" (having been removed from the list when they left for British Columbia), eleven Doukhobors who did not desire entry but who lived in the village (apparently Community sympathizers who did not want to go to British Columbia with the rest), and a Russian family of six (one of two families who had been told to vacate in May). Vosnisennie had only two families resident in November 1913.

A few villages actually had a larger population in November than in May. Simeonovo and Hlebedarnoe, bolstered by Doukhobors moving in from other villages and by a mix of non-Doukhobors, had populations of over 100 in November 1913, and seven other villages had populations of between forty and seventy. Simeonovo had a core population of thirty-seven Independents[5] belonging to the village, but they were outnumbered by seventy outsiders. Hlebedarnoe (formerly Spasovka) was home to the Wanderers, a collection of die-hard fanatics who, in the words of one government official

> are the remnants of people who have so often started out seeking the Saviour. Asylums, jails, pneumonia and chilblains may have made them less enthusiastic about parading in the nude. Owing to the Saskatchewan weather, the pilgrims may have found a religion they could practice with their clothes on for apparently the undress pilgrimages have ceased.[6]

In November 1913, about fifteen Wanderers occupied the lower part of the "twin" village of Hlebedarnoe, while the upper part of the village was home to ninety

---

individuals. "Outsiders," and even some returning Doukhobors who had been struck off the village census lists, are often listed only as families. In those cases, I have used a standard family size of five individuals to arrive at the estimated population.

5   Twenty-eight of the thirty-seven were not Independents in the full sense of the word, in that they did not want to make entry for the land, but according to the Commission, they were not Independent-Communists either (see notes 48 and 49, Chapter 11).

6   NA, RG15, V1164 F5404640, Landerkin to Hume, 19 November 1925, Hlebedarnoe Village File.

persons of mixed heritage: some "sensible" Doukhobors, four Russian families, and one "Galician" family.

With one exception — Troitzkoe, a village of Independents — the viable villages in 1913 occupied the heart of the North Colony along the Swan River and its tributary, Bearshead Creek, and all controlled good agricultural land. Troitzkoe and Oospennie were "complimentary" villages: Troitzkoe was established by Oospennie families who desired a more independent Doukhobor life, while Oospennie remained communal. Troitzkoe returned to the fold after Verigin's arrival (nearly 80 percent of the villagers belonged to the Community in 1905), but reverted to independence in 1909 when the Community members moved back to Oospennie. The consolidation of the Community members in Oospennie created one of the largest villages in the North Colony in 1909 (302 people), but, as with most of the Veriginite villages, it also foreshadowed the dramatic decline which would take place when the Community members relocated to British Columbia. While Troitskoe maintained its 1909 population of fifty-three in November 1913, Oospennie declined from 302 to twenty-eight in the same period.

As the Community membership declined and disappeared, so did the Community land base. In May 1913, the Community had nearly 8,200 acres under cultivation in the eleven village reserves recorded,[7] and in fact it is likely that the total was closer to 10,000 acres.[8] Large surpluses of land were reported in almost every village reserve, and the Commission recommended that the lands be thrown open for entry. In most cases, at least in the more favourable agricultural areas, this released land was taken up by Independent-Communists. By November 1913, the Community's land base was eliminated in the North Colony.[9]

In summary, the strongest CCUB villages were to experience the most dramatic decline as committed Community members moved *en masse* to British Columbia or to the Veregin Station heartland. Those villages which were less committed to the CCUB approach to communal living were able to maintain the semblance of village structure in 1913. In many cases, owing to favourable locations with respect to good agricultural land (and amount of cleared land), these villages actually grew in size from 1912 to 1913, although this was, in a sense, deceptive, as it was due largely to non-Doukhobor settlers moving into vacated houses in the villages. As far as the

---

[7] It is not always clear from the files what proportion of the cultivated land reported was on Community land and what proportion was on land in the village reserves allocated to the Independent-Communists.

[8] Two of the villages whose reserves were not recorded, Gromovoe and Perehodnoe, had significant populations of Community members (ninety and eighty-nine respectively) so it is likely that between them, they had another 1,000 to 1,200 acres under cultivation on their reserved land.

[9] The village files still note people on the list who did not wish to enter for homestead land, but they were identified as Independent-Communists or not classified at all. Since "Communists" or Community members are always identified by the November 1913 Commission in the South Colony villages, I assume that the absence of such identification means that those non-Independents left in the villages were not, in fact, part of the CCUB.

Doukhobor component of these villages is concerned, all but three appear to have been operating as Independent-Communist villages in November 1913.

The plans drawn from Fairchild's 1909 survey of the eighteen villages of the North Colony provide a good general overview of the villages at this time. He not only surveyed lot lines and roads but attempted, through unscaled drawings, to give an impression of the relative size and placement of the buildings within the village. In several instances he also indicated the type of building — machine shed, engine house, mill and so on. While an interval of four years could be expected to have modified these plans in some manner, it is reasonable to assume that the village structure portrayed then was largely unchanged in 1913. The general dismantling of village structures in many of the villages did not take place until after this date.

Despite a variety of orientations, each village was laid out on the traditional street-village plan which characterized all Doukhobor settlements from the beginning. Only Michaelovo was laid out differently, and even then, it was more a combination of traditional plans than a departure from them (see Figure 3, Chapter 2, and Chapter 3, "Michaelovo in 1899"). The strong communal element of the North Colony villages dictated a departure from the traditional village plan. Communal buildings tended to be grouped on larger lots near the centre of the village with the prominent community home on one side of the street and other assorted communal structures — barns, granaries, shops and sheds — on the other. This produced a distinctive core to the village structure and a focus for community activity (see Figure 36). The presence of a community home seems to have been critical; the structures, whether dwellings or communal buildings, of villages which lacked a community home were laid out on uniform lots. Only Procovskoe departed from this plan; the community home and other larger communal buildings were built on bigger lots at one end of the central street (see Figure 37).

The houses in the North Colony villages were truncated, traditional houses without the usual attached barn, and were arranged more or less uniformly along the central street. While most of the houses were of the high-lofted variety with, by now, shingled rather than thatched roofs, the most distinctive structure in thirteen of the eighteen villages was the community or prayer home. Built on the same plan as the houses, although usually somewhat larger, and having a distinct resemblance to them, they were distinguished by brick cladding and ornamentation — beautifully finished boxed gables with fancy railings, and ornate stamped-tin scrollwork on the gable ends and roof ridges (see Figures 12, 13, Chapter 2 and Figure 38). Narrow, double doors in bright blue opened into a rectangular entryway. To the front, another set of double doors led to the large common room; to the back, a set opened into a suite of rooms designed for overnight guests. Only four community homes remain to provide a reminder of things past in the present cultural landscape. Those of Oospennie, Procovskoe, and Vosnisennie remain on their original sites. Gromovoe's prayer home has been moved to Veregin and restored as part of the National Doukhobor Heritage Village.

In the fertile, well-drained areas of the North Colony, the cultural landscape of 1913 was not unlike that of 1905, at least superficially. Most of the farm villages were very much in evidence, and many of them were home to quite substantial numbers

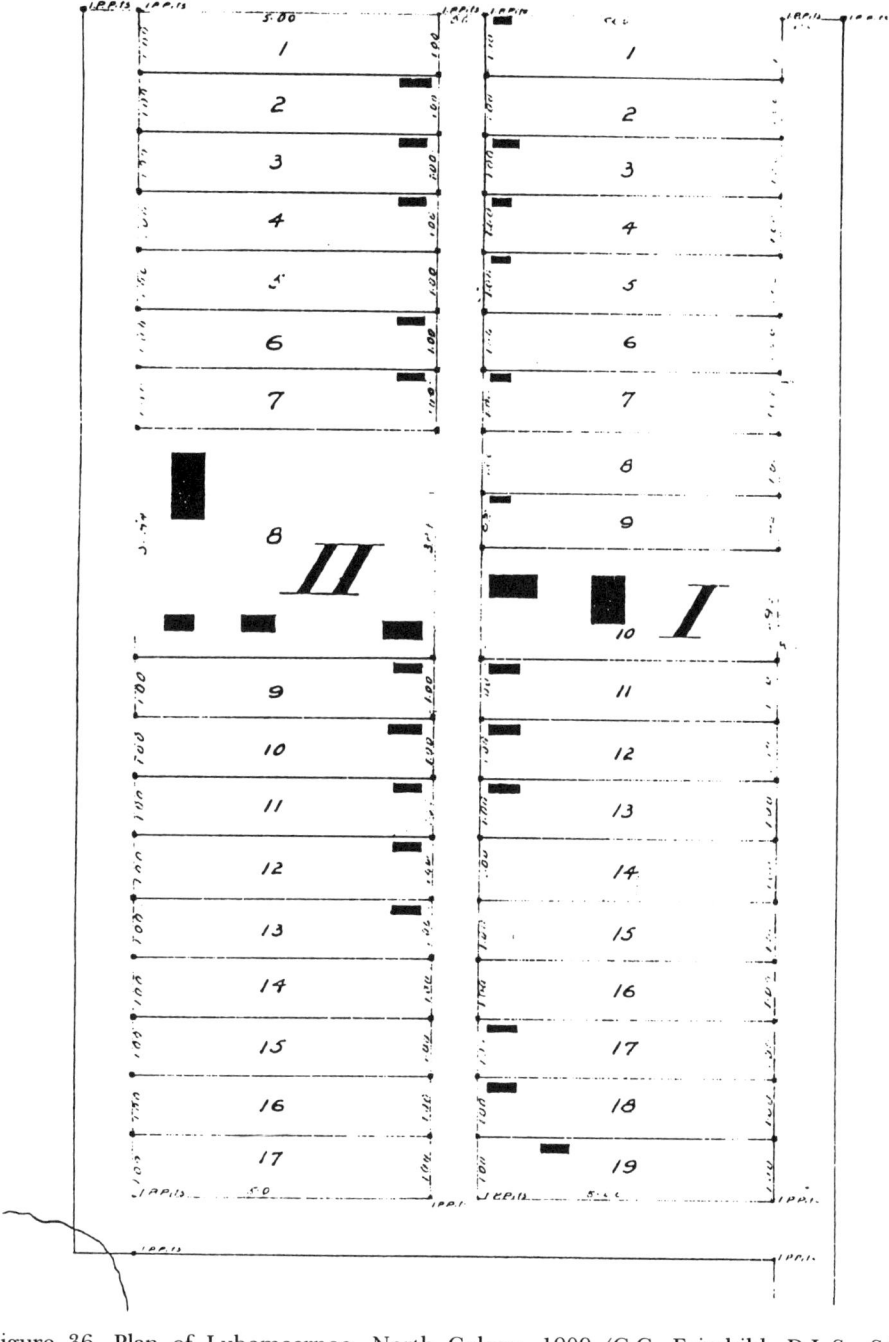

Figure 36. Plan of Lubomeernoe, North Colony, 1909 (C.C. Fairchild, D.L.S., SAB, Saskatoon).

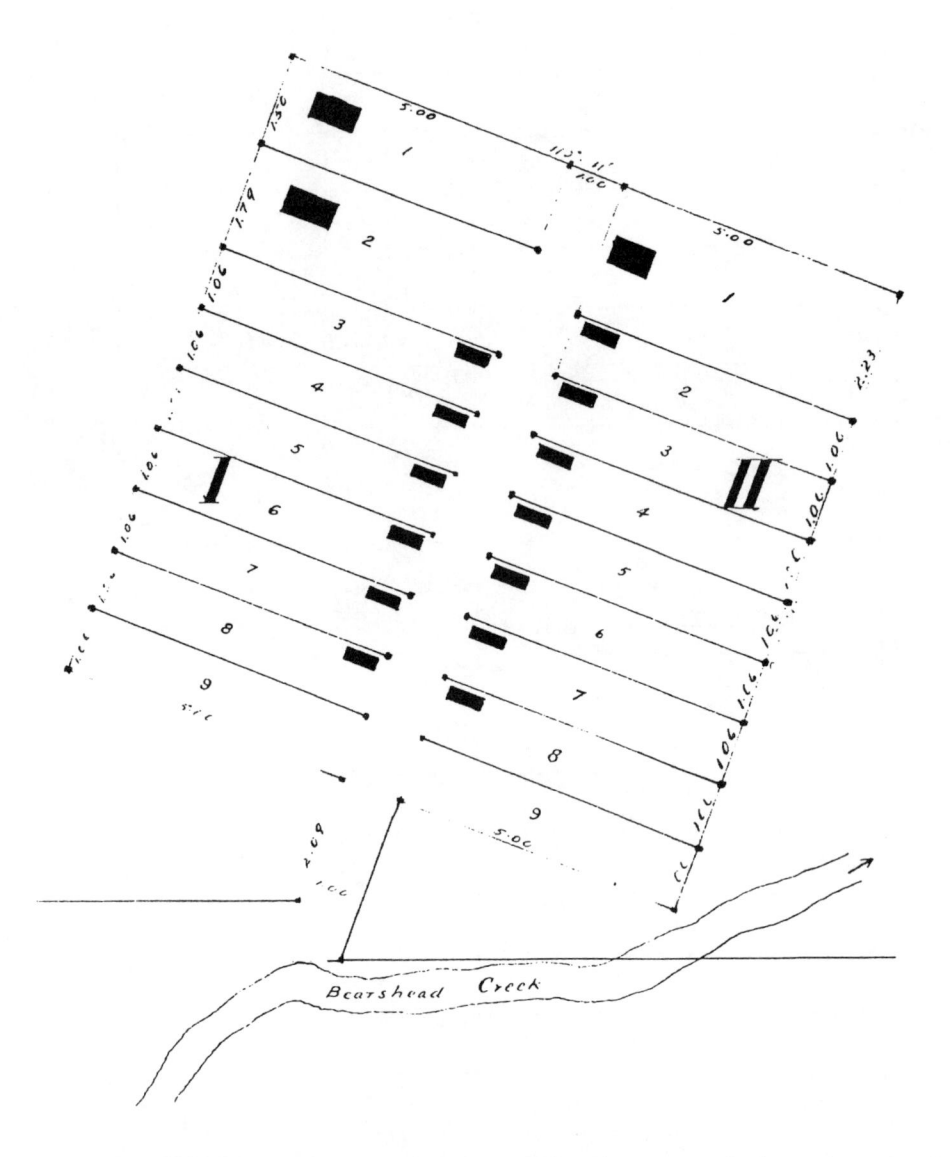

Figure 37. Plan of Procovskoe, North Colony, 1909. The community home is on Lot 1 of Block 2 (C.C. Fairchild, D.L.S., SAB, Saskatoon).

of actual, or intending, homesteaders. And, although an increasing number of non-Doukhobors had made their residence in the villages, Doukhobors still legally controlled village life. Some buildings within the village were either removed or torn down, but the original *strassendorf* pattern was still clearly evident. Fields around the villages were expanding as the land cultivated by the Community was taken over by non-Community Doukhobors, or by "outsiders."

Figure 38. Community home, Procovskoe, 1975 (author's photo).

In the less desirable agricultural areas, particularly in the northwest part of the reserve, the cultural landscape was undergoing significant changes. The villages which just a year before had bustled with activity were now almost completely abandoned. The structure of the *strassendorf* remained, but life in the village was more like life on adjoining homesteads, with only two or three families in each village. Some of these families were merely marking time until they could obtain land in some more favourable location. Unlike the other villages, there was little interest in the surrounding land, so their slide into obscurity was relatively unhindered.

Chapter 14
The South Colony and Annex - 1913

As the centre of Community activity, occupying the best agricultural lands, the South Colony fared better than the other settlements. But even here, village populations declined between the two Commission visits from 1,865 in May 1913 to 1,549 in November, a decline accounted for by the movement of Community members to British Columbia (see Table 20).[1] This figure would have been substantially greater had not outsiders moved into the villages, for approximately 550 Community Doukhobors left for British Columbia during this period. There was a significant reorientation of many of the remaining members from Communists to Independent-Communists, and from Independent-Communists to Independent homesteaders. Many of the Independents appeared to remain in residence in the villages, but some moved onto their homesteads in the summer; this latter movement appears to have been a minor factor in the overall decline.

By 1913, the Community in the South Colony had been scaled down to a working group which would remain fairly constant over the next five years (821 in late 1913, 825 in 1917).[2] It formed the core of the agricultural operations carried out on reserved government lands, purchased lands,[3] and those lands which would be purchased from the government and others in 1918-20. Of twenty-three South Colony villages in late 1913, ten had populations of fifty or more Community Doukhobors (Tomboscoe with eighty-nine "Communists" out of a total population of 108 had the largest number); all but two of these villages had some component

---

[1] All individual and cumulative village data are from the village files unless noted otherwise.

[2] These numbers refer to the Community population resident in the villages established by the Doukhobors on reserved land. There may well have been others who, in 1917, were living in newly established villages on purchased land.

[3] According to Tarasoff, the Community holdings by 1908 included fourteen square miles (8,960 acres) of purchased land around Veregin Station (*Plakun Trava*, 94). The Community also purchased small parcels of land near other villages, probably no more than an additional 1,000 acres by 1913.

Table 20
South Colony Village Populations

Village	1912	May 1913	November 1913	1917
Bisednoe	7 families	7 families	28 Independents	none
Blagodarnoe	60 IC	52 IC (plus 4 Russian and 4 Doukhobor families	98 Russians & homesteaders (including 19 Independents wanting homesteads)	18 IC; 24 others
Blagovishennie	126 C; 4 IC	46 C; 6 IC	58 C; 2 Independents	72 C
Efromovo	41 IC	11 IC; 20 Russians	65 homesteaders and outsiders	9 Independents; 9 Russians
Kapustina	162 C; 5 IC	120 C; 5 IC	69 C; 5 IC	92 C
Lubovnoe	87 C; 9 IC	60 C	35 C; 3 IC	21 C; 16 IC; 11 outsiders
Najersda	132 C; 2 IC	85 C; 9 IC	no information	67 C; 7 outsiders
Novoe	110 C; 5 IC	90 C; 4 IC	50 C; 4 IC	21 C; 23 IC
Oobezhdennie	an independent village - no information available			
Otradnoe	96 C; 25 IC; 24 P.A.[a]	no information	55 C; 23 IC; 3 Independents	43 C (23 absent in B.C. and Alberta
Petrovo	51 IC	5 C; 15 IC; 48 Independents; 77 Russians	5 C; 75 Russians, 64 others	13 C; 4 Independents; 60 Russians
Prokuratovo	45 Independents	5 village lots in use	6 Independent families	6 homesteaders, 3 others
Riduonovo	97 C; 29 IC	80 C; 31 IC	47 C; 20 IC	25 C; 20 IC
Savetnoe	147 C; 4 IC	106 C; 20 IC	52 C; 29 IC	58 C; 5 German-Russians
Smyrennie	74 C; 20 IC	54 C; 10 IC	31 C; 37 others	43 C
Spaskoe	141 C; 33 IC	119 C; 24 IC; 1 Russian family	69 C; 25 Independents; 41 others	70 C; 33 IC; 10 Wanderers[b]; 12 Russians
Terpennie	119 IC	97 IC	96 Independents	138 Independents[c]
Tomboscoe	166 C; 12 IC	138 C; 16 IC	89 C; 15 IC; 4 others	65 C; 11 IC
Troodoloobevoe	80 C; 34 IC; 2 Wanderers	66 C; 38 IC; 39 Russians; 1 Wanderer	39 C; 38 IC; 8 others	15 C; 6 Russians
Veregin Siding	63 C; 19 IC	55 C; 16 IC	40 C; 12 IC	40 C; 8 Independents
Vernoe	136 C; 8 IC; 13 P.A.	128 C; 7 IC	65 C	81 C
Voskrisennie	96 C; 10 IC	73 C; 8 IC; 12 Russians	52 C; 8 IC; 6 Russians	53 C
Vosziennie	122 C	100 C	63 C	46 C
Totals	1,835 C; 490 IC; 45 Independents; 39 others	1,325 C[d]; 358 IC; 48 Independents; 134 Russians[e]	819 C; 155 IC; 201 Independents[f]; 155 Russians; 219 others	825 C; 121 IC; 165 Independents; 94 Russians; 55 others

a) From the Prince Albert Reserve (Saskatchewan Reserve); b) Wanders (those who joined in the periodic marches of the "Sons of God"); c) of interest is that one entrant was away "at the war," a rare occurence for this pacifist group; d) does not include Otradnoe's population; e) includes several Russian families estimated at five members each; f) includes six Independent families estimated at five members each.

of Independent-Communists, Independents, and outsiders as well (see Map 12). Only Vosziennie and Vernoe were homogeneous Community villages. On the other hand, six villages had neither Veriginites nor Independent-Communists: Bisednoe, Blagodarnoe, Efromovo, Oobezhdennie, Pakrofka (or New Pakrofka, formed by the Independents of Prokuratovo when the Community members moved to Spaskoe in

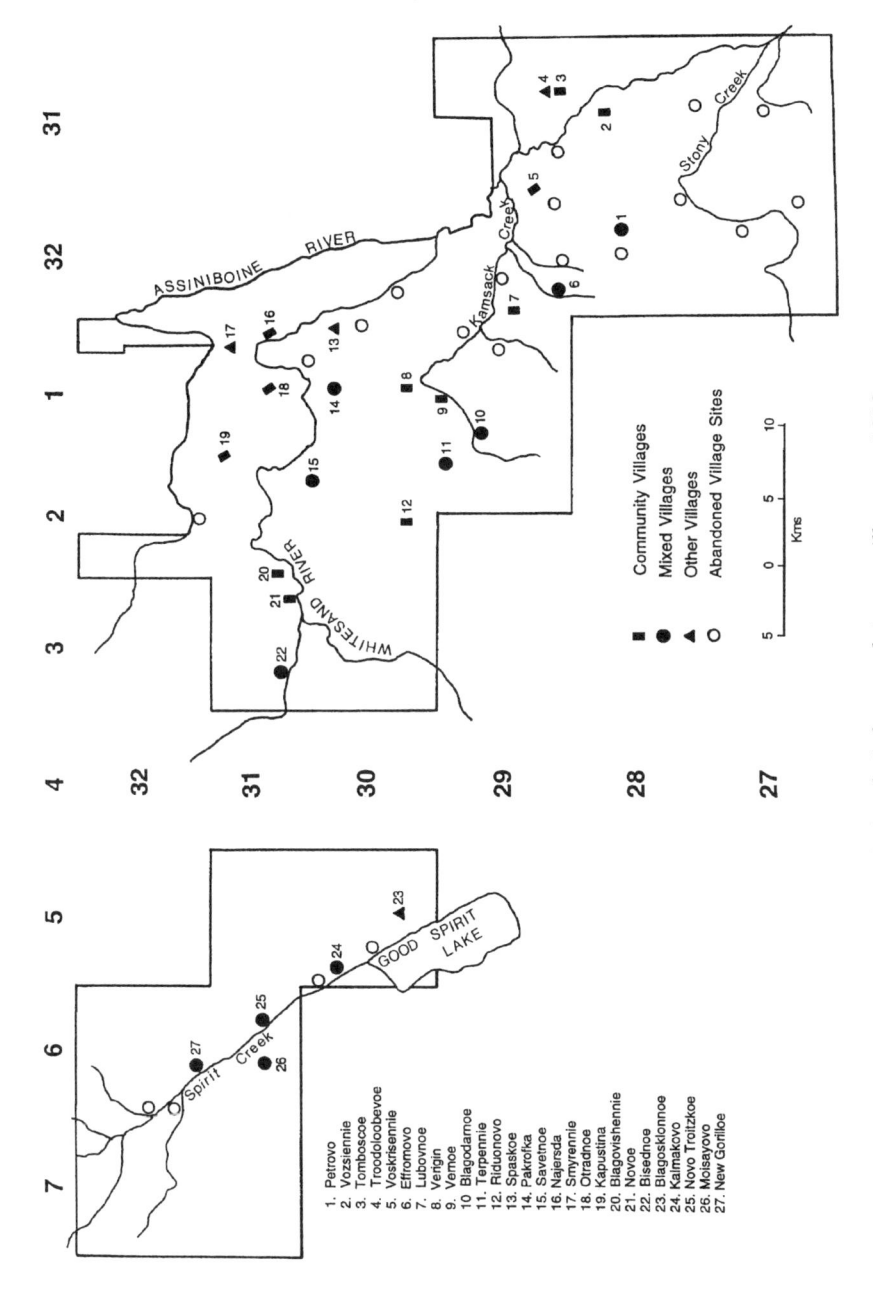

Map 12. South Colony and Annex villages — 1913.

1. Petrovo
2. Vozsiennie
3. Tomboscoe
4. Troodoloobevoe
5. Voskrisennie
6. Efromovo
7. Lubovnoe
8. Verigin
9. Vernoe
10. Blagodarnoe
11. Terpennie
12. Riduonovo
13. Spaskoe
14. Pakrofka
15. Savetnoe
16. Najersda
17. Smyrennie
18. Otradnoe
19. Kapustina
20. Blagovishennie
21. Novoe
22. Bisednoe
23. Blagoskionnoe
24. Kalmakovo
25. Novo Troitzkoe
26. Moisayovo
27. New Goriloe

Community Villages
Mixed Villages
Other Villages
Abandoned Village Sites

1907), and Terpennie had populations comprised only of Independents and outsiders. The largest village in the South Colony, the much-moved Petrovo (population 143), had only one family of CCUB faithful among its Russian "outsiders" and Independents. Novo Blagodarnoe, one of the larger communal villages begun in 1912 by fifty Communists from the village of Blagodarnoe and forty relocated Saskatchewan Colony Communists, does not appear in the 1913 lists. The village apparently moved *en masse* to British Columbia in the fall of 1912.

The "heartland" of Community village settlement in the South Colony in November 1913 was a more compact and less populated version of the Community heartland in 1905. Rather than establishing his headquarters in the midst of his most faithful followers in the North Colony or in the southern part of the South Colony, among the Cyprus, Orlovsky and Tambovsky Doukhobors, Verigin opted for a Saskatchewan community grounded in the economic opportunity afforded by the best agricultural lands and railway connections, and gathered around him here the remnant of his Saskatchewan faithful. The villages situated along the Whitesand River and on the lands drained by it in the central section of the South Colony[4] continued to be the population centre of the Community, with more than half of the South Colony Veriginites. Even here, a family or two of Independent-Communists were to be found in every village.

A few miles south of the older heartland, a more recent concentration of Community members at Veregin (the CCUB prairie headquarters) and nearby Vernoe made up the commercial core of the Community. The village population at Veregin originally was made up of people drawn from each of the Community villages, but by 1913, most of these had returned to their respective villages and their places were taken by people relocated from the Saskatchewan Colony. Most of the agricultural activity was on the purchased lands around these villages, but some cultivation was being done on what was known as the Post, or Prince Albert, Reserve — two sections of land reserved for another, smaller contingent of CCUB members from the Saskatchewan Colony. Not all the people farmed, of course. Some worked at the brick plant and others in the flour and gristing mill. Just over 100 CCUB members lived in Vernoe and on the Post Reserve and perhaps 150 more lived in nearby Veregin Station,[5] making up another 25 percent of the South Colony CCUB population.

A third component of the CCUB core was a "southeastern heartland" made up of four predominantly CCUB villages along the Assiniboine River south of Kamsack: Voskrisennie, Vosziennie,[6] and the twin Tambovsky villages of Tomboscoe and Troodoloobevoe. These four villages were home to another 248 Community members, about 25 percent of the total.

---

4   Otradnoe, Najersda (Terpennie Kars), Spaskoe, Smyrennie, Kapustina, Blagovishennie, Savetnoe, Riduonovo, and Novoe.

5   No figures are given for this village in 1913, but in 1911 the population was given as 182.

6   Vosziennie was built on land purchased from the Winnipeg Western Land Corporation Ltd (NA, RG15, V1166 F5412425, Vosziennie Village File, 12 April 1907 Report).

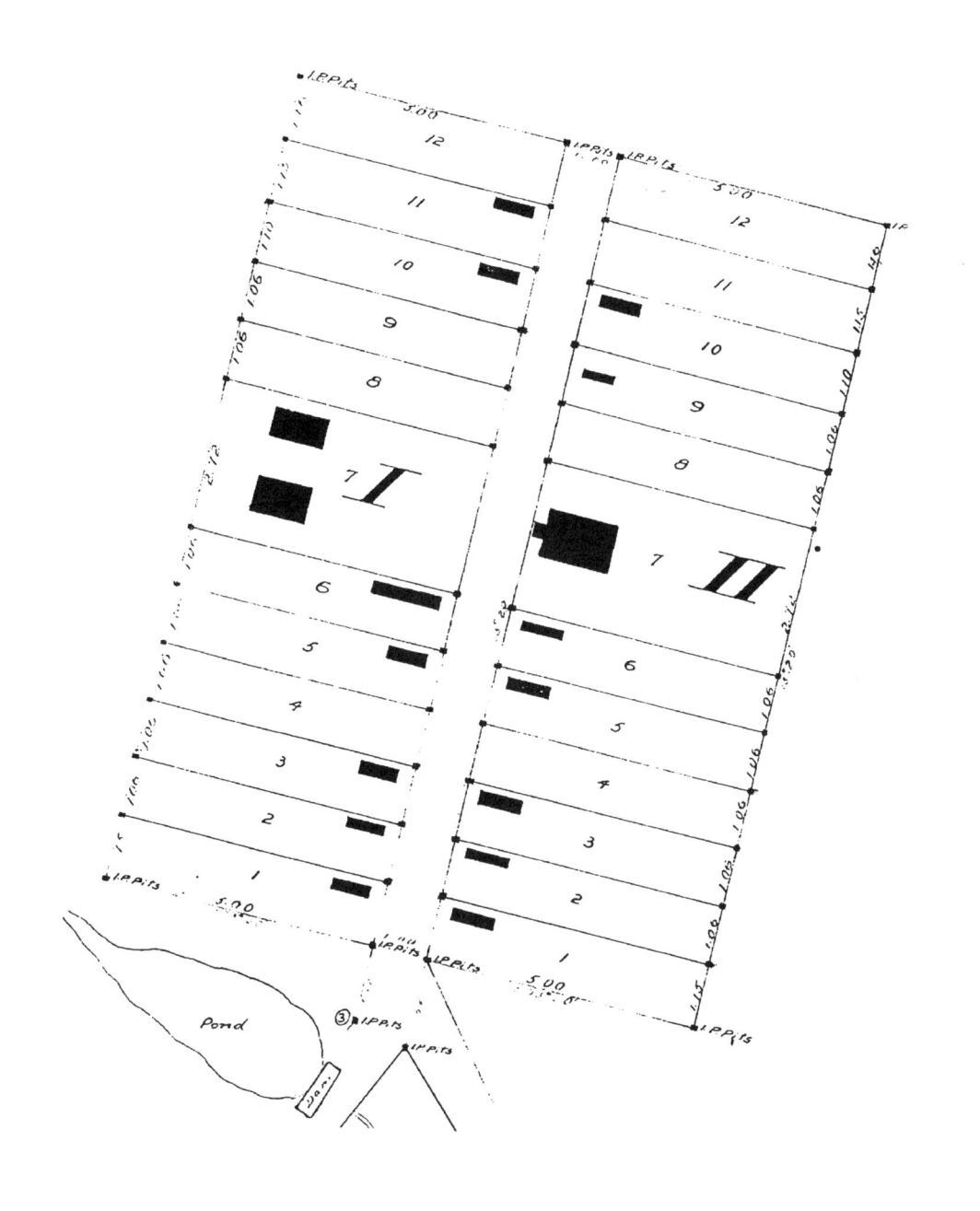

Figure 39. Plan of Blagovishennie, South Colony, 1909 (C.C. Fairchild, D.L.S., SAB, Saskatoon).

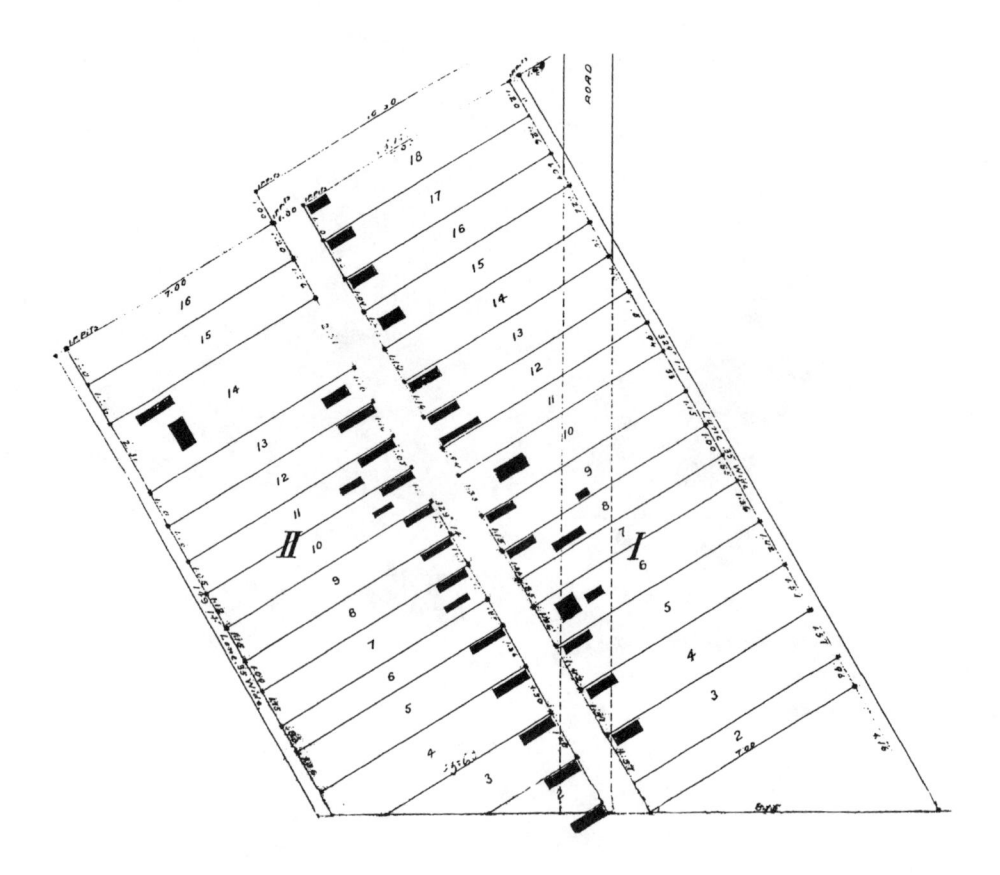

Figure 40. Plan of Blagosklonoe, South Colony, 1909 (C.C. Fairchild, D.L.S., SAB, Saskatoon).

The structure and appearance of the villages can be determined from the plans produced from Fairchild's 1909 survey of the South Colony villages. There would have been little modification of these villages in the years between the survey and 1913, particularly in the core areas. Here, as in the North Colony, the traditional plan of the village and the architecture of the buildings were modified by the communal organization of the village. A core of communal buildings at the centre of the village was common to most villages, especially those with a community home (see Figure 39). In a few of the villages, the communal buildings grouped more to the end of the street (as in Blagosklonoe; see Figure 40), and in Otradnoe, Peter Verigin's home village, the community home sat overlooking the village from a site at the end of the central street (see Figure 41). It would shortly fall victim to the arson of the Sons of Freedom.

The houses in most of the villages were generally of the high-lofted variety, with their gable ends facing the central street. However in villages like Savetnoe and

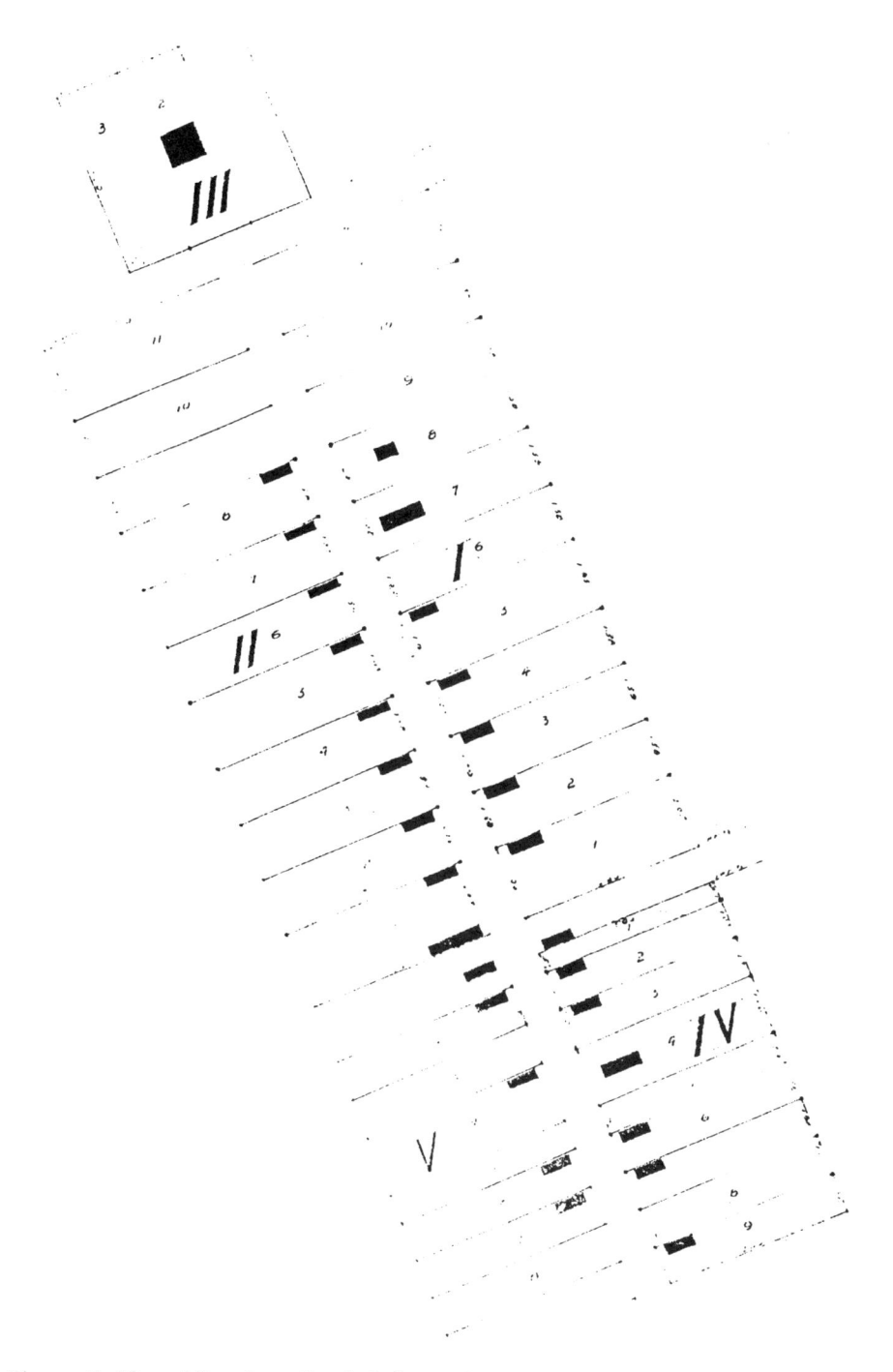

Figure 41. Plan of Otradnoe, South Colony, 1909 (C.C. Fairchild, D.L.S., SAB, Saskatoon).

Blagodarnoe, the houses were oriented parallel to the street (as were some individual structures in the other villages — see Figure 25, Chapter 4). The community homes were the most distinctive buildings in eight of the villages. They were nearly identical to the North Colony prayer homes, varying slightly in size and ornamentation. The community homes of Voskrisennie and Vosziennie have survived, providing solid evidence as to what these structures were like.

The consolidation of the CCUB, which took place between 1905 and 1912 as a result of movements within the reserves and out of the reserves to other CCUB lands, produced a cultural landscape in the South Colony that was a compact version of the vital village settlements of 1905. The perimeter of Community control had contracted around the cores of early village strength and the more recent concentration around Veregin Station on the railway. Some villages were abandoned outright as CCUB faithful moved to core villages and as Independents moved out to residences on their own homesteads. Other villages were depleted of the core of Community members that held the fabric of village life together. In these villages, the external form was maintained by Independent-Communists, by Independent Doukhobors who maintained residences in the village while cultivating their homestead lands individually, and by outsiders who were marking time until they could avail themselves of homestead land when it became available.[7]

The Community agricultural base on government land also continued to dwindle as CCUB members left for British Columbia or for purchased land in Saskatchewan, each removing their fifteen-acre allotment from the village lands. Those who decided to farm as Independent Doukhobors or who withdrew from the larger Community to farm communally on individually entered lands also withdrew land from the "per capita" reserve.[8] The 821 Communists remaining in South Colony villages in late 1913 (as many as 150 more may have been resident at Veregin Station), were eligible for 12,315 acres, although the actual reserves amounted to about 35,600 acres, a surplus of approximately 23,250 acres (the only deficit reported was 105 acres in the Troodoloobevoe village reserve). In any case, the extent of Community holdings on government land in Saskatchewan declined from

---

[7] Many of the Independents were also marking time: "There were 7 other applicants [for homesteads] but they all refused to take land now thinking that their chances would be better for the selection of a good parcel of land after the next trek of the community to BC" (NA, RG15, V1166 F5412447, Spaskoe Village File, 12 December 1913 Report). Some were also waiting because there was insufficient land in the village reserve to give full homesteads to every legitimate applicant. Such was the case at Terpennie which needed 5,280 acres to satisfy all thirty-three applicants but with a reserve of only 2,080 acres (NA, RG15, V1166 F5412443, Terpennie Village File, 5 December 1913 Report), and some were waiting for lands to be released in other reserves: "Andrey Potapoff and Iwan Gritchin want land at Verigin where they originally were on the list and belonged, resided. Told they may get land when the community all go away from that reserve" (NA, RG15, V1167 F5412489, Riduonovo Village File, 9 December 1913 Report).

[8] It should be emphasized that my concern here is to trace the decline of the Community settlements and lands in Saskatchewan. The "losses" I am detailing at this stage are losses to the Community only, and in many (perhaps most) cases this "lost" land was taken up by Independents or Independent-Communists, and remained in Doukhobor hands.

a maximum of 372,800 acres in 1905 (representing 2,330 homestead entries by Community members) in the three colonies, to 122,800 acres in 1907 (fifteen acres per capita for 8,175 Community members), to just over 12,000 acres in the fall of 1913, all in the South Colony.

It is impossible to determine how much of this reserve land was cultivated as the reports of the visits of the Commissions in the fall of 1913 rarely gave this information. In May, the Commission reported a cultivated acreage of just over 14,300 acres in the thirteen villages which had some Community members, but some of this would have been done by the Independent-Communists of eleven of these villages. If we assume that the cultivated land was distributed in proportion to the populations of the two groups — a somewhat dubious assumption, given the fact that the Independent-Communists were taking over land previously controlled and cultivated by the Community — the cultivated land on Community holdings would have amounted to approximately 12,600 acres.[1] If the decline in the amount of cultivated land was proportional to the decline in these villages of CCUB members between May 1913 and November/December 1913 (a decline of about 40 percent), then the cultivated acreage in fall 1913 would have been approximately 7,560 acres, a "loss"[11] of about 5,040 acres.[12]

Good Spirit Lake Annex

In the Good Spirit Lake Annex, the Community ceased to exist for all practical purposes by 1912 (see Table 21). No Community members were reported in any of the villages in that year. The villages of Old Gorilloe, Ootishennie, and Kyrillovo were already homogeneous Independent villages by this time, and the inhabitants of the other villages were either Independents or Independent-Communists. In the consolidation of Community members in the Annex, Moisayovo had taken in Community members from Ootishennie, New Gorilloe and Novo Troitzkoe, but it, like the other "stronghold" village of Blagosklonoe, was emptied of its Community members in a wholesale move to British Columbia in 1912. The people who remained in the villages were designated as Independent-Communists and were made up of those who never left for British Columbia, and those who had returned after spending some time there.[13] Blagosklonoe, with a population of 151 "Communists" in July 1911, was reduced to a single family of Independent-Communists the following year.

---

9   There is no cultivation information for Otradnoe, Spaskoe and Veregin in May 1913.

10 The Community population was 1,146 or 88 percent of the 1,301 people in the thirteen villages, disregarding Independents and outsiders.

11 In some cases, the Commission allowed continued cultivation of per capita land lost in the move to British Columbia, or on reserve land entered by Independent-Communists or Independents (NA, RG15, V1166 F5412437, Tomboscoe Village File, 2 November 1913 Report).

12 The two sets of data are not quite comparable as the November 1913 Commission did not report on one of the thirteen villages. The loss of land would probably be slightly higher if Najersda would have been included.

13 See NA, RG15, V1165 F5404642, Moisayovo Village File, May 1913 Report.

Table 21
Good Spirit Lake Annex Village Population

Village	1912	May 1913	November 1913	1917
Blagosklonoe	8 IC	4 C; 19 Independents	10 C; 10 Independents	24
Gorilloe	10 IC (2 families)	10 IC	10 IC	empty
Kalmakovo	41 IC	40 IC	79 Independents	18 Independents
Kyrillovo	very few here	1 Independent	1 Independent	1 Independent
Moisayovo	121 IC	6 C; 106 IC	99 IC	11 Independents (1 family)
Old Gorilloe	17 Independents	17 Independents	12 Independents	12 Independents
Ootishennie	empty, removed to Kalmakovo	7 Independents (homesteader family)	12 Independents*	empty
Novo Troitzkoe	5 families	10 IC; 18 Independents	10 IC; 13 Independents	5 Independents (homesteader family)

* Includes a family of five which occupied a house in the village in winter only.
Source: Village Files.

Community members reappeared in the two previously communal villages by May 1913. A family of four returned to Blagoskonoe and a family of six to Moisayovo. It is likely that these families returned from British Columbia and decided to maintain their Community attachment. They must have felt quite alone among the 213 Independents and Independent-Communists in the Annex, and the family in Moisayovo apparently sought to alleviate the loneliness by joining the other Community family at Blagosklonoe in the summer. Although formal reserves were still on the books in the fall of 1913, the Community had no land in the Annex at this time.[14]

Fairchild's plans for the eight villages of the Good Spirit Lake Annex suggest a good deal more variety in the village landscape here than in the previous colonies. Whether as a result of moulding the village layout to nearby Good Spirit Lake or Spirit Creek, or as a result of the individualistic tendencies of the villagers, the forms of many of the villages were much less regular in plan and building orientation. As well, three of the villages were already independent at the time of Fairchild's survey so changes were no doubt more evident there. In these independent villages — Kyrillovo, Gorilloe, and Old Gorilloe — as well as in Ootishennie, a village of Independents and Independent-Communists, the traditional *strassendorf* regularity was not much in evidence, with buildings scattered over the lots almost randomly. However, in what had been the core Community villages of Moisayovo, Kalmakovo, and Blagosklonoe, the village layout and the village architecture was very uniform (see Figure 28, Chapter 4). Not surprisingly, each of these villages had a community home as a dominant part of the village landscape.

---

14 Although there were no Community members reported (other than the two families noted), Community cultivation was reported for some of the villages as late as November 1913. I assume that this cultivation was noted so as to determine the amount of compensation paid to the Community if the land was being entered by an Independent. If it was being entered by an Independent-Communist, it appears that the cultivated land was considered to be part of the package, since the entrants were part of the Community that did the original cultivation.

Summary

It seems clear that the erosion of Community people and lands in the South Colony and Annex came in the main from people leaving for the British Columbia communities. But a substantial additional cause was the retreat of many of the Community members to what appears to have been an intermediary state of communalism (Independent-Communists, see note 10, Chapter 10) represented by withdrawal from the larger Community to practice a form of communalism free of Verigin's control on lands for which the individual families made entry. This seems to have given way over the next few years to complete independence; in fact, as noted above, it appears that some of these "Independent-Communists" were really Independents masquerading under that name in order to assure themselves of a piece of the reserved land for their use.

As in the other reserves, the South Colony landscape gave evidence of these changes and, like the North Colony, there were considerable differences between the peripheral landscapes and the "core" areas of Verigin's prairie operations. In the outlying parts of the South Colony, villages were either declining rapidly or in a holding pattern. Most had only two or three families of Independent-Communists and Independents, bolstered, in the better areas, by varying numbers of outsiders. The fields around the villages were being enlarged, either by Doukhobors who had left the Community, or by non-Doukhobor outsiders. Many of the villages in the heartland, on the other hand, continued to be functioning agricultural settlements, but even here went about their farm operations not knowing if and when they would be moving to British Columbia. Here too, the cultivated land was declining, and the fields which the Community had brought into production over the course of a decade, were being taken over and expanded by others.

Chapter 15
The Saskatchewan Colony ~ 1913

The Saskatchewan Colony, containing the most individualistic of all the Doukhobors, had lost any expression of Community identity in either land or people by 1912. The exodus of approximately 665 Community members to the North and South Colonies and a further exodus of 200 to British Columbia effectively eliminated the Community presence (see Map 13). Those Community members who for various reasons returned (many did) abandoned the CCUB and most also abandoned any form of communal structure. This was true even of the earlier centres of Community strength. Bodenofka, the destination of the only sizeable flow of Community members from the eastern core area to this peripheral colony, and Spasofka, the gathering place for the Community faithful of the Saskatchewan Colony, both had become villages of Independent-Communists by 1912, and by 1913, most had entered for individual homesteads. Karilowa also continued to maintain a sizeable Independent-Communist population (see Table 22) and about half of these continued to refuse to make entry for land because of the oath of allegiance, although apparently they too rejected any practical identification with the CCUB.

The Saskatchewan Colony villages were scarcely affected by the problem of "outsiders," so as the village population declined, village structure was rarely maintained artificially by non-Doukhobors. Buildings were removed or torn down, and gradually the village disappeared or was reduced to the farmstead of the homestead entrant to the village quarter section, with perhaps a few of the outbuildings left from other lots which the homesteader used. A notable exception was Petrofka village which had a large and rather mixed population of Germans, Bulgarians, Russians and English, in addition to homesteading Doukhobors. The "outsiders" here were not only moving into vacant houses, but were building houses

---

[1] Some forty-five to fifty Community people from Terpennie village in the South Colony relocated here in 1908 (NA, RG15, V1166 F5412443, Terpennie Village File, January 1908 Report).

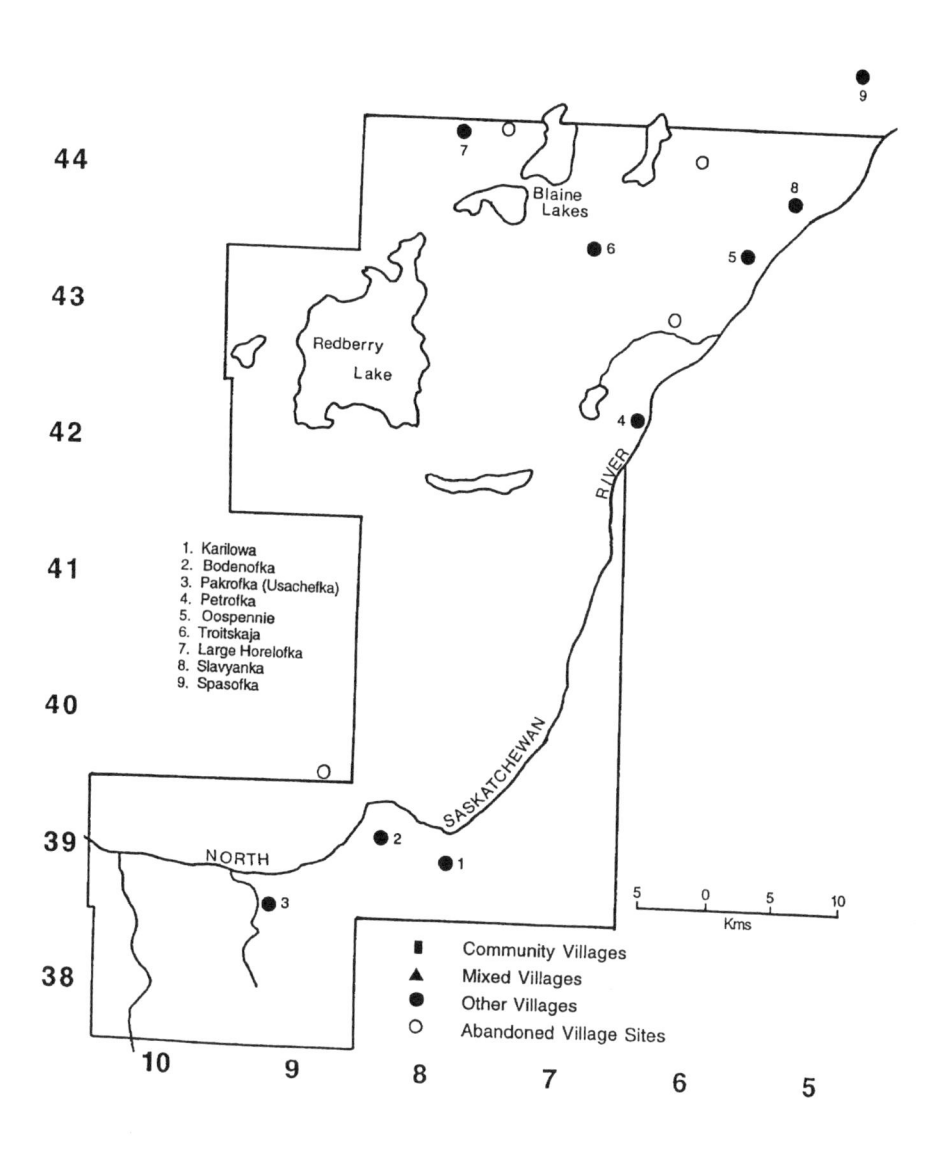

Map 13. Saskatchewan Colony Villages — 1913.

Table 22
Saskatchewan Colony Village Population

Village	1912	Spring 1913	Fall 1913	1917
Bodenofka	116 IC	115 IC	96 IC	26
Karilowa	98 IC	90 IC; 7 outsiders	85 IC	22 (1915)[a]
Large Horelofka	n/a	70 Independents	36 Independents	5 (1 family)[b]
Oospennie	62 Independents	81 Independents	64 Independents; 5 outsiders	13 Independents (2 families)
Pakrofka	75 Independents	n/a	5 Russian families and "some Doukhobors"[c]	51[d]
Pasariofka	10 Independents	10 Independents	11 Independents	empty (1915)
Petrofka	61 Independents	67 Independents[e]	51 Independents; 22 non-Doukhobors	80 (including 12 Germans)
Slavyanka	27 Independents	33 Independents	32 Independents; 1 English female	13
Small Horelofka	4 families	5 (homesteader family)	n/a	empty (1915)
Spasofka	35 IC	33 IC	34 IC	1 family (1915); 7 (1917)
Terpennie	2	no information	n/a	n/a
Troitzkaja	16 IC	17 IC	5 IC; 33 Independents	8 IC; 11 Independents
Totals	265 IC; 237 Independents (and 4 families)	255 IC; 266 Independents and many non-Doukhobors	220 IC; 227 Independents and many outsiders	231 total (most not categorized)

a) Apparently includes those who moved back into the village in winter; b) in temporary occupance; c) individual count not given; d) includes four Russian families; e) may include some non-Doukhobors.

Source: Village Files.

on vacant lots, a situation that kept it viable as a village settlement long after the other villages had been abandoned. That raised problems for the authorities in closing out the village reserve. Petrofka's location near the ferry crossing on the North Saskatchewan River no doubt contributed to its longevity. Pakrofka, at the opposite end of the Colony, also experienced an influx of non-Doukhobors: "The houses are being filled with Russians as they are vacated." Slavyanka was the only other village in the Saskatchewan Colony which had a non-Doukhobor resident — an English lady who was in charge of Kimberley Post Office in the village. Oospennie had five "outsiders" but they belonged to a family of Doukhobors from nearby Large Horelofka, and hence were "outsiders" only in the sense of "belonging" to another village.

It is evident from the data in Table 22 that the villages of the Saskatchewan Colony were in various stages of decline in 1913. Small Horelofka had already been abandoned by all but the family homesteading the village quarter, Pasariofka had

---

2   NA, RG15, V1164 F5391335, Petrofka Village File, 28 October 1913 Report.
3   NA, RG15, V1166 F5404690, Pakrofka Village File, 19 September 1912 Report.

only two families in addition to the homesteading family (eleven persons in all), and the Terpennie village site had been purchased earlier, so no population is given by the Commission Report (although it notes one person eligible for land in the village reserve). While these villages were either abandoned or in the last stages of dissolution, several other villages had sizeable populations, two, as has been noted, bolstered by non-Doukhobors or by ineligible Doukhobors. Petrofka, in April 1913, had only six legitimate residents (those on the village list who "belonged" to this village). However, the Report of October 1913 indicates that of a total village population of seventy-three, seventeen were legitimate residents, thirty-four held licenses of occupation but were either on their own farms or away elsewhere, and twenty-two (Russians, Germans and English) were living in houses purchased from the Doukhobors, but were required to leave. The Commission Reports of 1913 do not give population totals for Pakrofka, but the April report notes the presence of four Russian families residing in houses purchased from the Doukhobors; they were told to leave and to take their houses with them. An additional Russian family joined the others by October, and all five families were told to vacate. It would seem that these directives (or requests) were not taken very seriously. Seventy-eight people were still residing in the village in 1917, and John Bowes recommended that the village site be sold at $3 per acre to the purchaser of the homestead since he not only lived in the village but wanted the other residents to stay there as well.[4]

The Independent villages of Large Horelofka, Oospennie, Slavyanka, Troitzkaja and Pakrofka were shrinking in population owing to families leaving the village to establish farms on their homesteads. Some of these villagers were "part-time" residents, however, independent farmers who maintained some sort of dwelling on their homestead land for the six-month residence requirement, but who lived in their village houses during the winter months. The whole population of Large Horelofka — seventy people — engaged in these seasonal moves,[5] and there is frequent mention of this activity in other Independent villages as well. As a result, these village populations fluctuated considerably from year to year.

Very little land in the Saskatchewan Colony remained in the village reserves by the end of 1913. Bodenofka was reported to have 1,020 acres "worked to seed" on a reserve of seven quarter sections in October 1913, but the Commission took entries for all seven quarters (except the village site) at that time, which closed out the reserve. Similarly, Karilowa had a reserve of eleven quarter sections in October 1913, but entries were made for all reserve land except the village site. Reserves had been closed out earlier in all the other villages except Troitzkaja, where a reserve of forty acres was being held for one additional year in order to allow the crop to be taken off. In the Colony as a whole, then, only the village sites were left as reserved land,

---

[4] NA, RG15, V1164 F5391335, John Bowes to Secretary, Department of the Interior, 8 June 1917, Petrofka Village File.

[5] NA, RG15, V1167 F5412487, Large Horelofka Village File, 18 April 1913 Report.

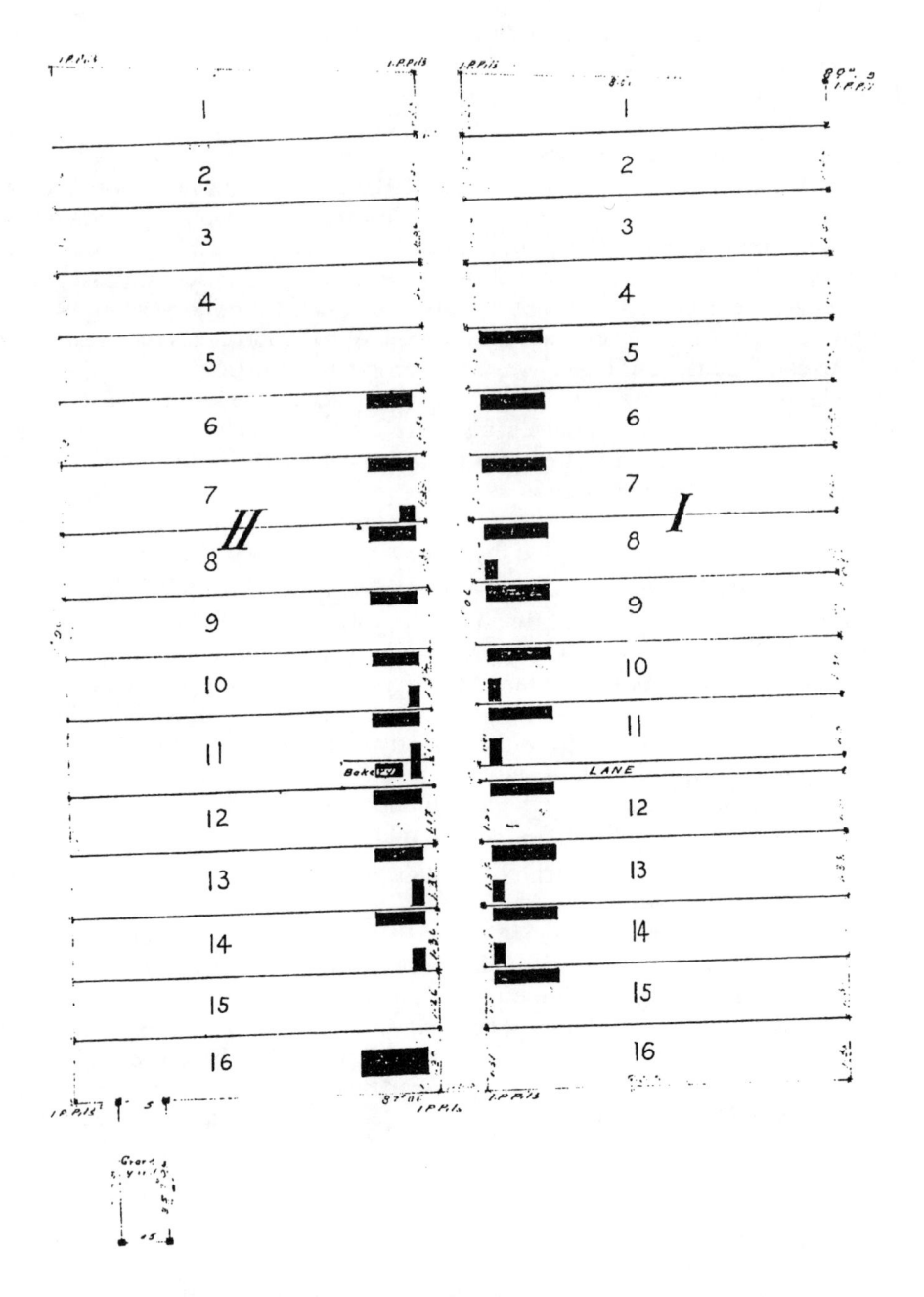

Figure 42. Plan of Bodenofka, Saskatchewan Colony, 1909 (C.C. Fairchild, D.L.S., SAB, Saskatoon).

and they were to be added to the homesteads of the appropriate entrants as quickly as the resident villagers could be moved out onto their own land, or elsewhere.

The destinations given for the forty-four intransigent members of Bodenofka village indicate the range of possible choices for those who refused to enter for homesteads because of the oath of allegiance:

> 29 represent those who are buying land, 8 reported going to British Columbia, 2 may go to Oregon and the other 5 are working out in the vicinity of the reserve.[6]

It is clear that by 1913, the Community presence had disappeared for all practical purposes. Fairchild's 1909 plans probably bear the least resemblance to the remnant villages of 1913, since the glue that held the structure together had disappeared. Nonetheless, the unmodified traditional street-village most characterized the villages here, and although much of the substance of the village landscape had disappeared with the settlers, the regular outlines were still in place (see Figure 42). Here, where strict allegiance to Peter Verigin was renewed after the villages had been built, community homes were absent, and house-barn combinations of the low-lofted, double purlin type were the norm. In villages where Doukhobors and non-Doukhobors were maintaining fairly sizeable populations — Bodenofka (ninety-six persons), Karilowa (eighty-five persons), Petrofka (seventy-seven persons), and Oospennie (sixty-nine persons) — even the substance remained.

Saskatchewan Colony villages were surrounded by sizeable areas of cultivated land, but most of that land was now in the hands of Doukhobors who had rejected the leadership of Peter Verigin and had left his Community. We have, then, a cultural landscape comprised of villages from which the communal vitality was drained, but whose structure was propped up by Doukhobors and "outsiders" who were not committed to maintaining this form of settlement. The villages were no longer held together by common purpose and common activity, but existed solely for the temporary convenience of settlers either waiting for homestead land or waiting for a convenient time to build farmsteads on their individual quarters.

---

6   NA, RG15, V1165 F5404664, Bodenofka Village File, October 1913 Report.

Chapter 16
Dissolution - 1913-1918

The processes and adjustments which created the pattern of village settlement in 1913 — the abandonment of Community lands for individual quarter sections for Independents and Independent-Communists, the movement of Community members to British Columbia, and the consolidation of Saskatchewan Community members in villages at the core of the South Colony — continued to erode village populations in all but the South Colony. The populations of individual villages tended to fluctuate considerably, inflated, or at least maintained, by intending Independents or Independent-Communists waiting for better land as Community members continued to relocate in British Columbia, leaving more of the village reserves open to homesteading, and by non-Doukhobors waiting for any land at all. Overall, however, village population continued to decline.

Tracing the absolute decline of village populations is made more difficult by the fluctuations in populations caused by non-Doukhobors occupying the vacated buildings in many villages and by the return of Doukhobors from British Columbia (which appears to have been limited to the South and Saskatchewan Colonies). Overall, the population in the villages declined from 3,103 in the fall of 1913 to 1,870 in 1917,[1] but both totals include a fairly significant component of "outsiders" — about 12 percent of the 1917 total. Unfortunately, the reports do not always distinguish between Doukhobors and non-Doukhobors, although they frequently note the presence of Russian, German and "Galician" families designated as "outsiders" and complain of the problem of keeping people out of the vacant houses in the village in order to dispose of the village sites.[2] For these reasons, some villages

---

1   Individual and cumulative village data are taken from the village files unless noted otherwise. The Commission visited all the extant villages in October 1917. No colony totals are available for 1918 since the census taken that year was restricted to those South Colony villages with a Community component.

2   An additional problem is that those labelled "outsiders" by the Commission often included Doukhobors who were from another village reserve, or who had been on a particular village per

remained as small settlements for several years after the main body of the Doukhobors had abandoned them, and some South Colony villages were important components of the prairie Community until 1918 and beyond.

The farm village, as part of the cultural landscape, declined more rapidly in some areas than others. The North Colony village population dropped from 722 in late 1913 to 326 in 1917, and nearly 20 percent of that total were outsiders. In eight of the villages, the only residents were the family members of the settler whose homestead included the village quarter section. Only three of eighteen villages had more than two or three families; Hlebedarnoe (seventy-seven persons including seven Russian families) and Simeonovo (fifty persons, including three Russians) were the largest. Michaelovo remained divided to the last. In 1917, the three families remaining were those of Ivan Ivin, the redoubtable Independent who was finally moving to his homestead that year, the homesteading family, and a family of five who were "returning to the Community." These lone Community members of the North Colony appear to have been among the eleven Independent-Communists recorded in 1913, but they had decided to rejoin the larger Community.

Village population in the Saskatchewan Colony declined from 505 in October 1913 to 231 in 1917, with well over half that population in the Independent villages of Petrofka and Pakrofka (see Table 22, Chapter 15). In these cases, Independent farmers who lived in the village — in some cases for only six months of the year — and worked on their homestead or on purchased land in the vicinity of the village, maintained the structure of the village if not its community life. Four villages were abandoned by this time, and four others had only two or three families. One of the two families at Spasofka had returned from British Columbia, but had decided to leave the Community.

The Annex villages, too, had been largely emptied by this date. Blagosklonoe and Kalmakovo had two or three families, one of which in Blagosklonoe may have been the only Community family in the Annex. Two other villages were abandoned completely and the remaining four had only the homesteading family of each village quarter section in residence.

While most of the villages built initially by the Doukhobors were abandoned as viable settlements by 1917 (and in several cases, the village land itself had been added to the homestead quarter on which it had been located), the Community Doukhobors maintained the "heartlands" in the South Colony. The total village

---

capita list, but had been struck from it when they left for British Columbia. This is a problem only for determining the village population; the Community component of each village is almost always clearly identified.

3   The distinction between Independents, Independent-Communists and Community members was occasionally flawed, both by the sometimes arbitrary distinctions between Community and non-Community members, and by individuals moving into and out of the Community: "Both Fred and Alex claim they are Communists, but are noted by us in the Records as Independents" (NA, RG15, V1167 F5412475, Maber Memorandum, 11 January 1918, Archangelskoe Village File).

Table 23
Village Populations by Colony — 1917

Colony	Independent	Independent-Communist	Community	Other	Total
North	186[a]	56	5	79[b]	326
South	157	121	838[c]	134	1,250
Annex	61	—	10	—	71
Saskatchewan	168	26[d]	—	37	213
Total	572	203	853	250	1,860

a) Includes eighty-one who are not clearly identified and could be Independent-Communists; b) includes eighteen Doukhobors who could be either Community or Independent-Communists; c) includes twenty absent in British Columbia and Alberta, and ten Wanderers; d) includes eighteen Doukhobors whose status is not clearly identified.

Source: Village Files.

population declined by nearly 350 between late 1913 and 1917, but the Community population actually increased slightly (see Table 20, Chapter 14 and Table 23). People continued to return from the Second Community in British Columbia, some to take up their places in the Saskatchewan Community and some to take up homesteads as Independents. Of the twenty-two villages for which information is available,[4] eighteen still had sizeable populations in 1917, although in most cases they were mixed populations and included substantial proportions of "outsiders." Twelve of the eighteen had Community majorities, and ten of these were either wholly or primarily comprised of Community members. Six villages had populations greater than seventy-five people in 1917; the largest, Terpennie, was occupied by ninety-six Independents and forty-two "others." Spaskoe had perhaps the most interesting array of residents, reporting seventy Community members, thirty-three Independent-Communists, twelve Russians and ten "Wanderers." The population of Petrovo was dominated by several families of non-Doukhobor Russians and many other villages had populations bolstered by non-Doukhobors.

Between 1917 and 1918, the Community population actually residing in Saskatchewan declined to about 730 (see Table 24).[5] Even in the "heartland," there

---

[4] Since the government Commissions were concerned only with lands under their control, they had no interest in lands acquired by the Doukhobors by purchase or in former reserve lands which had been entered by individuals under the normal homestead conditions. Oobezhdennie, occupying purchased land, was such a village.

[5] Some of those "temporarily absent" in British Columbia had been gone only a few months, but if the Community did not report them, or, as in some cases, apparently gave the Commission false information about them, they lost their "acres." Two men went to British Columbia leaving their families in Najersda but "the Commission called while they were gone and the Community told us they had left for good and their families would follow them [they were gone only four months] but they are all here again and are Independent now. There is another family of Communists here Fred Zarichoff but the Community use him as one of their own and keep him. His family is not on the list either. If possible these three men should be restored as they have worked all those years and now is [sic] turned out without a dollar to start them in life and a family to support" (NA,

Table 24
South Colony Community Villages and Cultivation — 1918

Village	In Village	At Veregin[b]	Community British Columbia/ Alberta	Cultivated Acres	Independent-Communists[a] Population	Cultivated Acres
Blagovishennie	33	10	25	924	—	—
Kapustina	44	53	9	1,011	—	—
Lubovnoe	13	—	14	260	16	200
Nadejda	71	—	—	590	3	25
Novoe	20	10	10	643	30	330
Otradnoe	17	—	40	290	17	315
Riduonovo	34	—	23	417	17	—
Savetnoe	21	27	—	570	22	235
Smyrennie	43	—	—	620	—	—
Spaskoe	53	—	25	510	37	510
Tomboscoe	42	31	15	902	18	300
Troodoloobevoe	12	—	24	230	9	130
Veregin	54	6	—	560	7	90
Vernoe	90	—	—	1,090	—	—
Voskrisennie	17	—	22	147	30	240
Vosziennie	19	9	42	784	11	100

a) Although Casakoff notes the non-Community members of the village as "Independents," these would be regarded as Independent-Communists, as they were entitled to acres in the village reserve. The population and cultivation statistics are given only for those villages which had some Community members; b) those temporarily absent from the village who were working on the Community lands around Veregin.

was a continuing slide to independence: some of the Community members of the old stronghold villages of Otradnoe, Najersda, Voskrisennie, and Vosziennie, had apparently taken the first step toward independence by becoming Independent-Communists by 1918.[6]

The Community land base also continued to decline, even in the South Colony. As noted in previous chapters, each individual leaving the Community, for whatever

---

RG15,V1167 F5412459, Bowes to Cory, 1 April 1918, Najersda Village File). At this late date, this ploy, in direct contrast to the normal practice of keeping these non-resident members on the list for as long as possible so as to maintain the size of the village reserve, may have been designed to keep uncertain Community members in line. If they returned as Independents, they not only lost their labour on Community projects, but lost out on the possibility of obtaining homestead land in Saskatchewan.

6 As I have noted before, the uncertainty of the status of the Independent-Communists makes it impossible to make an unqualified statement. Looking at the Commission reports over a series of years, there certainly seems to be a progression from "Communist" to "Independent-Communist" to "Independent," but the distinction between the latter two is not clear. Some of the Independent-Communists appear to have continued to maintain some connection with the CCUB (witness the fact that many of the mortgages undertaken by them were co-signed by the CCUB) and some apparently had the intention of deeding the land to the CCUB when they finally obtained title to it.

reason, reduced the village reserves by fifteen acres, so as the Community population in the villages declined, so did their land base. In May 1913, the Community was using some 17,200 acres of cultivated land; the 1917 Commission reported 10,451 acres cultivated (Kapustina, Otradnoe, and Veregin acreages were not given); and the 1918 census reported just under 9,600 acres of Community cultivation.

The 1918 census was used to determine the portion of the village reserves to be allocated to the Community on the per capita basis; these lands were sold to individual Community members at $10 per acre, but the Sun Life Assurance Company mortgages for the funds were cosigned by M.W. Cazakoff, Vice-President and Secretary for the CCUB.[7] It is not clear whether those purchasers intended to deed their land back to the Community after acquiring title to the quarter section. I have found no convenient way of determining how much village reserve land made its way into the purchased land base of the Community in this manner. According to a 1926 newspaper report, the CCUB had disposed of 50,000 acres of land in the Kamsack district because of the possible return of 2,500 Doukhobors to Russia.[8] The bulk of this land would have been purchased directly by the CCUB but some of it must have been land that was acquired in the way just described. The rest of the land in the reserve (approximately 23,000 acres in 1917) was either homesteaded, leased (6,250 acres were rented for the 1918 season), or reserved for the Soldiers' Settlement Board.

The last land to be disposed of was the village site, a block of land usually occupying twenty to thirty acres, and often containing land in two or more quarter sections. Beginning in 1910, after Fairchild had provided the legal outlines of the villages lots with his 1909 survey, licenses of occupation for village lots had been given as an intermediary step between Community use and either homestead entry or sale. Licenses of occupation gave usage rights to a piece of land — village lots or surrounding agricultural land — and particularly in villages where Doukhobors of different "classes" coexisted, the licenses were apparently given to keep the peace between them. If the village was populated by all Communists or all Independents, licenses of occupation were not needed:

> The inhabitants [of Lubomeernoe] were told that as there was only one class of people in the village no license of occupation would be issued as it was only necessary to take such action where there were two or more [classes] of doukhobors [sic] occupying lots in the village site.[9]

As the reserves and villages were phased out, the licenses were cancelled so the whole village site could be sold as a block. At least this was the course of action finally adopted. In 1913, in cases where a village had become Independent through either the departure or change of heart of the Community members (thus terminating the

---

7   Some seventy mortgages were registered for Community lands in the South Colony (NA, RG15, V1165 F5404644, Cory Memorandum, 17 November 1919, Kapustina Village File).
8   NA, RG15, V1165 F5404670, Landerkin to Hume, 9 March 1926, Blagovishennie Village File.
9   NA, RG15, V1167 F5412461, Commission Report, May 1909, Lubomeernoe Village File.

village reserve), the intent was to have the families purchase their village lots. This rarely occurred except in one or two unusual cases where the village lot adjoined the homestead of the lot occupant. Where the license of occupation was for land outside the village site, the license holder usually had the "best right" to purchase that land.

The most common course of action was to add the village site to the homestead of whoever had entry to the rest of the quarter section, either by making it part of the homestead entry or by sale at $3 per acre. Although this figure was much below the current value of land at the time, Michael White, the government-appointed investigator of Doukhobor village sites, argued that the price was fair:

> first in order to facilitate settlement, and second because these deserted villages sites require much labour before they could be made use of. Practically all house [sic] had sod roofs and wall [sic] of mud, and where the houses stood great piles of baked clay remain requiring hundreds of dollars to clear. Besides there are other obstructions, such as old well [sic], cellars, etc.[10]

A meeting house left on the village site complicated these arrangements. Since the meeting house belonged to the CCUB in all but three villages, the Department required it to be sold before the land itself could be disposed of, and this process could delay the transfer of title for several years. The meeting houses in Voskrisennie, Troodoloobevoe and Spaskoe were built cooperatively by Independents and the Community, which complicated matters further. The Independents wanted to continue using these "for Church purposes" and therefore needed to have title to the lots on which they sat and the roads leading to them.[11] This seems not to have been a problem in disposing of the other Community-owned village structures (barns, workshops, stables, and so on). Presumably these smaller and less valuable buildings were disposed of more readily before the demise of the village. Of course, if the villages were on purchased land, as in the case of Vernoe and Novo Blagodarnoe, the Community could dispose of the site in any manner it chose.

Nine quarter sections of reserved land remained in the Good Spirit Lake Annex in 1917, three in the Kalmakovo reserve and six in the Blagosklonoe reserve. In 1918, two of the nine were reserved for hay, five were reserved for the Soldiers' Settlement Board and two were sold.

Except for the village sites, some of which were already disposed of, only three quarter sections of reserved land remained in the North Colony in 1917 and these were used for stock-raising by the residents of Hlebedarnoe. The land was reserved for the Soldiers' Settlement Board in 1918. No reserved land remained in the Saskatchewan Colony except for the village sites (usually twenty acres, but eighty acres in the case of Petrofka), and these were in the process of being added to the homesteads of the appropriate entrant.

---

10   NA, RG15, V758 F494483, Pt. 5, Report of Michael White, 6 August 1918.
11   NA, RG15, V1165 F5404680, Troodoloobevoe Village File.

Summary

The Community's presence in the areas originally allocated to the Doukhobors had totally disappeared in all but the South Colony by 1917. Shortly after the census of 1918 all village lands were sold, leased, homesteaded, or reserved for the Soldiers' Settlement Board. The only lands remaining were the village lots themselves, whose disposition, in a few cases, was delayed by complications in the sale of the community homes still standing on village sites.

The focus of Community attention in Saskatchewan now turned to the lands purchased by Verigin and the Community in the years since 1903. Several "villages," usually comprised of one or two large multifamily houses and a few outbuildings, were established on these lands while the remaining original villages were eventually abandoned. So, although the Community population in the villages on government lands steadily declined, that is not the whole picture. The total population of Community Doukhobors in Saskatchewan clearly was much larger, and the Doukhobor population in Saskatchewan — including Independents and those who were practicing some form of communal living outside the organizational framework of the CCUB — was much larger yet.

Chapter 17
Conclusion

The drama of initiation, development, and decline of the distinctive cultural landscapes of the Community Doukhobors was played out in less than two decades. Initially, the Doukhobors were welcomed as thrifty and industrious farmers by a government eager to fill the largely unsettled lands of the Canadian West and by a public largely sympathetic to the plight of a group which had suffered much hardship and loss. But there were problems almost immediately. The Doukhobors refused to follow the most basic Canadian regulations: they would not provide information on births and deaths, nor would they register for homesteads individually. And while the government was willing to accommodate the communal village settlement of the Doukhobors by means of the Hamlet Clause, it insisted that the Doukhobors conform to the accepted norms of western settlement — individualistic homesteading — by requiring individual application for each homestead. Just as this stalemate was about to reach crisis proportions, Peter "Lordly" Verigin, the Doukhobors' exiled leader, joined his followers from Russia. He persuaded the Community that individual registration for homesteads was a pragmatic formality rather than a conflict of values. This strategic move, plus a cultivation concession by Clifford Sifton, smoothed the way for a temporary period of relative tranquility in which the Doukhobor Community developed and expanded rapidly. But changes in the context of agricultural settlement in the West created further conflicts. Sifton's successful immigration campaign put good homestead land at a premium and competition for land made compromise of the individualistic, free-enterprise economic model increasingly remote. Then Clifford Sifton was replaced in 1905 by Frank Oliver, a man decidedly antagonistic to special homestead concessions, especially to Slavic immigrants. He set aside the cultivation concession granted by Sifton and demanded that the Doukhobors indicate their intentions to become good Canadian farmers by swearing allegiance to the Crown. This raised the level of conflict from pragmatism to principle and neither side was willing to compromise. Peter Verigin realized that if the Community was to survive it would have to do so from a different land base, so he purchased land in British Columbia and relocated the majority of his followers there. The thousands of Community Doukhobors occupying more than fifty villages were reduced to a few hundred faithful living in a small clutch of villages.

While this drama can be sketched out in a few words, it involved thousands of people in a conflict which was costly in economic terms and in human suffering. And questions remain. Who was to blame? Could the conflict have been avoided? Was a successful outcome possible?

I believe that the preceding discussion of the initiation, development and decline of the villages and fields of this unique group sheds some light on these questions and enriches our understanding of the ways in which the values of an immigrant group can both mould the landscape into its own image and lead to its abandonment. Several points are worth highlighting in this concluding section.

To begin with, the perspective presented in the literature is one of a group establishing, under great hardship, the fifty-seven original villages, then going on in subsequent years to establish a few more villages. These developed into an increasingly prosperous Community under the capable leadership of Peter Verigin. What is missing here is the near-continuous change in the village pattern. The cultural landscape of the Community Doukhobors was in almost constant flux during the time under consideration. Old village sites were abandoned and new villages established at a quite remarkable pace. No fewer than thirty such village moves were made. Rather than the sixty-one villages noted by most sources, the Doukhobors built in excess of ninety villages in the prairies and parklands of Saskatchewan. Considering that the bulk of this activity was carried out when draught animals were in extremely short supply, that many of the men were engaged in work outside the reserves, and that land was broken and sown (and abandoned when the villages moved) in addition to the work in the villages, the magnitude of change is remarkable, and the human labour involved is staggering.

But this was not just an exercise in human exertion. The changing village pattern suggests that Verigin had a carefully conceived plan to consolidate the Community faithful around a centrally located, accessible core of good agricultural lands. Peripheral villages in the South Colony moved closer to the core. Saskatchewan Colony Veriginites moved to the North and South Colonies to become a more cohesive part of the Community. Later, when most of the Community members moved to British Columbia, Veriginites moved from "mixed" villages to consolidated Community villages in the core. In general terms, the consolidation of the villages geographically reflected the consolidation of the bulk of the Doukhobors organizationally under Verigin's leadership. The process also marked an increasingly clear distinction, geographically and socially, between the Community and non-Community Doukhobors.

The early pattern of consolidation suggests that Verigin had some hopes of establishing a strong Saskatchewan Community base in the North and South Colonies as late as 1905-06. Although the issue of naturalization was being raised, Verigin apparently felt that some compromise would be reached as it had with the cultivation issue. When it became clear in 1906 that there would be no compromises on either issue, Verigin continued the strategy of consolidation, focussing now on the core lands of the South Colony. This made good sense. These were the most productive lands, and they would provide the most rapid returns which were needed to finance the newly established colonies in British Columbia. They were also adjacent to the Saskatchewan lands Verigin had purchased earlier, so the transition from the reserved lands to the purchased lands could take place efficiently. The Canadian Northern Railway provided efficient exchange of commodities produced in Saskatchewan and British Columbia. The constant changes in the components of the cultural landscape reveal energies and strategies not immediately apparent in the existing literature.

Second, although I noted in the "Introduction" that changing the public image of the Doukhobors was not my major concern, I would hope this study has helped to dispel the notion that Doukhobors in general paraded in the nude and burned buildings on a whim. Such a caricature is inaccurate and unfair to the large majority of the early settlers. Other persistent errors appear from time to time in the literature, however. Two can be dispensed with quite quickly. As Woodcock and Avakumovic point out, there is a persistent belief among some Doukhobors that Queen Victoria gave her personal assurance that they could live in Canada under their own laws for ninety-nine years.[1] This belief makes the government's actions in taking back land in the reserves especially heinous: either Queen Victoria was duplicitous, or the Canadian government carried out a renegade decision against its own sovereign. A second error, found in several instances in the literature, is that the village reserves constituted an allotment of fifteen acres per *family* rather than fifteen acres per person. This gives a misleading impression of the severity of government action and of the magnitude of the land lost in 1907.

The exaggeration of the amount of land lost in the decision of 1907 leads into a much more widespread error which has persisted because of lack of data. It is commonly held that much, if not most, of the land lost in 1907 was improved (cultivated) land. The error appears to be based on the 1914 evaluations of M.W. Cazakoff, manager for the CCUB. He claimed that the government took from the Doukhobor community 2,300 "improved" farms of some 380,000 acres, worth, on average, $30 per acre, for a total value, including buildings, of $11,400,000.[2] It must be noted that of the nearly 2,500 homesteads cancelled, 766 were returned as village reserves, and 384 were reserved for entry by Doukhobors who wished to go along with individual ownership. Even if the latter quarter sections were included, the number of farms lost was 1,734, representing just under 278,000 acres. Even accepting the 2,300 "improved" farms,[3] the acreage would amount to 368,000, rather than the 380,000 claimed. The editor, L.I. Strakhovsky, also provides an exaggerated estimation of cultivated land lost, claiming "over 100,000 acres of choice farm land, cleared, worked, and improved by the Doukhobors, reverted to

---

1 Woodcock and Avakumovic, *The Doukhobors*, 134.

2 "Doukhobor Claims for Compensation," *Canadian Slavonic Papers* I (1956), 1-15 (documents from the papers of J.E. Mavor with an editorial note by L.I. Strakhovsky).

3 It is unclear what Cazakoff meant by the term "improved" farms. It is clear from the village files that many of the "farms" (homestead quarter sections) had no improvements of any kind.

the Government."[4] Even Peter Verigin's estimate of the cultivated land in this same group of documents was only 50,000 acres.[5]

When one considers that the Doukhobors were involved in the choice of lands to be retained in the village reserves, and that even according to government documents, the land in the reserves was to be allocated in such a way as to retain as much cultivated land as possible, it would seem that these claims are exaggerated. Since the total cultivated acreage in 1906 was between 40,000 and 45,000 acres, and since the greatest proportionate loss of cultivated land was about 40 percent (in the South Colony), it would seem reasonable to assume that the cultivated acreage lost in 1907 was no more than 25,000 acres and, quite likely, considerably less.

Not all the land lost to the Community was lost in 1907, of course. There was a continual dwindling of the village reserves which reduced the land base, and an increasing amount of this land would have been cultivated. But it is somewhat questionable to consider this land as part of the equation, for after 1907 it was quite clear to the Community that any further improvements on government land were in danger of being lost.

No matter what the actual figure was, it represented to the Doukhobors a huge loss in the investment of capital and labour; of more fundamental importance, it represented broken promises and rekindled long-held fears of governments which could not be trusted.

Third, the questions of why the distinctive cultural landscapes disappeared so quickly, after so much effort expended by Doukhobors and non-Doukhobors alike, and who was to blame for their disappearance, are more difficult to answer since they raise issues of interpretation based on uneven factual data. What documentation exists is almost wholly from non-Doukhobor sources. We have little documentation of the Doukhobor perspective (not surprising since the group was largely illiterate): the cryptic and enigmatic statements by Verigin in his letters, some translated interviews with Doukhobor representatives, and very little else. Any interpretation of what was going on in Verigin's mind and in the minds of his followers must be based almost wholly on their activities, and the insights that can be gleaned from what was happening in the villages and fields.

On the surface, it would appear that the scenario at the beginning of this section — conflict, compromise, concession, progress, new conflict, final stalemate, abandonment — adequately traces the Doukhobor problem. The early promise of success based on concession and compromise in early 1903 was increasingly endangered by a series of new conflicts until the final confrontation over allegiance left neither side room to maneuver. It would appear, however, that even as he was persuading his followers that registering for homestead land was a mere formality, Verigin knew

---

4   "Doukhobor Claims," 2. He also repeats the error that the village reserves comprised land based on an allotment of fifteen acres per family.

5   Ibid., 7.

that the question of allegiance would be the critical issue, and that there would be no compromise on the part of his followers.[6]

Why, then, would Verigin organize his followers into an efficient Community whose progress after the "understanding" of February 1903 was dramatic? A letter to Tolstoy infers that the compromise reached in 1903 was to buy time.[7] Perhaps Verigin thought that sustained progress in the three years left before patent would become an issue that would convince the government to waive the citizenship requirement. Alternatively, perhaps he knew that relocation was inevitable, and the acceleration in activity was to bankroll the move. I have noted support for both of these interpretations, and it is possible that both were true.

That Verigin continued to exert the Community's energies on village reserves after 1907, reserves that were constantly dwindling owing to the departure of Community members for one reason or another, suggests either that he was confident he could maintain a core community on the remaining village lands for some time to come (until 1918 in the South Colony, as a matter of fact), or that this was the most efficient way of raising much-needed cash for the Second Community in British Columbia and for the purchase of additional land in Saskatchewan (the Kylemore and Kelvington settlements in 1918).

While the above may explain the continued expansion of Community interests, economically if not geographically, the question of the ultimate cause of the failure remains. Woodcock and Avakumovic attribute the final failure primarily to political expediency bolstered by a rigid commitment to an individualistic settlement model.[8] Adelman argues persuasively that it was a basic conflict between economic models: collective ownership of land as opposed to the independent, owner-occupant homestead model of land holding.[9] He holds the government responsible for the failure since,

> although officials were eager to see staple-producers populate the grass-lands, which was why the refugees were offered land in the first place, these same officials would not countenance a system of property relations which did not cohere with the homestead model.[10]

Other studies also lay stress on the economic aspects of the conflict as an outgrowth of different ideologies.[11]

---

6   Donskov, *Tolstoy-Verigin Correspondence*, 64, 83.

7   Ibid., 64.

8   Woodcock and Avakumovic, *The Doukhobors*, 217-24.

9   Adelman, "Early Doukhobor Experience on the Canadian Prairies," 111.

10   Ibid., 113. Woodcock and Avakumovic also hold the government responsible, not only for the moral (if not legal) lapse in reneging on Sifton's concession, but for the failure to "yield gracefully" on the necessity of taking the oath of allegiance (*The Doukhobors*, 221-22).

11   For example, see A. Kershaw, "Ideological Conflict, Assimilation, and the Cultural Landscape: A Case Study of the Doukhobors in Canada," in Waters, ed., *Aspects of Human Geography*, 9-26.

The ultimate sticking point, however, was not communal ownership but swearing allegiance to the Crown. That the government desired the Community members to adopt an individualistic model is not in doubt. That Frank Oliver used a strict interpretation of the cultivation and residence requirements to force a more individualistic model on the Doukhobors is equally clear. But there is absolutely no evidence that had the Doukhobors compromised their beliefs and taken the oath of allegiance, they could not have continued their communal operations on patented land (which they did on purchased land in Saskatchewan). In fact, the government made clear on several occasions that after patent, the Doukhobors could do what they liked with the land. If indeed the government of the day could not tolerate communal ownership of land for political and economic reasons, it seems to have been counting on the Doukhobors' commitment to their beliefs to help dismantle it.

Two things seem clear. In the complimentary desires of the Doukhobors to escape persecution and the government to fill the West with experienced agriculturalists, both either overlooked, or ignored, essential details of land settlement. The government had the greater responsibility in clarifying these. It clearly retreated from both the intent and the letter of an agreement made by Clifford Sifton regarding the communal cultivation of land. While this was not necessarily the final hindrance to the Community taking up land, the "betrayal" of the government on this issue certainly made it more unlikely that they would accept any compromise (although none seems to have been offered) on the matter of swearing (or affirming) allegiance to the Crown.

It is necessary to remember the context within which these conflicts were played out, however. The government could hardly ignore, nor could it modify, the spirit of the times. A mystical, communal people, given special concessions unavailable to the ordinary (and particularly the Anglo-Saxon) settler was not likely to gain the sympathy of either the government or the public. In this context, it would seem the Doukhobors could not hope to avoid the unmodified requirements of the Homestead Act. It is a tribute to the Community Doukhobors that they would abandon hard-won lands rather than submit to requirements which ran counter to their basic beliefs.

This study has been concerned with the distinctive cultural landscapes created by the Community Doukhobors on reserved government land in what is now the province of Saskatchewan. The story of this Community did not end with the closing out of the last of the reserves in 1918. It continued on purchased land adjoining the reserves and in the new settlement areas near Kylemore and Kelvington. The original villages and fields were abandoned, and eventually time erased all but the faintest traces of their presence. But new villages were built. They differed from the old villages in form and architecture, but they were home to faithful CCUB members and part of an economic empire that included newly settled lands in Alberta as well as headquarters in British Columbia. A detailed study of the location and development of the prairie component of the CCUB on purchased lands is the focus of a future study.

Epilogue

Time has wasted this distinctive cultural landscape of Old World villages and communal fields which once dominated some half-million acres of Saskatchewan prairie and parkland. But tantalizing reminders of its richness remain: exotic brick-clad meeting houses, Russian inscriptions marking long-forgotten graves in overgrown cemeteries, the suggestion of old village lots and the foundations of houses and mills, and the memories of children's children woven from grandparents' tales and yellowed photographs.

At Oospennie, a brick-clad meeting house serves as a granary, and a solitary log house settles back on its haunches, its overhung gable pointing toward the sky. The fringe of dadoes along the eaves are punctuated with gaps like an old man's smile, and the scrolled metal that once decorated the ridge of the *dom* lies in strips on the ground. Another meeting house, with its wooden frame showing through patches of scaling brick, stands staring blankly at the traffic passing by on the highway south of Kamsack. The stone foundation of Michaelovo's *dom* stands in an open field, while thick second growth hides that of Libedevo, only a few steps from the grid road. A group of mud-plastered log buildings quietly disintegrates in a scruffy clearing behind the foundation. The central street of Vosnisennie remains as a faint trace in the grass and a truncated meeting house sits facing the trace. A log farmhouse leans into the wind on the first site of Osvoborsdennie; a few others stand isolated and oddly awkward on abandoned farm sites. A line of trees marks the central street of Otradnoe and an open square of trees at the head of the street surrounds the site of Verigin's house, an early casualty of the fiery indignation of the Sons of Freedom.

But there is even less to mark the passing of most of the villages. Parallel patches of grey clay on black summerfallowed fields mark building sites in some. In others, a stubble field gives up a few shards of glass and pottery, a scrap of scrolled copper from the roof ridge of a *dom*, a gingerbread spread of broken brick.

It took only four decades to dissolve Verigin's vision of a utopia based on primitive Christianity, and less than two to eliminate the extensive and distinctive cultural landscape it created in Saskatchewan. Were the Community and the landscape it created victims of a government bent on squeezing all elements of the West into a central Canadian mould, or victims of a fanatical faith that refused to adapt to the norms of Canadian society? Was the government the tool of the power brokers of central Canada, or the oft-tried benefactor of a group of poverty-stricken dissidents, controlled by the whims of an autocratic leader?

Whatever the carefully qualified answers to these questions, from the vantage point of nearly a hundred years of material progress, multiculturalism, and occasional racial hysteria, Canada's experience with the Doukhobors is a cautionary reminder of the need for tolerance and understanding in the recognition both of basic beliefs and the rule of law.

A Note on Sources

Original Material

A fortuitous byproduct of the sometimes radical discontent of the Doukhobors with the norms of Canadian life, and in particular with the demands of the Canadian government with respect to land registration and ownership, was the detailed data compiled by various surveys and commissions as the government sought to keep track of details of location, population and cultivation of the Doukhobor villages. The earliest schedule of villages is Leo Sulerzhitsky's list of 9 July 1899,[1] but while it gives population, stock and a general indication of total land seeded, it does so only for the thirteen villages of the North Colony. William Harvey's November 1899 schedule is the earliest complete survey of the original fifty-five villages in the three colonies.[2] He noted such things as population, number of houses, acres ploughed, stock, and so on. Unfortunately, village locations are not given, and variations in spelling and change of village names often make it difficult to make connections between this and later schedules. Hugh Harley's report on the North Colony villages in June and November 1900 provides another reference point for assessing changes in the villages of that reserve.[3] His report on the status of the villages after the "mania" of 1902 gives some interesting detail but the information given is not consistent for all villages.[4] The schedules of two homestead inspectors in the summer of 1902 are more detailed and complete, but it appears that only the villages of the North and South Colony were investigated.[5]

The most detailed record of the Doukhobor villages was compiled by homestead inspectors in 1905 (see Bibliography for a complete list of sources). They visited all the villages and recorded the names, ages and sex of every Doukhobor (although

---

1   NA, RG15, V 755 F494483, Pt. 1, McCreary to Pedley, 12 August 1899.
2   NA, RG76, V184 F65101, Pt. 5, "Schedule of Doukhobor Villages and Statistics," "Prepared by William B. Harvey, during his visit in the Eleventh Month of 1899."
3   Ibid., Report of Hugh Harley.
4   NA, RG76, V184 F65101, Pt. 6, Harvey to Speers, 26 November 1902.
5   NA, RG15, V754 F494483, Pt. 2, Schedule of Thomas Young; ibid., Schedule of N.G. McCallum.

some refused to give their age and some parents gave false ages for their sons), as well as the location of each homestead entered upon, the amount of cultivation on each quarter, and the number and kinds of buildings, stock and equipment. Subsequent surveys by the various Doukhobor Commissions beginning in 1906 were not as detailed, but village populations, population movements, and individual land entries are given quite consistently for 1906, 1909, 1910, 1911, 1912, and for two visits in 1913. Since most of the villages were abandoned by this last date, the information in the village files documents in detail the decline of the villages from their peak in numbers and prosperity. All of these records are located in the Doukhobor village files of the Department of the Interior, National Archives of Canada, Ottawa.

The extensive photographic collection assembled by Koozma Tarasoff and housed in the Provincial Archives of British Columbia in Victoria, together with the photographs assembled by the Saskatchewan Archives Board (Regina and Saskatoon), Provincial Archives of Alberta (Edmonton), and the Glenbow-Alberta Archives (Calgary) contain a wealth of visual evidence relating to Doukhobor culture and activity. These images not only supplement the text, but provide rich detail about architecture and village format, and give glimpses into a way of life long past.

The original surveyors' notebooks include detailed notations about vegetation cover which were used for the reconstruction of vegetation at the time of settlement. They also contain the original surveys of the villages in 1909 (a few villages were surveyed earlier), from which the large linen plans of the villages were drafted. These were indispensable for locating the last site and orientation of the villages for field work in 1973, 1975, 1989, and 1992. (Appendixes A and B give complete lists of the surveyors' notebooks and village plans.) These visits to the original village sites provided information on relict features and a feel for the site and the surrounding landscape. In addition, I used 1949 air photos to investigate inaccessible sites, and to check for evidence of villages in locations mentioned in the early documents but not identified in the more complete schedules and maps.

Published Sources

Although the problems and peculiarities of this group have generated perhaps more journalistic ink than any other in western Canada, the body of literature attempting to provide a balanced and dispassionate treatment of its development and decline is quite modest. Contemporary observers produced only a few comprehensive accounts. Aylmer Maude's first-hand account (*A Peculiar People*) is the most informed of these. Not only was he the major liaison for the Doukhobors in their choice of lands in Canada, but he was fluent in Russian and, as translator of Tolstoy's works into English, was well versed in the close ties between Tolstoy's ideology and the developing Doukhobor idealism. Joseph Elkinton (*The Doukhobors*) wrote out of his experience with the Quaker support of Doukhobor relocation and his personal encounters with the Doukhobors themselves on visits to their settlements in western Canada. James Mavor, Canadian supporter of Doukhobor immigration and advocate of their cause in the subsequent problems surrounding the land question, recorded his experience and assessment in his larger autobiographical work, *My Windows on the Street of the World*. Two recent translations of contemporary material are Leopold Sulerzhitsky's *To America with the Doukhobors* (originally published in Russian in 1905) and Andrew Donskov's *Leo Tolstoy-Peter Verigin Correspondence*. The first recounts Sulerzhitsky's experiences with the North and South Colony Doukhobors and provides description and assessment of the form and life of these settlements from a sympathetic but astute observer intimately involved with the early life of the Doukhobors in Canada. The second sheds some light on the Doukhobor-government conflict from the leader's perspective. A host of contemporary observations and assessments were recorded in newspapers, journals and travel accounts as the curious and concerned were drawn to the Doukhobor settlements.

Of the more recent comprehensive studies, Jim Wright's *Slava Bohu* is the earliest, and, although written in a journalistic style and lacking the usual documentary citations (an omission he intended to rectify in a planned revision of the work), provides a most evocative account of the inner workings of Doukhobor leadership. *The Doukhobors*, by George Woodcock and Ivan Avakumovic, is a model of thorough scholarly analysis and literary elegance and, although not without its weaknesses, stands as the most complete work on the Doukhobors in Canada. Koozma Tarasoff has probed Doukhobor consciousness and activity with an insider's insight and understanding in several extensive and diverse works (the unpublished three-volume typescript, "In Search of Brotherhood," as well as his books *A Pictorial History of the Doukhobors*, and *Plakun Trava*). William Janzen's concern in *Limits on Liberty* is more restricted: to evaluate government response to certain accommodations the Doukhobors (as well as the Hutterites and Mennonites) required in order to maintain viable communities separate from mainstream society. Other book-length treatments were undertaken — see the Bibliography for a more complete listing — but are of more limited use either because of their journalistic excess or their narrow perspective. In addition to these, the various government commissions provide assessments of the Doukhobor "problem" from the supposedly dispassionate perspective of public inquiries.

Beyond these more comprehensive treatments, the literature is limited to shorter studies of specific problems, and these are usually more concerned with the sociological and economic aspects of the Doukhobors. Fewer scholars have explored specifically geographical themes related to their settlement — Thorsteinson, 1917; Bockemuehl, 1963; Gale, 1973; Tracie, 1975, 1976; Gale and Koroscil, 1977; Mealing, 1984 — and generally they have concentrated on the later settlements in British Columbia. This is a curious neglect considering the distinctive, though ephemeral, cultural landscapes the Doukhobors created on the prairies and forest fringes of Saskatchewan.

Appendix A
Doukhobor Villages ~
Legal and File Location[*]

North Colony

Archangelskoe (NW16-35-31 W1) RG15 V1167 F5412475
Boghumdanoe (SE16-35-30 W1) RG15 V1165 F5404662
Gromovoe (SW33-34-31) RG15 V1165 F5404654
Hlebedarnoe (SE13-34-31 W1) RG15 V1164 F5404640
Lubomeernoe (NW2-34-31 W1; SE2-34-31 W1) RG15 V1167 F5412461
Michaelovo (NW36-34-30 W1) RG15 V1167 F5412457
New Kaminka (SE23-33-30; NW23-33-31) RG15 V1165 F5404676
Old Libedevo (NW32/NE31-33-31 W1)
New Libedevo (NE20-33-31 W1) RG15 V1167 F5412465
Old Bogdanofka (NW1-34-32 W1) RG15 V1167 F5412477
Oospennie (SW3-36-30) RG15 V1167 F5412453
Osvoborsdennnie (NW6-34-31 W1; NE5-34-31 W1) RG15 V1167 F5412455
Pavlovo (NE3-35-31 W1) RG15 V1167 F5412493
Perehodnoe (SE7-35-31 W1) RG15 V1168 F5412973
Pocrovskoe (NW21-34-30 W1; SW9-34-30) RG15 V1167 F5412481
Simeonovo (SE14-43-30 W1) RG15 V1166 F5412449
Teehomeernoe (SE28-33-30 W1) RG15 V1166 F5412435
Tehomerofka (SE1-34-32 W1) RG15 V1167 F5412471
Troitzkoe (SW1-36-30 W1) RG15 V1165 F5404672
Vera (NE24-34-30 W10) RG15 V1165 F5404682
Vosnesennie (NW22-34-30 W1) RG5 V1166 F5412439

---

[*]   Department of the Interior Files, National Archives of Canada (spelling as in the files).

Saskatchewan Colony

Bodanofka (NW20-39-8 W3) RG15 V1165 5404664
Karilowa (NW14-39-8 W3) RG15 V1167 F5412463
Large Horelofka (SW35-44-8 W3) RG15 V1167 F5412487
Oospennie (SE1-44-6 W3) RG15 V1168 F5412499
Pakrofka (NW/SW4-39-9 W3) RG15 V1166 F5404690
Pasariofka (SW27-44-6 W3) RG15 V1166 F5404692
Petrofka (NW30-42-6 W3) RG15 V1164 F5391335
Slavyanka (NE17-44-5 W3) RG15 V1167 F5412495
Small Horelofka (NW31-44 W3) RG15 V1165 F5404648
Spasofka (centre of 14-45-5 W3) RG15 V1166 F5412429
Terpennie (SW22-43-6 W3) RG15 V1166 F5412441
Tonbofka (SE2-40-9 W3) RG15 V1166 F5412433
Troitzkaja (NW/SW2-44-7 W3) RG15 V1166 F5412445

South Colony and Annex

Bisednoe (NW17-31-3 W2) RG15 V1165 F5404658
Blagodarnoe (SE/SW30-29-1 W2) RG15 V1165 F5404656
Novo Blagodarnoe (location not given) RG15 V1165 F5404656
Blagosklonoe (SE9-30-5 W2) RG15 V1167 F5412479
Blagovishennie (NW18/SW19-31-2 W2) RG15 V1165 F5404670
Kalmakovo (SE30-30-5 W2) RG15 V1165 F5404646
Kyrillovo (NW7-32-6 W2) RG15 V1165 F5404666
Najersda (Terpennie Kars) (NW24-31-1 W2) RG15 V1167 F5412459
New Gorilloe (NW4-32-6 W2) RG15 V1165 F5404650
Novo Troitzkoe (Resbehileovo) (NW23-31-6 W2) RG15 V1168 F5412501
Novoe (NE14/NW13-31-3 W2) RG15 V1168 F5412497
Obezhdennie (NE7-30-32 W1) RG15 V1166 F5404686
Old Gorilloe (NE17-30-5 W2) RG15 V1165 F5404652
Old Kaminka (SE21-27-31 W1) RG15 V1167 F5412485
Old Lubovnoe (SE23-29-1 W2) RG15 V1165 F5404674
Lubovnoe (NE13-29-33 W1) RG15 V1165 F5404674
Old Moisayovo (Section 3-33-34 [probably 33-33-4]) RG15 V1165 F5404642
Moisayovo (NE21-31-6 W2) RG15 V1165 F5404642
Old Petrovo (SW27-27-32 W1) RG15 V1167 F5412491
Petrovo (NW21-28-32 W1; NW22-28-32 W1) RG15 V1167 F5412491
Old Riduonovo (Section 5-29-31 W1) RG15 V1163 F5412489
Riduonovo (SE9-30-2 W2) RG5 V1163 F5412489
Old Slavenka (NW25-29-1 W2) RG15 V1165 F5404644
Kapustina (NE/NW36-31-2 W2) RG15 V1165 F5404644

Old Terpennie (NE11-27-32 W1) RG15 V1166 F5412443

Terpennie (NW36-29-2 W2) RG15 V1166 F5412443

Old Voskrisennie (NE2/SW11-29-32 W1) RG15 V1167 F5412469

Voskrisennie (NW12-29-32 W1) RG15 V1167 F5412469

Ootishennie (SW31-30-5 W2) RG15 V1166 F5412451

Otradnoe (NE/SE27-31-1 W2) RG15 V1167 F5412467

Pokoratovoe (NE34-30-1 W2) RG15 V1167 F5412483

New Pakrofka (NE28-30-1 W2) RG15 V1167 F5412483

Savetnoe ([NW14-31-2 W2]NW35-30-2 W2) RG15 V1166 F5404688

Slavnoe (NE4-32-2 W2) RG15 V1165 F5404678

Smyrennie (SE35-31-1 W2) RG15 V1166 F5412431

Spaskoe (NE25-30-1 W2) RG15 V1166 F5412447

Tomboscoe (SE/NE3-29-31 W1) RG15 V1166 F5412437

Troodoloobevoe (NE3/SE10-29-31 W1) RG15 V1165 F5404680

Trusdennie (SE5-29-32 W1; SW20-29-32 W1) RG15 V1165 F5404660

Efromovo (NW6-29-32 W1) RG15 V1165 F5404660

Verigin Station (SE9-30-1 W2) RG15 V1166 F5412427

Vernoe (NW/SW33-29-1 W1) RG15 V1165 F5404668

Vosziennie (NE21-28-31 W1) RG15 V1166 F5412425

Appendix B
Surveyors' Notebooks

North Colony

#6041 — J.C. DesMeules, 1898
#6120 — J.A. Belleau, 1899
#7072 — C.F. Aylsworth, 1900
#7395 — C.F. Aylsworth, 1900
#7397 — C.F. Aylsworth, 1900

#6118 — J.A. Belleau, 1899
#6213 — E.W. Hubbell, 1898
#7073 — C.F. Aylsworth, 1900
#7396 — C.F. Aylsworth, 1900
#14423 — G.P.J. Roy, 1913

Saskatchewan Colony

#2662 — J. Doupe, 1883
#2664 — J. Doupe, 1883
#3470 — J.K. McLean, 1883
#3825 — R.C. Laurie, 1883
#3861 — W.C. Eaton, 1883
#4106 — H.W. Selby, 1884
#4239 — J. Fefresne, 1884
#4510 — F.L. Foster, 1884
#4512 — F.L. Foster, 1884
#4514 — F.L. Foster, 1884
#8455 — W. Beatty, 1903
#8457 — W. Beatty, 1903
#8461 — W. Beatty, 1903

#2663 — J. Doupe, 1883
#2770 — A.G. Cavana, 1883
#3824 — R.C. Laurie, 1883
#3827 — R.C. Laurie, 1883
#4077 — F. Vincent, 1884
#4107 — H.W. Selby, 1884
#4509 — F.L. Foster, 1884
#4511 — F.L. Foster, 1884
#4513 — F.L. Foster, 1884
#4515 — F.L. Foster, 1884
#8456 — W. Beatty, 1903
#8458 — W. Beatty, 1903
#8462 — W. Beatty, 1903

South Colony and Annex

#1091 — A.L. Russell, 1880
#1597 — J. McLatchie, 1880
#1704 — W. Wagner, 1882
#1957 — W. Wagner, 1882
#2120 — R.W. Lendrum, 1882
#2186 — R.W. Lendrum, 1882
#4944 — J. McLatchie, 1890
#4962 — W.J. Thompson, 1890
#4966 — W.R. Burke, 1890
#5027 — J. McLatchie, 1889
#5462 — F. Vincent, 1890
#5923 — C.C. Duberger, 1897
#6196 — A.J. Brabazon, 1899 (missing)
#6198 — A.J. Brabazon, 1899
#6206 — C.F. Aylsworth, 1898
#6209 — C.F. Aylsworth, 1898
#6247 — A.F. Martin, 1899
#6289 — A.F. Martin, 1899, 1900
#6294 — A.F. Martin, 1899
#8707 — C.J. Aylsworth, 1905
#10578 — W.J. Deans, 1907

#1596 — J. McLatchie, 1880
#1703 — W. Wagner, 1882
#1954 — W. Wagner, 1882
#1958 — W. Wagner, 1882
#2184 — R.W. Lendrum, 1882
#4826 — T.R. Hewson, 1889
#4954 — J. McLatchie, 1890
#4963 — W.T. Thompson, 1890
#4968 — W.R. Burke, 1890
#5028 — J. McLatchie, 1889
#5567 — J.E. Woods, 1893
#6101 — C.F. Aylsworth, 1898
#6197 — A.J. Brabazon, 1899
#6202 — C.F. Aylsworth, 1898
#6207 — C.F. Aylsworth, 1898
#6210 — C.F. Aylsworth, 1898
#6251 — A.F. Martin, 1899
#6291 — A.F. Martin, 1899
#6296 — A.F. Martin, 1899, 1900
#9334 — C.F. Aylsworth, 1905

Bibliography

Adelman, Jeremy. "Early Doukhobor Experience on the Canadian Prairies." *Journal of Canadian Studies* 25, no. 4 (Winter 1990-91): 111-28.

Ballantyne, James. "The Doukhobors." *The Westminster* 18, no. 2 (February 1911): 113-19.

Barcroft, Joseph. "The Doukhobors." *The Friends Quarterly Examiner* (April 1900) (cited in Elkinton (1903), 11).

Bell, Archie. "What Would Jesus Do?" Chapter 15 in Bell, *Sunset Canada: British Columbia and Beyond*. Boston: The Page Co. 1918.

Bellows, John. *Letters and Memoirs*. Edited by his wife. London: Keagan Paul, 1904.

Bernard, Lally [May Fitzgibbon]. *The Canadian Doukhobor Settlements*. Toronto: William Briggs, 1899.

Blaine Lake School. "Our Historical Blaine Lake." Mimeographed typescript, 1957.

Blakemore, William. *Report of the Royal Commission on Matters Relating to the Sect of Doukhobors in the Province of British Columbia*. Victoria: King's Printer, 1913.

Bockemuehl, Harold W. "Doukhobor Impact on the British Columbia Landscape: An Historical Geographical Study." M.A. thesis, Western Washington State College, 1963.

Bondoreff, John I. "Ospennia 'Dug-Out' Hut Village, 1899-1904." In *Bridging the Years*, 22-24.

——. "Slavanka Village." In *Bridging the Years*, 26-27.

Bradley, A.G. "The Doukhobors." In Bradley, *Canada in the Twentieth Century*, 297-303. London: Constable, 1905.

Bridging the Years, Era of Blaine Lake and District, 1790-1980. Blaine Lake, SK: Town of Blaine Lake and Rural Municipality of Blaine Lake #434, 1984.

Brown, Robert C. and B. Ramsey Cook. *Canada 1896-1921: A Nation Transformed*. Toronto: McClelland and Stewart, 1974.

Buyniak, V.O. "Place Names of the Early Dukhobor Settlement in Saskatchewan." In *Slavs in Canada*, edited by C.S. Jaenen, vol. 3, 143-149. Proceedings of the Third National Conference on Canadian Slavs. Toronto: Ukrainian Echo, n.d.

——. "Doukhobors, Molokans and Skovoroda's Teachings." In *Roots and Realities Among Eastern and Central Europeans*, edited by Martin L. Kovacs, 13-23. Edmonton: Central and East European Studies Association of Canada, 1983.

Canada. *Census of the Prairie Provinces*. 1906.

——. *Papers Relating to the Holding of Homestead Entries by Members of the Doukhobor Community; Being Part of a Return Laid on the Table of the House of Commons on April 17, 1907; With the*

Final Report of the Commission Appointed to Investigate and Adjust the Claims of Doukhobors as to Residence and Improvements. Ottawa: Government Printing Bureau, 1907.

———. *Reports and Maps Relating to Lands Held Under Homestead Entry by Doukhobors and the Disposition of Same*. Ottawa: Government Printing Bureau, 1907.

Copping, A.E. *Canada Today and Tomorrow*. London: Cassell, 1911.

Cormie, J.A. "Will the Doukhobor Survive?" *University Magazine* 10 (1911): 589-96.

Dafoe, John W. *Clifford Sifton In Relation to His Times*. Toronto: Macmillan, 1931.

Dawson, C.A. *Group Settlement: Ethnic Communities in Western Canada*. Toronto: Macmillan, 1936.

Donskov, Andrew, ed. *Leo Tolstoy-Peter Verigin Correspondence*. Ottawa: Legas, 1995.

"Doukhobor Claims for Compensation." Documents from the papers of J.E. Mavor with an editorial note by L.I. Strakhovsky. *Canadian Slavonic Papers* 1 (1956): 1-15.

Doukhobor Research Committee. *Doukhobors of British Columbia*, edited by Harry Hawthorne. Vancouver: University of British Columbia, 1955.

"The Doukhobors in Canada." *New Order* 6, no 26 (April 1900): 60.

Elkinton, Joseph. *The Doukhobors, Their History in Russia, Their Migration to Canada*. Philadelphia: Ferris and Leach, 1903.

Ewashen, Larry A. *Peter V. Verigin 1859-1924, An Appreciation*. Creston, BC: Great Western Publishing, 1988.

Ewashen, Larry A. and Koozma J. Tarasoff. *In Search of Utopia: The Doukhobors*. 2nd revised and enlarged edition. Veregin, SK: Living Word Corporation, 1990.

Ferguson, Emily. *Janey Canuck in the West*. 3rd. ed., London: Cassell and Co., 1910.

Fitzgibbon, May. See Lally Bernard.

Ford, Arthur R. "The Doukhobors in Canada." *The Westminster* 12 (April 1908): 219-24.

Friesen, John W. and Michael M. Verigin. *The Community Doukhbors: A People in Transition*. Ottawa: Borealis Press, 1989.

Gale, D.T. "Belief and the Landscape of Religion: The Case of the Doukhobors." Master's thesis. Simon Fraser University, 1973.

Gale, D.T. and Paul M. Koroscil. "Doukhobor Settlements: Experiments in Idealism." *Canadian Ethnic Studies* 9, no. 2 (1977): 53-71.

Gibbon, J. Murray. "Russian and Canada," Chapter 16 in Gibbon, *Canadian Mosaic*, 364-79. Toronto: McClelland & Stewart, 1938.

Gruchy, Lydia E. *The Doukhobors in Canada*. Toronto: Committee on Literature, General Publicity and Missionary Education of the United Church of Canada [1930].

Hall, D.J. *Clifford Sifton*, Vol. 1, *The Young Napoleon 1861-1900*. Vancouver: University of British Columbia Press, 1981.

Haxthausen, Baron von. *The Russian Empire, Its People, Institutions, and Resources*. Reprint trans. Robert Farie. 1856; London: Frank Cass & Co. Ltd., 1968.

Hawkes, John. *Saskatchewan and Its People*. 3 vols. Regina: S.J. Clarke Publication Co., 1924.

Hayward, Victoria. "Doukhobors: A Community Race in Canada." In Hayward, *Romantic Canada*, 225-35. Toronto: Macmillan Co., 1922.

"Houses with Flowering Roofs." *Touchstone* 7 (April 1920), 26-29, 72.

"Interview with Dr. J.I. Pereverseff." *Mir* 2, nos. 1 & 2 (May 1974): 12.

Jackson, S.J. "Report." Appendix 19 to the Report of the Surveyor General. Department of Interior. *Sessional Papers*. 3-4 Edward VII, 1904.

Janzen, William. *Limits on Liberty*. Toronto: University of Toronto Press, 1990.

Kershaw, Adrian. "Ideological Conflict, Assimilation, and the Cultural Landscape: A Case Study of the Doukhobors in Canada." In *Aspects of Human Geography: The Kelowna Papers, 1981*, edited by Nigel M. Waters, 9-26. BC Geographical Series No. 34. Vancouver: Tantalus Research Ltd. 1982.

Leacock, Stephen. *My Discovery of the West*. New York: Hale, Cushman and Flint, 1937.

Lindsay, Corporal. "NWMP Reports." *Sessional Papers*. No. 15, 63 Victoria A. 1900, 75-7.

Lyle, G.R. "Eye Witness to Courage." *Saskatchewan History* 20, no. 3 (Autumn 1967): 81-107.

Lyons, John E. "A History of Doukhobor Schooling in Saskatchewan and British Columbia 1899-1939." M.A. thesis, University of Calgary, 1973.

Lyons, John E. "The (Almost) Quiet Evolution: Doukhobor Schooling in Saskatchewan." *Canadian Ethnic Studies* 8, no. 1 (1976): 23-37.

Maloff, Peter. "The Christian Community of Universal Brotherhood." Typescript. Peter Maloff Papers, UBC Special Collections, 1948.

Maude, Aylmer. *A Peculiar People: The Doukhobors*. New York and London: Funk and Wagnall's Company, 1904.

Mavor, James. *Report to the Board of Trade on the North West of Canada with Special Reference to Wheat Production for Export 1904*. London: His Majesty's Stationery Office, n.d. [1905].

———. *My Windows on the Street of the World*. 2 vols. Toronto: J.M. Dent & Son, 1923.

McCormick, P.L. "The Doukhobors in 1904." *Saskatchewan History* 31 no. 1 (Winter 1978): 12-19.

Mealing, F. Mark. *Doukhobor Life: A Survey of Doukhobor Religion, History, & Folklife*. Castlegar: Kootenay Doukhobor Historical Society/Cotinneh Books, 1975.

———. Review of "In Search of Utopia —The Doukhobors" (film, directed by Larry Ewashen and narrated by Koozma Tarasoff, GEMINI Cooperative Inc., Toronto). *Canadian Ethnic Studies* 12, no. 1 (1980): 113-14.

———. "Doukhobor Architecture: An Introduction." *Canadian Ethnic Studies* 16, no. 3 (1984): 73-88.

Miller, James R. *Skyscrapers Hide the Heavens* (rev. ed.). Toronto: University of Toronto Press, 1991.

National Archives of Canada. Department of the Interior Papers. Record Group 15, Volumes 754-758, File 494483; Volumes 1163-1168, Files 5391335, 5404640-5404692, 5412425-5412501, 5412973.

———. Topographical Surveys Branch Papers. Record Group 15, Volume 760, File 5020904.

———. Immigration Branch Records. Record Group 76, Volume 183, File 65101, parts 1-7.

Owram, D. *Promise of Eden*. Toronto: University of Toronto Press, 1980.

Palmer, Howard. "Strangers and Stereotypes." In *The Prairie West*, edited by R.D. Francis and H. Palmer, 309-333. Edmonton: Pica Pica Press, 1985.

Papove, W.N. "The Doukhobor Saga." Submitted to the Ethnic Organizations Sub-Committee of the British Columbia Centennial '71 Committee, November 1970.

Reid, Ewart P. "The Doukhobors in Canada." M.A. thesis, McGill University, 1932.

"Report of General Meeting of the Doukhobor Community Held at Veregin, January 25th, 1910." *Saskatchewan History* 24 (1972): 73-75.

Rhoads, Jonathan. *A Day With the Dukohobors* [sic]. Philadelphia: William H. Pile and Sons, 1900.

Serhienko, Peter J. "Settlement of the Petrofka Village." In *Bridging the Years*, 24-26.

——. "Radouga Creek" and "Radouga Creek Flour Mill." In *Bridging the Years*, 33.

Snesarev, Harry (Harry Trevor). "The Doukhobors in British Columbia." Report for the University of British Columbia. Vancouver, 1931.

Stoochnoff, John Philip. *Toil and Peaceful Life*. Privately printed, n.d.

——. *Doukhobors As They Are*. Privately printed, 1961.

Stupnikoff, Sam George. *Historical Saga of the Doukhobor Faith, 1750-1990s: Toil and Peaceful Life*. Privately Printed, 1992.

Sulerzhitsky, L.A. *To America With the Doukhobors*. Trans. Michael Kalmakoff. Regina: Canadian Plains Research Center, 1982.

Szalasznyj, Kathlyn Rose Marie. "The Doukhobor Homestead Crisis." M.A. thesis, University of Saskatchewan, 1977.

Tarasoff, Koozma J. "In Search of Brotherhood." 3 vol. typescript. Vancouver: UBC Special Collections, 1963.

——. *A Pictorial History of the Doukhobors*. Saskatoon: Prairie Books, 1969.

——. *Plakun Trava*. Grand Forks, BC: Mir Publication Society, 1982.

——. "The Western Settlement of Canadian Doukhobors." In *Visions of the New Jerusalem*, edited by Benjamin G. Smillie, 121-36. Edmonton: NeWest Press, 1983.

Thorsteinson, Elina. "The Doukhobors in Canada." *Mississippi Valley Historical Review* 4, no. 1 (June 1917): 3-48.

Tracie, Carl J. "Ethnicity and Settlement in Western Canada: Doukhobor Village Settlement in Saskatchewan." In *Western Canadian Research in Geography: The Lethbridge Papers*, edited by B.M. Barr, 67-76. BC Geographical Series No. 21. Occasional Papers in Geography. Vancouver: Tantalus Research, 1975.

——. "Ethnicity and the Prairie Environment: Patterns of Old Colony Mennonite and Doukhobor Settlement." In *Man and Nature on the Prairies*, edited by R. Allen, 46-65. Regina: Canadian Plains Research Center, 1976.

Woodcock, G. and I. Avakumovic. *The Doukhobors*. Toronto: Oxford University Press, 1968.

——. *Odysseus Ever Returning*. New Canadian Library No. 71. Toronto: McClelland and Stewart, 1971.

Woodsworth, J.S. *Strangers Within Our Gates*. 1909; Toronto: University of Toronto Press, 1972.

Wright, J.F.C. *Slava Bohu*. New York: Ferrar & Rinehart, 1940.

Zubek, J.P. and P.A. Solberg. *Doukhobors at War*. Toronto: Ryerson Press, 1952.

Index

N = North Colony
S = South Colony and Good Spirit Lake Annex
SK = Saskatchewan Colony

Alberta xi, 167, 170, 212
Archangelskoe (N) 46, 47, 133, 175
Archer, Herbert 40, 41, 53, 58, 99, 106, 110, 111, 128, 149
Ashworth, John 53, 64, 80, 114
Assiniboia, District of 6, 8, 122
Assiniboine River 13, 14, 18, 20, 67, 68, 82, 186
Aylsworth, C.F. 30, 48, 50, 54, 69, 142

Bearshead (Bear Head) Creek 11, 46, 177
Beatty, Walter 15
Beaver Lake 5
Belleau, J.A. 30
Bernard, Lally 31, 36, 40, 48, 58, 61
Bisednoe (S) 184
Blagodarenovka (see Blagodarnoe)
Blagodarnoe (S) 78, 138, 154, 163, 165, 184, 186, 190, 205
Blagosklonoe (S) 143, 144, 164, 188, 191, 192, 201, 205
Blagovishennie (S) 162
Blaine Lake 15
Bodenofka (SK) 84, 91, 147, 150, 164, 194, 197, 199
Bodyansky, Alexander 99, 108
Bogdanofka (N) 30, 46, 49, 53, 61, 116, 128, 131
Boghumdanoe (N) 46, 131
Bowes, John 171, 197
Brandon 17
British Columbia ix, xi, 153, 159, 161, 162, 163, 164, 166, 167, 170, 171, 172, 175, 176, 177, 183, 186, 190, 191, 194, 200, 202, 207, 208, 209, 211, 212

Canadian Northern Railway 137, 209
Canadian Pacific Railway 6
Carrot River 6, 15
Caucasus 1, 11, 67, 138
Cazakoff, M.W. 204, 209
Christian Community of Universal Brotherhood (CCUB) 122, 127, 141, 162, 167, 169, 171, 172, 175, 177, 186, 190, 194, 204, 205, 209, 212
Clark, E.C. 102
Cormie, J.A. 24, 78
Cory, W.W. 101
Côté Indian Reserve 11, 13
Cowan 8, 11, 17

Deans, W.J. 69
Deville, E.G. 21, 22, 46, 48
Dewan, Thomas 120
Dixon, FitzRoy 101, 103
Dominion Lands Act 24, 156
Duck Lake 19, 84, 86, 92
Duck Mountain 8, 14

Eagle Creek 86, 91
Edmonton 5, 6
Efromovo (S) 184

Fairchild, C.C. 49, 50, 64, 69, 87, 89, 159, 169, 178, 188, 192, 204
Fast, Hermann 112, 113
Fisher, Fred 11
Fort Pelly 8, 102

Good Spirit Lake (Devil's Lake) 13, 14, 21, 68, 82, 122, 192
Gorelovka (see Old Gorilloe)
Gorilloe (S) 192
Great Bogdanofka (see Teakomeernoe)
Gromovoe (N) 37, 133, 149, 150, 175

Harley, Hugh 112, 120, 161
Harvey, Philip 106
Harvey, William B. 31, 58, 61, 64
Hilkoff, Prince 5, 6, 15
Hlebedarnoe (N) 117, 128, 131, 176, 201, 205
Homestead Act 100, 212
Horelofka (SK) 86, 91, 92, 94, 145
Hubbell, E.W. 13, 17, 18, 21, 22
Hudson's Bay Company 15, 20, 50, 67, 116, 117, 153

Ivin, Ivan 40, 57, 58, 201

Jackson, S.J. 54

Kalesnikoff, Sam 87
Kalmakovo (S) 79, 141, 143, 164, 170, 192, 201, 205
Kalmykova, Luker'ia 2
Kaminka (N) 44, 46, 47, 128, 131
Kaminka (S) 30, 31, 44, 77, 78, 79
Kamsack 186, 204, 213
Kamsack Creek 138
Kapustina (S) 118, 162, 170, 204
Karilowa (SK) 84, 147, 150, 194, 197, 199
Kelvington 211, 212
Kerelovka (S) 117
Key Indian Reserve 13
Keyes, P.G. 100
Khristianovka (S) 141
Kirilovka (SK) 145
Kirilowa (S) 69
Kylemore 211, 212
Kyrillovo (S) 164, 191, 192

Langham 19, 149, 165
Large Horelofka (SK) 118, 147, 164, 196, 197
Leather River 6
Libedevo (N) 46, 128, 133
Lindsay, Corporal 91
Lubomeernoe (N) 46, 54, 59, 116, 117, 130, 158
Lubovnoe (S) 117, 137, 165

MacDougall, John 156, 157
Mahortoff, Ivan 139
Maloneck Creek 46
Manitoba 8, 62, 105
Manitoba & North Western Railway 17

Maude, Aylmer 5, 10, 23, 99
Mavor, James 3, 4, 5, 10, 14, 17, 23, 113, 114
McCallum, N.G. 118, 155
McCreary, William 6, 18, 53, 64, 77, 80
McMunn's Camp 18
McVey's Camp 8, 62, 117
Mealing, Mark 36
Michaelovo (N) 11, 17, 40, 44, 49, 57, 58, 62, 64, 80, 117, 128, 131, 133, 134, 175, 176, 178, 201, 213
Milky Waters 2
Minnedosa 105
Moisayovo (S) 69, 117, 141, 162, 164, 170, 191, 192
Molochnaya River 2

Nadjesda (see Najersda)
Najersda (S) 77, 162, 165, 203
New Gorilloe (S) 141, 144, 164, 191
New Kaminka (N) 46
New Pakrofka (S) 184
Nickolaievka (S) 69, 118, 135, 137
Nikon, Bishop 1
North Saskatchewan River 7, 15, 17, 19, 20, 84, 86, 87, 91, 118, 196
Novo Blagodarnoe (S) 163, 164, 165, 186
Novo Petrofka (S) 137
Novo Slavanska (S) 118
Novo Slavyanka (S) 69
Novo Troitzkoe (S) 69, 71, 78, 80, 141, 142, 191
Novoe (S) 135, 163, 165
Novotroitzkoe (see Simeonovo)

Old Bogdanofka (N) 128
Old Efromovo (S) 117, 165
Old Gorilloe (S) 78, 141, 191, 192
Old Kaminka (S) 117, 135, 137, 165
Old Libedevo (see Stradaevka)
Old Petrovo (S) 117, 118, 135, 137, 138, 165
Old Riduonovo (S) 117, 137, 165
Old Slavenka (S) 117, 165
Old Terpennie (S) 117, 135, 137
Old Voskrisennie (S) 117, 165
Oliver, Frank 103, 127, 153, 155, 156, 157, 207, 212
Oobezhdennie (S) 165, 184
Oospennie (N) 30, 36, 37, 40, 44, 50, 53, 54, 57, 58, 131, 164, 177, 178
Oospennie (SK) 86, 87, 89, 94, 115, 118, 146, 196, 197, 199, 213

Ootishennie (S) 78, 143, 144, 191, 192
Osvoborsdennie (N) 46, 48, 49, 57, 59, 61, 116, 131, 132, 213
Osvobozhdenie (see Osvoborsdennie)
Otradnoe (S) 78, 135, 137, 138, 140, 159, 162, 164, 188, 203, 204, 213

Pakrofka (S) 135, 165, 184
Pakrofka (SK) 84, 89, 91, 115, 148, 164, 170, 196, 197, 201
Pakrovka (N) 41
Pasariofka (S) 69, 77
Pasariofka (SK) 86, 92, 118, 145, 164, 170, 196
Pavlovo (N) 57, 128, 131, 149, 175
Peaker, James 100
Perapolkin, Ivan 106
Perehodnoe (N) 46, 47, 133, 149, 175
Petrofka (S) 118, 135
Petrofka (SK) 86, 89, 112, 115, 118, 146, 148, 164, 170, 194, 196, 197, 199, 201, 205
Petrovo (S) 68, 137, 138, 165, 186, 202
Pipestone 6
Planidin, Pavel 102, 153
Porcupine Hills 8
Poterpevshe (see Otradnoe)
Prince Albert 6, 100
Procovskoe (N) 37, 41, 46, 61, 178
Prokuratovo (S) 135, 165, 184

Queen Victoria 209

Redberry Lake 15, 17, 86, 106, 120
Reiben, Simeon 102, 153
Rhoads, Jonathon 87, 91
Riduonovo (S) 162
Roblin, Duff 105
Russia xii, 2, 40, 109, 154, 204, 207
Russian Orthodox Church 1, 2

Saskatchewan ix, xi, 62, 125, 127, 190, 209, 213
Saskatoon 19, 84, 106
Satz, A.A. 64
Savetnoe (S) 188
Schoukin (Shukin), Ivan 142
Seale, John 41
Selkirk 17, 19, 86
Sifton, Clifford ix, xii, 6, 100, 101, 102, 103, 105, 127, 131, 139, 147, 155, 207, 212

Simeonovo (N) 36, 117, 120, 128, 131, 132, 133, 164, 167, 176, 201
Slavnoe (S) 118, 135
Slavyanka (SK) 89, 118, 164, 196, 197
Small Horelofka (SK) 118, 164, 170, 196
Smart, James 6, 18
Smirenovka (see Troodoloobevoe)
Smith, J. Obed 48, 101
Smyrennie (S) 165
Soldiers' Settlement Board 204, 205
Sons of Freedom x, 109, 188, 213
Sons of God 109, 167
Spaskoe (S) 138, 165, 184, 202, 205
Spasofka (SK) 15, 84, 86, 89, 92, 165, 194, 201
Spasskoe (N) 117, 128, 131
Spirit Creek 13, 67, 192
St. John, Arthur 99
Stone Creek 137, 138
Stradaevka (N) 46, 54, 128
Stradenofka (see Trusdennie)
Strakhovsky, L.I. 209
Sulerzhitsky, L.A. 6, 8, 10, 17, 18, 48, 50, 58, 59, 61, 62, 64, 67, 68, 80, 99, 154
Swan River 6, 8, 10, 11, 20, 40, 46, 49, 53, 58, 62, 121, 122, 131, 175, 177

Tambofka (see Tomboscoe)
Tarasoff, Koozma 23, 61
Teakomeernoe (N) 30, 46, 47, 48, 49, 53, 61, 116, 128
Techomeerovka (see Teakomeernoe)
Terpennie (S) 77, 78, 79, 81, 105, 110, 135, 141, 164, 165, 186
Terpennie (SK) 86, 87, 89, 92, 170, 197, 202
Thorsteinson, Elina 31, 77
Thunder Hill 8, 10, 49, 62
Tiflis (Tbilisi) 2, 11
Tolstoy, Lev 2, 114, 211
Tomboscoe (S) 69, 77, 139, 183, 186
Tonbofka (SK) 89, 118, 120, 149, 150, 163, 170
Transcaucasia 2, 14, 19, 48
Troitska (S) 117
Troitskaja (SK) 86, 89, 106, 197
Troitzkoe (N) 30, 36, 40, 44, 50, 53, 54, 58, 133, 164, 177
Troodoloobevoe (S) 69, 139, 186, 190, 205
Troozshdanie (see Trusdennie)
Trusdennie (S) 77, 118, 135, 165

Usachefka (see Pakrofka)

van Horne, William 22
Velichkina, Dr. Vera 64
Vera (N) 40, 49, 61, 81, 133, 164
Veregin 37, 135, 149, 170, 175, 178, 186, 204
Veregin Station (Siding) 135, 137, 139, 148, 149, 163, 165, 170, 177, 186, 190
Verigin, Peter V. ix, x, 2, 5, 24, 25, 29, 68, 71, 96, 97, 101, 102, 103, 107-115, 119-122, 125, 127, 135, 137, 138, 141, 146, 148, 150, 153, 154, 155, 159, 161, 163, 167, 177, 186, 188, 199, 207, 208, 210, 213
Vernoe (S) 164, 165, 184, 186, 205
Verovka (see Vera)
Voskrisennie (S) 37, 78, 79, 138, 141, 163, 165, 186, 190, 203, 205
Vosnisennie (N) 17, 37, 41, 44, 49, 50, 62, 64, 117, 128, 130, 131, 175, 176, 178, 213
Vosoyanie (see Vosziennie)
Vosziennie (S) 37, 68, 118, 138, 170, 184, 186, 190, 203

Wet Mountains 2, 19,
Wetaskiwin 6
White, Michael 205
Whitebeech Creek 46
Whitesand River 13, 14, 20, 67, 82, 186
Woody River 11, 46

Yorkton 6, 17, 65, 67, 100, 105, 106, 107, 113, 119, 131, 164
Young, Thomas 41

Ziebaroff, Nikolai 175